Michigan Studies in International Political Economy

SERIES EDITORS: Edward Mansfield and Lisa Martin

Michael J. Gilligan
Empowering Exporters: Reciprocity, Delegation, and Collective Action in American Trade Policy

Barry Eichengreen and Jeffry Frieden, Editors
Forging an Integrated Europe

Thomas H. Oatley
Monetary Politics: Exchange Rate Cooperation in the European Union

Robert Pahre
Leading Questions: How Hegemony Affects the International Political Economy

Andrew C. Sobel
State Institutions, Private Incentives, Global Capital

Roland Stephen
Vehicle of Influence: Building a European Car Market

William Bernhard
Banking on Reform: Political Parties and Central Bank Independence in the Industrial Democracies

Banking on Reform

Gretchen Casper

Banking on Reform

Political Parties and Central Bank Independence in the Industrial Democracies

William Bernhard

Ann Arbor

The University of Michigan Press

Published in the United States of America by
The University of Michigan Press
Manufactured in the United States of America
∞ Printed on acid-free paper

2005 2004 2003 2002 4 3 2 1

A CIP catalog record for this book is available from the British Library.

Library of Congress Cataloging-in-Publication Data applied for
ISBN 0-472-11254-6

For Jen

Contents

Figures

Tables

Acknowledgments

This project evolved from my graduate work at Duke University. My greatest intellectual debt goes to my dissertation advisor, Peter Lange. Peter has shaped this project in innumerable direct and perhaps more significantly, indirect ways. I thank him for his guidance, advice, and above all, patience. Bob Bates and Herbert Kitschelt also strongly influenced my intellectual development. Their research and teaching exemplify what political science should be. Special thanks are also due to William Bianco and Emerson Niou, who provided invaluable assistance during the process both as dissertation committee members and more importantly, as friends. Other (past and present) Duke faculty members who offered advice, encouragement, and criticism include John Aldrich, John Brehm, Paul Gronke, Tom Havrilesky, and Beth Simmons. While I was at Duke, the project also benefited from a dynamic and collegial cohort of graduate students: Clark Gibson, Dean Lacy, Brian Loynd, Howard Lubert, Layna Mosley, Phil Paolino, Matt Schousen, Patrick Sellers, Regina Smyth, and Ned Walpin.

Although many people have contributed to this project, a few individuals have gone above and beyond the call of duty. Kathryn Firmin-Sellers, Rob Franzese, Jim Granato, Torben Iversen, and David Leblang merit special thanks for their kind and gracious assistance. Each has read the entire manuscript at least once and offered extensive comments and recommendations.

In addition, I have received helpful advice and encouragement from Jim Alt, Alison Alter, Lawrence Broz, Kelly Chang, William Clark, Maria Green Cowles, Mark Crescenzi, William Downs, John Freeman, Jeff Frieden, Matt Gabel, Mark Hallerberg, John Huber, Erik Jones, Karl Kaltenthaler, William Keech, Kate McNamara, Burt Monroe, Irwin Morris, Thomas Oatley, Sofia Perez, Ron Rogowski, Andy Sobel, David Stasavage, and Daniel Verdier. Seminar participants at Harvard University, the Political Economy Program at

Harvard University, Franklin & Marshall College, Indiana University, and the University of North Texas also made valuable comments.

My colleagues at both Dartmouth College and the University of Illinois also deserve thanks for their time and advice. At Dartmouth, Darren Hawkins, Jim Hentz, Dave Kang, Catherine Shapiro, Joao Resende-Santos, and Jim Shoch provided intellectual stimulation. At Illinois, Lee Alston, Bear Braumoeller, Brian Gaines, Gerry Munck, Larry Neal, Bob Pahre, Brian Sala, and Richard Snyder made comments and suggestions. The University of Illinois Department of Political Science and the University Research Board provided the resources necessary for the completion of the project.

Fieldwork was made possible by a Fulbright Grant to the European Communities. As a Visiting Research Fellow at the Centre for European Policy Studies, I interacted with Peter Ludlow and Daniel Gros. Ivo Maes of the National Bank of Belgium also deserves thanks for helping me acclimate to the world of central banking in Europe.

I thank Robert Franzese, Torben Iversen, David Leblang, Adam Posen, and Dennis Quinn for sharing data. Chad Atkinson and Sang-Hyun Lee provided able research assistance.

Chapter 1

Political Parties and Central Bank Independence

Central banks stand at the intersection of economics and politics. These bureaucratic institutions implement monetary policy by regulating the supply of money and credit to the economy. Both academic and popular accounts emphasize how a country's central bank significantly shapes its economic destiny (e.g., Beckner 1996; Deane and Pringle 1995; Greider 1987; Marsh 1992). In many countries, opinion polls and newspaper stories recognize central bankers as the most influential nonelected public officials.

Although central banks perform a similar function across the industrial democracies, their institutional structures—their levels of independence—differ across systems. The structure of an independent central bank restricts the government's ex-ante and ex-post influence over monetary policy, often by limiting the number of cabinet appointees on a bank's governing board, by preventing the cabinet from vetoing the bank's policy decisions, and by prohibiting the cabinet from punishing central bankers through dismissal or budget cuts. A dependent central bank, on the other hand, places few limitations on the government's authority.

In the 1970s and 1980s, only a few central banks were independent; the majority of industrial democracies had dependent central banks. In the 1990s, however, this distribution shifted significantly as many countries legislated more independence for their central banks. Most dramatically, European Union (EU) member states agreed to a single currency under the administration of an independent central bank. In this book, I explain these patterns of central bank independence.

Central Bank Independence: The Reform Trend

Throughout most of the post–World War II period, only a few industrial democracies, including Germany, Switzerland, and the United States, possessed independent central banks. The German Bundesbank, for example, is generally recognized as one of the most independent central banks in the world (Deutsche Bundesbank 1989; Goodman 1992; Kennedy 1991; Marsh 1992; Sturm 1989). The German federal government appoints only a minority of the Central Bank Council, the bank's main decision-making body. Further, the government cannot veto the bank's decisions, although it may delay for two weeks the implementation of a bank decision.

In countries such as Britain, Italy, and France, on the other hand, the government retained full control over the central bank's policy actions. In Britain, for example, the government appointed the entire governing board and could veto the bank's policy decisions. The Treasury dictated the Bank of England's policies (Fay 1988). Nigel Lawson, a former chancellor of the Exchequer, described the relationship between the government and the bank in this way, "I make the decisions and the Bank carries them out" (*The Economist,* 10 February 1990).

Many economists and policymakers argue that an independent central bank insulates monetary policy from political influences to produce more stable and predictable monetary policies and as a result, lower levels of inflation. Indeed, countries with an independent central bank generally had better inflation performance during the 1970s and 1980s than countries with a dependent central bank. Yet during this time, no country moved to make its central bank more independent.

In the late 1980s and 1990s, however, a wave of central bank reform swept across the industrial democracies. Politicians in Italy and New Zealand made the earliest efforts to grant their central banks more independence. In Italy a 1981 administrative decree freed the Bank of Italy from its obligation to purchase unsold public debt, an act known as the "divorce" of the Bank of Italy (Epstein and Schor 1989; Goodman 1991, 1992; Tabellini 1987, 1988). After the divorce, the Bank of Italy was less willing to finance budget deficits, forcing the government to pay for its debt through higher taxes and lower spending. Throughout the 1980s and 1990s, Italian politicians granted the bank widened authority over monetary policy, including control over the discount rate in February 1992 (Padoa-Schioppa 1987).

In New Zealand politicians reformed the central bank in 1989. Under the new law, the government determines the inflation objectives, and the central bank governor is charged with implementing monetary policy to achieve that goal. Uniquely, the reform links the bank's policy performance with the central bank governor's tenure: the governor can be dismissed if the bank does not achieve the inflation target (Dalziel 1993; Walsh 1995b). Additionally, the governor must report to the Parliament regularly about the government's economic policy choices.

Perhaps the most spectacular monetary reform occurred in December 1991, when the EU member states committed themselves to an audacious experiment: the creation of an Economic and Monetary Union (EMU) with a single currency for all participating countries. The Maastricht Treaty established deadlines for the transition to a single currency and an institutional blueprint for the management of EU monetary policy. Under the plan, a European central bank, independent of direct political control, would administer the currency. Modeled after the Bundesbank, the bank's governing board is composed of six individuals unanimously appointed by the Council of Ministers and by one appointee from each participating member state. Board members are supposed to receive no instruction from their national governments. Finally, the bank's mandate requires the board to focus solely on price stability in determining monetary policy.

Member states also agreed to make their central banks independent as a precondition to participation in the final stage of EMU. Belgium, France, Spain, and Portugal moved promptly to follow through on this commitment.

However, not all industrial democracies moved so quickly to initiate central bank reform, even within the EU. In Britain, for example, the Conservative government thwarted reform efforts in the early 1990s. Not until 1997 did a newly elected Labour government increase the Bank of England's independence, granting the bank institutional authority over interest rates and reforming the bank's decision-making procedures. Moreover, several countries continue to have dependent central banks. Australia and Norway, for instance, have not increased the independence of their central banks.

The Puzzles of Central Bank Independence

Central bank institutions have obvious substantive importance—they affect monetary-policy choices and overall economic performance. But the issues surrounding central bank independence also inform larger debates in political economy concerning the relationship between politicians and bureaucrats, the influence of the international economy on domestic policy autonomy, the institutional consequences of electoral change, and the balance between economic optimization and democratic accountability. The following puzzles illustrate these issues.

Cross-National Variations in Central Bank Independence

The cross-national variation of central bank independence in the 1970s and 1980s raises some interesting questions about bureaucratic design and delegation. Given that central banks perform similar functions across countries, why did some countries have independent central banks while others possessed dependent central banks? Why were politicians in some countries willing to limit their control of monetary policy with an independent central bank?

Many political economists have noted an association between federalism and central bank independence. Prior to the 1990s, independent central banks tended to be found in federal systems, including Germany, Switzerland, and the United States (Banaian, Laney, and Willett 1983). Unitary systems—Britain, New Zealand, France—usually had dependent central banks. What explains this relationship? How does federalism affect the choice of central bank institutions?

The Commitment to an Independent Central Bank

A second set of questions concerns politicians' commitments to an independent central bank. An independent central bank limits the government's ability to manipulate monetary policy for its own short-term gain. In certain instances, conflict between an independent central bank and the cabinet can even cause the government to collapse (Berger 1997; Marsh 1992). Yet politicians in countries with an independent central bank have remained committed to those institutions.

The German Bundesbank's independence, for instance, allows it to pursue economic policies that run counter to the government's wishes, which occurred most visibly during the Social Democratic–led government of the 1970s and early 1980s. The program of the Social Democratic party, which became the senior party in government in 1969, emphasized the goal of full employment. In 1973–74, however, the bank implemented a restrictive monetary policy to combat the effects of the first oil crisis. Although this policy kept inflation in check, it cost thousands of jobs, despite the Social Democrats' employment objectives (Scharpf 1987). The government and the Bundesbank clashed again in the late 1970s. In 1978 Social Democratic Chancellor Helmut Schmidt decided to pursue expansionary macroeconomic policies in a coordinated effort with the United States to ignite the sluggish world economy. The advent of the second oil crisis, however, threatened unacceptably high levels of inflation. In response, the Bundesbank pushed interest rates to their highest postwar levels, effectively derailing the "German locomotive" before it left the station. These actions negated the government's ability to maintain employment levels, hurt the Social Democrats' popularity, and hastened their fall from government (Goodman 1992; Kennedy 1991; Marsh 1992; Scharpf 1987; Sturm 1989).

The Bundesbank's independence appears to limit the ability of German governments to produce the types of economic outcomes they prefer. Why did the Social Democratic–led government not change the institutional status of the bank to provide the policies it desired? Why have German politicians remained committed to an independent Bundesbank?

The Wave of Central Bank Reform

Patterns of central bank stability and reform across the industrial democracies also raise questions about the relationship between the international economy and domestic politics. With a few exceptions, central bank institutions changed infrequently from the 1950s to the early 1980s. Then in the late 1980s and 1990s, country after country adopted a more independent central bank. What can account for these trends?

The stability of central bank institutions in the 1970s and early 1980s warrants explanation, especially given the dramatic economic shocks of this period. First, the Bretton Woods international monetary system collapsed in the early 1970s. After World War II most industrial countries pegged their exchange rates to the U.S. dollar. The system operated smoothly through the 1950s, but strains appeared in the 1960s, when the commitment to a fixed exchange rate with the United States forced countries to "import" inflationary policy from the United States. In 1972 the Nixon administration abruptly ended this system and initiated a system of floating exchange rates. Many countries welcomed the floating exchange rate regime because it promised greater monetary-policy autonomy. One might have expected these states to reform their domestic monetary institutions in order to take advantage of this new autonomy.

Second, the energy shocks touched off high inflation in the industrial countries. In 1973–74 the oil-producing countries increased oil prices over 400 percent almost overnight. Uncertainty about the Iran situation in 1979–81 again increased oil prices. As a result, inflation entered double digits in many countries, levels not seen since the immediate postwar period. Central bank reform might have helped quell these crises, but again, no state made central bank independence a priority during this period. What factors account for the remarkable stability in central bank institutions during the 1970s despite the enormous changes in the international economic environment?

In turn, why did the wave of central bank reform take place across the industrial democracies in the late 1980s and 1990s? The temporal proximity of these reforms suggests that they shared a common cause. Changes in the international economy are a possible culprit. The size and pace of the international economy continued to grow during the 1980s and 1990s, as both technological changes and regulatory liberalization increased cross-border capital mobility. How did these developments influence the choice of central bank institutions? What are the mechanisms that link increased economic openness to domestic institutional change?

Variations in the Timing of Central Bank Reform

While some countries embraced central bank reform, other countries were slower to adopt independent central banks. And some countries have not increased the independence of their central banks. What explains these cross-national differences in the timing and nature of reform?

Britain, for instance, would have seemed an ideal candidate for early central bank reform. In the late 1970s, inflation in Britain was out of control, reaching 18 percent in 1980. Public discontent with the Labour government's economic performance swept the Conservatives into power in 1979. Under Margaret Thatcher the government implemented a drastic program designed to halt inflation. The government raised interest rates and announced strict monetary targets, hoping to limit the growth of the money supply. These measures plunged the economy into a recession. Unemployment quickly doubled and remained above 10 percent throughout most of the 1980s. But the recession had its intended effect; by 1986 inflation had fallen to less than 4 percent.

An independent central bank could have helped the Conservatives demonstrate their commitment to sound monetary policies and perhaps lowered the employment costs of disinflation. Additionally, an independent Bank of England might have prevented future Labour governments from manipulating monetary policy for their own electoral gain. Finally, an independent central bank, insulated from the short-term political pressures of Britain's antagonistic parties, could have provided greater policy stability, creating an environment in which economic agents could plan and invest for the future. Despite these potentially beneficial economic and political consequences, the Thatcher government never moved to grant the bank more independence. Why?

Central Bank Reform and Institutional Reform

Interestingly, central bank reform has coincided with the implementation of broader political reforms in several industrial democracies. For example, in Italy, just as the central bank received greater policy autonomy from the government in the early 1990s, the political system disintegrated under the weight of corruption scandals, increasing regional disparities, and voter dissatisfaction with the ruling parties, particularly the Christian Democrats. In a series of referenda, Italian voters approved a new mixed proportional representation–majoritarian electoral system. In Britain the Labour government announced the 1997 reform of the Bank of England amid plans for other institutional changes, including regional devolution and the exploration of electoral reform. Finally, in New Zealand the adoption of an independent central bank in 1989–90 occurred just prior to major electoral reform. In 1992–93 New Zealand voters rejected the majoritarian electoral system in favor of mixed-member proportional representation. What, if anything, explains the coincidence of central bank reform and these other institutional changes? Are both the result of an underlying cause?

The European Union's Commitment to the Single Currency

The Maastricht Treaty established the goal of an economic and monetary union for member states, a major step toward political integration. By signing the treaty, Europe's leaders hoped to build on the popular enthusiasm surrounding the completion of the single market by January 1993. Yet plans for a single currency immediately met with skepticism and mistrust. Many economists were wary of the scheme, noting that Europe did not yet constitute an optimal currency area and that European political institutions were probably not strong enough to handle the task. Although European business interests generally supported the project, they did not rally around the single currency as they had done with the 1992 project. The public response was apathetic, if not hostile, especially in Germany and northern Europe. Indeed, the ratification process did not go smoothly. In referenda Danish voters initially rejected the treaty and French voters passed it by only a thin margin. As a result, the future of the single currency remained in doubt throughout much of the 1990s.

Despite this lack of public support, most politicians in Europe continued to advocate the Maastricht plans for a single currency. And in January 1999, the euro came into existence. Why were Europe's politicians so committed to the single currency? Why were they willing to tolerate the short-term political costs associated with the transition to the euro? What does the euro imply for the EU's democratic deficit?

The questions raised by the patterns of central bank independence extend beyond issues of economic performance and speak to deeper debates concerning the nature of the relationship between markets and governments, capitalism and democracy, and accountability and representation. Explaining central bank reform can provide insight into how politicians balance political concerns and economic priorities, as well as international pressures and domestic goals.

Conventional Explanations

Simple political economy arguments do not provide satisfactory explanations for the choice of central bank institutions. Political economists, for example, often assume that governments are overridingly concerned with reelection, making them myopic manipulators of economic policy (Cukierman and Meltzer 1986; Nordhaus 1975; Rogoff and Sibert 1988; Tufte 1978). An independent central bank, however, limits the government's ability to manage monetary policy for its own short-term benefit. Consequently, the government may be prevented from generating economic booms around election time. If an independent central bank restricts the policy options available to the government, why would self-interested politicians ever agree to an independent central bank?

A second group of political economists contends that the economic objectives of the governing party shape monetary policy (Alesina 1989; Alesina and Sachs 1988; Havrilesky 1987; Hibbs 1987). Partisanship theories typically assume that Right parties place a priority on price stability, whereas Left parties emphasize employment and income redistribution. Given the empirical relationship between central bank independence and inflation performance, these theories imply that Right parties will institute independent central banks, whereas Left parties will choose dependent central banks (Goodman 1991). Yet central bank independence does not correlate with government partisanship. In Britain, for example, the Conservative government during the 1980s retained a dependent central bank, whereas in Germany the Social Democratic government of the 1970s remained committed to an independent Bundesbank. In addition, central bank reforms in France, Belgium, New Zealand, Italy, and Spain enjoyed cross-partisan support.

Explanations that focus on the economic consequences of central bank independence, electoral opportunism, or government partisanship cannot account for the variation of central bank institutions. They do not tell us why some countries were quicker to adopt independent central banks while monetary reform was delayed or thwarted in others. These arguments cannot explain the association between federalism and central bank independence or the coincidence of monetary reform and other institutional reforms.

To better explain the variation of central bank independence, I focus on the politics surrounding the choices of these institutions, particularly the role of political parties. In particular, I contend that the choice of central bank institutions reflects the potential for intraparty conflicts over economic and monetary policy.

Political Parties and the Supply of Central Bank Institutions

Traditional partisan and opportunistic models assume that political parties are unified actors. But parties are more than just sets of policy priorities. And winning elections requires more than just producing good economic outcomes around election time. Instead, political parties organize choices for voters, putting together packages of policy alternatives. Parties translate citizen demands into public policy, coordinate the legislative process, and in parliamentary systems, determine the composition of the cabinet. In short, parties are central to every step of the policy process: elections, legislation, and governance.

Political Parties and Elections

Political parties represent teams of politicians—politicians who sometimes have diverse preferences and incentives about the party's policy program (Aldrich 1995; Downs 1957). Although individual party politicians want to attain office themselves, they also have an interest in ensuring that other members of their political party hold office as well; many rewards of office are contingent on the electoral success and cooperation of other party members. Politicians need fellow party members to pass legislation. Additionally, the distribution of leadership positions in the legislature and the cabinet often reflects the party's overall electoral performance.

Differences between an individual candidate's objectives and the party's electoral goals, however, can create conflict within the party, especially in the area of economic and monetary policy. Individual party politicians, for instance, may have to appeal to constituents with opposing preferences over monetary policy. Or they may run for election nonconcurrently, giving them different incentives over policy sequencing. The intraparty divergence of these policy incentives can lead to conflicts—conflicts that can threaten the ability of the party to attain and remain in office.

Political parties therefore must balance the different interests of party politicians in order to ensure the party's success. Electorally, the party must make strategic choices about which sets of voters to pursue and then must design policies to appeal to those constituents (Boix 1998; Kitschelt 1994; Przeworski and Sprague 1986). The process of building and maintaining social coalitions is critical not only for the party's electoral viability but also for managing intraparty conflicts over economic and monetary policy.

Political Parties and Governance

Political parties also structure the composition of the cabinet (president, prime minister, cabinet ministers).[1] Party legislators usually delegate policy responsibility to leaders who in turn serve as cabinet ministers. In a multiparty government, parties delegate responsibility for policy areas to their coalition partners.[2] Typically, the executive handles policy implementation and develops new policy initiatives.

The delegation of monetary-policy authority to cabinet ministers creates a principal-agent relationship between backbench legislators, coalition partners, and the cabinet.[3] The cabinet potentially possesses a great deal of discretion of over monetary policy; that is, cabinet ministers may take certain policy decisions without formal approval from the legislature. Ministers also enjoy two informational advantages over backbench legislators and coalition partners, affording them a greater opportunity to manipulate policy for their own benefit. First, cabinet ministers are in a better position to develop the policy expertise necessary to predict the relationship between policies and outcomes. Second, they can shroud their policy choices in secrecy, hiding them from backbench legislators and coalition partners.

These information asymmetries may contribute to conflicts between backbench legislators, coalition partners, and government ministers. Because the reelection of party legislators and coalition partners depends in part on the government's economic policy, they must decide whether to trust the government to implement policies that reflect their interests. If party politicians (and coalition partners) face a variety of incentives over monetary policy, they are likely to distrust cabinet ministers. For instance, if the party appeals to constituents with diverse preferences over monetary policy, the cabinet's policy decisions will likely benefit certain constituents while hurting others, contributing to the potential for conflict within the party.

Backbench legislators and coalition partners, however, possess the ability to punish cabinet ministers. If the cabinet's policy choices produce unacceptable outcomes, backbench legislators and coalition partners may attempt to punish the government by removing the cabinet from office or thwarting its policy agenda. The information asymmetries of the policy process, therefore, can threaten the party's ability to remain in government, especially if party legislators and coalition partners face divergent incentives over monetary policy.

Central Bank Independence and Political Parties

It is my contention that an independent central bank can help overcome potential intraparty conflicts over monetary policy. Although the cabinet retains ultimate responsibility for economic and monetary policy, an independent central bank restricts the cabinet's discretion. An independent central bank controls monetary-policy instruments, removing day-to-day policy management from the direct control of the cabinet (Debelle and Fischer 1994; Fischer 1995; Grilli, Masciandaro, and Tabellini 1991; Havrilesky 1994b). Furthermore, an independent central bank can publicize its disputes with cabinet ministers (Berger 1997; Fair 1979; Goodman 1992; Havrilesky 1994b). Central bankers possess information about the cabinet's policy choices and their economic consequences—information that party legislators and the public need to monitor the cabinet. The structure of an independent bank protects central bankers from the cabinet's authority, allowing them to reveal that information. An independent central bank can therefore provide credible information about economic and monetary policy.

Such information can aid parties both in winning election and surviving in office. First, an independent central bank's credibility can help parties assemble and maintain electoral coalitions across constituents with diverse policy preferences. An independent central bank allows potential party supporters, financial markets, and the public to monitor the government's policy choices (Clark 1999; Maxfield 1997; Simmons 1994). It also provides assurances that cabinet ministers are unlikely to manipulate policy for short-term electoral or partisan gain, helping parties appeal to inflation-averse economic sectors (Hall and Franzese 1998; Iversen 1999). Finally, an independent central bank's credibility with financial markets may help keep long-term interest rates relatively low (Franzese 2000). Low interest rates reduce the cost of servicing public debt, giving the parties in government extra fiscal policy flexibility, which they may use to compensate different actors in their social coalitions.

An independent central bank can also help parties remain in office by drawing attention to situations in which cabinet ministers pressure the central bank—either directly or indirectly—to manipulate policy in ways that deviate from policy objectives. Party legislators and coalition partners can use that information to ensure that the cabinet does not pursue policies with harmful electoral consequences. Faced with a veto threat, government ministers in turn will not make policy choices that do not reflect the interests of their legislative principals.

Additionally, an independent central bank can verify that cabinet ministers attempted to achieve certain economic outcomes, even if those policy choices had unintended consequences unacceptable to their legislative and coalition supporters. Party legislators and coalition partners, therefore, will be less likely to withdraw their support from the government in the face of negative economic outcomes. The credibility of an independent central bank, therefore, prevents intraparty conflict. As a result, parties remain in office longer, even if party politicians have different incentives with respect to monetary policy.

Explaining Central Bank Independence

An independent central bank therefore can help parties win and hold office. The credibility of an independent central bank can help parties build and maintain social coalitions by signaling the government's commitment to monetary-policy stability. By publicizing disputes with the cabinet over monetary policy, it can also help prevent potential intraparty conflicts over monetary policy from shortening the government's tenure in office.

I contend that these political functions critically shape the choice of central bank institutions. In particular, politicians will choose an independent central bank when potential conflicts over monetary policy threaten the ability of the governing party(ies) to remain in office. These conflicts are likely when (1) party politicians have divergent incentives over monetary policy (if, for example, the party's constituents hold diverse policy preferences) and (2) backbench legislators and coalition partners can credibly threaten to punish government ministers. When party politicians have relatively similar monetary-policy incentives or when the intraparty divergence of monetary-policy incentives does not jeopardize the governing party's ability to hold office, the bank will be less independent of government control. Differences in these variables across systems and over time can explain the puzzles of central bank independence.

Cross-National Variation in the 1970s and 1980s

Systemic differences in the potential for intraparty conflict over monetary policy can explain the cross-national variation of central bank independence in the 1970s and 1980s, particularly the association between federalism and central bank independence. Federal systems are likely to create more potential for intraparty conflict. In large federal systems, politicians face a variety of incentives over monetary policy. Constituents possess a range of preferences over economic policy in part because of regional differences in economic activity. Additionally, the political institutions of federalism—powerful regional offices, bicameral legislatures, and so on—compel party politicians to appeal to different sets of constituents and to run for office at different times. Consequently, the possibility of conflict over monetary policy is high in federal systems, giving politicians an incentive to choose an independent central bank.

The Wave of Central Bank Reform in the 1990s

I argue that the wave of central bank reform in the 1990s reflects developments in the party systems of the industrial democracies over the previous 20 years—developments that have increased the potential for intraparty conflicts over economic and monetary policy. In particular, changes in the patterns of electoral support for the main governing parties and decreases in the capability of cabinet ministers to deliver promised policy outcomes have hurt the ability of the main governing parties to attain and retain office.

First, the traditional social coalitions of many parties in the industrial democracies have eroded. Voter dealignment has contributed to increased electoral volatility and less-predictable electoral outcomes. Furthermore, economic developments have changed constituent demands over economic and monetary policy. Because of increases in economic openness, the rise of the service sector, and higher levels of wealth, new divisions over economic policy have replaced traditional class-based demands—divisions between exposed and sheltered sectors, between manufacturing and service sectors, between rising and declining sectors, between the private and public sectors, and between owners of mobile and specific assets. Where once parties could depend on blocks of voters for electoral support, these parties now have to appeal to constituents with more varied demands over economic and monetary policy. The diversity of these demands increases the potential for intraparty policy conflict.

At the same time, the capacity of cabinet ministers to deliver promised outcomes to party legislators and constituents has also decreased. The emergence of high public debt in many industrial democracies during the 1970s limited the flexibility of fiscal policy, pushing cabinet ministers to rely on monetary policy to manage the macroeconomy. But established monetary-policy choices no longer produced predictable outcomes. The combination of high inflation and high unemployment in the 1970s undermined confidence in the traditional policy trade-off between inflation and unemployment. Increased levels of economic openness exacerbated the problems of policy management, making national economies more vulnerable to external shocks and limiting national policy autonomy. Decreased policy effectiveness made it more difficult for cabinet ministers to satisfy party legislators, coalition partners, and constituents.

The electoral volatility of the 1970s was an early signal of these fundamental changes to party systems in the industrial democracies. The political fallout of the 1970s, however, could easily be attributed to exogenous economic shocks, limiting the urgency of institutional reform in many countries. But the persistence of intraparty conflicts over economic policy through the 1980s indicated that these developments had far-reaching impact on the ability of parties to compete for and hold office. Therefore, many political parties altered their electoral strategies and policy priorities in the 1980s and 1990s to balance conflicting interests, rebuild social coalitions, and maintain electoral viability (Boix 1998; Kitschelt 1994).

I argue that this strategic repositioning included monetary reform. In both Italy and Britain, for example, monetary reform took place as the governing parties sought to reposition themselves in the political space, indicating that these reforms reflected political as well as economic calculations. In Italy the decisions to enter the European Monetary System (EMS) and initiate the divorce of the Bank of Italy in the late 1970s and early 1980s occurred during a period when the Christian Democratic Party was reassessing its electoral and policy strategies. The British Labour Party's decision to support more independence for the Bank of England in 1997 represented a desire to appeal to both markets and more-moderate constituents.

Variations in the Timing of Reform

Political calculations can also help explain variations in the timing of central bank reform. Where intraparty conflicts over monetary policy threatened the ability of the governing parties to remain in office, politicians had incentives to adopt an independent central bank. By preventing conflicts over monetary policy, an independent central bank could extend the viability of the established governing parties, despite changes in the policy preferences of their traditional constituent bases. In contrast, where the configuration of domestic institutions prevented intraparty conflict from hurting the ability of parties to remain in office, politicians had fewer incentives to adopt an independent central bank. In these systems, politicians delayed or entirely put off central bank reform.

Again, the Italian and British examples provide illustrations. Although the Christian Democrats remained the largest party in Italy during the 1970s, their position at the end of the decade appeared increasingly vulnerable. The party itself was divided over how best to deal with the power of the labor unions and the economy. Voters were exasperated with the party's indecisiveness and factionalization. Electoral support for the Communist Party, the Christian Democrats' main rival, had increased substantially throughout the 1970s. Without some sort of reform measures, the Christian Democratic Party was in danger of losing office. As a result, the Christian Democratic government initiated central bank reform in 1981, along with other reforms in the area of regional policy, fiscal policy, and industrial policy.

In Britain, on the other hand, the Conservatives' position in office remained secure throughout the 1980s and early 1990s, even though the party itself was sharply divided over economic policy (and later, policy toward Europe). The institutions of the Westminster system provided strong disincentives for dissatisfied backbench legislators to challenge the government. Party leaders could discipline rebellious backbench members of Parliament (MPs). In addition, because opposition MPs have almost no policy influence, party MPs were less willing to risk their own status as members of the governing party by withdrawing support from their own cabinet. These institutions muted internal party divisions, ensuring that the government saw no threat to its ability to hold office. As a result, the Conservative government did not reform the Bank of England. Indeed, it blocked a bill to grant the central bank more independence in 1993–94.

Central Bank Reform and Institutional Reform

The development of intraparty conflicts and the erosion of the social coalitions underpinning the traditional parties can account for the coincidence of central bank reform and other institutional reforms, including devolution and electoral reform. In part these reform experiments represent efforts by the governing parties to respond to new constituent interests and electoral volatility. Faced with changing constituent demands, less-committed electoral support, and new political challengers, these parties are searching for ways to revitalize their electoral base and protect their political fortunes. Central bank reform represents one of these strategic experiments.

Social Coalitions and the Single Currency in the European Union

Politicians' commitment to the euro also reflects their perception that delegating monetary policy to the European level would help manage intraparty conflicts over economic policy and allow them to rebuild social coalitions at the domestic level. Monetary integration could enhance their political fortunes in a variety of ways. First, the single currency removed a potentially divisive issue from the domestic political agenda. With monetary policy off the table, politicians could use other issues to foster agreement and support among constituents. Second, the single currency would solidify the single market and presumably lead to stronger economic growth, providing higher tax revenues and increased job creation. Third, monetary union would insulate national politicians from the political consequences of international currency and financial markets. Finally, the Maastricht Treaty's convergence criteria helped politicians pursue fiscal retrenchment by providing specific goals and incentives for deficit reduction.

To enjoy these benefits, politicians in the member states would have to give up national control over monetary policy. But under the European Monetary System, monetary-policy autonomy was already limited: member states had to mimic German monetary policies to maintain the value of their currencies against the D-mark. Although the single currency means that no country will have monetary-policy autonomy, the structure of the European central bank does allow national representatives (in the form of central bank governors) to participate in the formulation of European monetary policy.

An examination of the problems and incentives of political parties, therefore, helps to explain Europe's commitment to the single currency, even though it entailed enormous risks and popular apathy. The single currency promised politicians in the EU an opportunity to rebuild and reshape their electoral coalitions. The challenge for Europe's politicians will be to incorporate those sectors that are hurt by the single currency into social coalitions that support not only the current configuration of political and economic institutions but also further European integration.

Overview

In the following chapters, I examine in more depth the issues raised here. In chapter 2, I define the dependent variable, central bank independence, and discuss the variation of central bank independence across systems and over time. I also review how the macroeconomic, international political economy, and bureaucratic delegation literatures have approached the choice of central bank institutions.

In chapter 3, I develop an explanation for the choice of central bank institutions that focuses on the principal-agent relationship between party legislators, coalition partners, and cabinet ministers. I argue that politicians will choose an independent central bank to alleviate the conflicts created by the information asymmetries of the policy process. The argument provides implications about (1) the patterns of policy disputes between governments and independent central bankers, (2) the cross-national variation of central bank independence between 1970 and 1990, and (3) the durability of cabinets in systems with an independent central bank. The following four chapters explore those implications.

In chapter 4, I examine several episodes of potential conflict between German politicians and the Bundesbank to illustrate how central bankers behave strategically in the policy process. Even in countries with an independent central bank, the formulation of monetary policy depends on the strategic interaction between politicians and central bankers. The formal institutions of an independent central bank mean that central bankers are responsible to multiple principals, allowing them to challenge the cabinet's policy choices. Party politicians and constituents can learn about the cabinet's behavior from this interaction.

I discuss in chapter 5 the correlation between federalism and central bank independence in the 1970s and 1980s. First, I delineate the conditions under which politicians will choose an independent central bank, focusing on the potential for intraparty conflict over monetary policy. I examine how the configuration of political institutions and the distribution of voter preferences shape the relationship between party legislators, coalition partners, and cabinet ministers. I then use these variables to examine episodes of central bank choice in Germany and Britain. Finally, I test the relationship between incentive divergence, the threat of punishment, and central bank independence statistically on the cross-national variation of central bank independence in 18 industrial democracies.

In chapter 6, I assess whether an independent central bank can help prevent conflicts between backbench legislators, coalition partners, and government ministers by testing the effect of central bank independence on cabinet durability in 16 parliamentary democracies. If an independent central bank prevents these conflicts, then cabinets in parliamentary systems will survive longer than cabinets in similar systems with dependent central banks. The results indicate that an independent central bank increases cabinet durability under conditions of economic openness—precisely where one would expect more intraparty conflicts over monetary policy. The statistical results in turn provide predictions about the conditions under which politicians will find it in their interest to adopt an independent central bank.

I examine in chapter 7 central bank reform in Italy and in Britain. In both countries, the economic developments of the 1970s and 1980s increased the potential for conflict over economic policy within the main governing parties. In Italy these conflicts threatened the position of the Christian Democrats as the dominant party, giving them an incentive to support a more-independent central bank. In Britain the Labour Party's decision to grant the Bank of England more independence reflects a desire to maintain its potentially fragile electoral coalition—a coalition that includes constituents with heterogeneous economic-policy preferences. Moreover, in both cases, central bank reform was only one of a series of other policy and institutional reforms.

In chapter 8, I discuss the transition to the single currency in the EU, focusing on the uncertainties and doubts of the process during the 1990s. Politicians' commitment to the euro reflects in part the domestic political benefits of a single currency.

I conclude by discussing in chapter 9 the relationship between central bank independence and democratic governance.

Chapter 2

What Is Central Bank Independence?

In the 1990s, central bank independence became a universal catchphrase for economists, international agencies, and policymakers interested in improving economic performance. Nevertheless, the term *independence* meant different things to different people (e.g., de Haan 1997; Forder 1998b; Mangano 1998; Prast 1996; Waller 1995). Political economists often use the concept of independence in two distinct, if related, ways (Hall and Franzese 1998).

One set of political economists equates central bank independence with a bias in monetary policy directed toward price stability. Many models of monetary policy-making, for example, assume that an independent central bank emphasizes controlling inflation at the expense of other objectives. Drawing on Rogoff (1985), these political economists argue that the "conservative" policy preferences of the central banker represent the key aspect of independence. This interpretation implies that the bank's legislated policy mandate should emphasize price stability as the primary, if not sole, policy objective.

A second set of political economists contends that central bank independence refers to the amount of influence that politicians exert on monetary policy. That is, a central bank acts "independently" when it takes a policy decision without pressure from politicians or even against the policy preferences of government leaders. Central bank dependence indicates the situation whereby government ministers determine policy directly.

The fundamental problem with these conceptions of central bank independence is that both policy bias and political influence over policy are endogenous to the policy process (Forder 1996). Monetary policy and the political influence over policy result from the strategic interaction between central bankers and politicians—interaction that takes place within the legal framework of the central bank and the configuration of domestic policy institutions.

Critics have in fact sought to address these problems. First, some political economists have pointed out the difficulty of legislating a conservative policy bias. The bank's political principals, for instance, may not be able to gauge the policy preferences of prospective central bankers. Or central bankers' policy preferences may change once in office (de Haan 1997; Mangano 1998; Walsh 1993). These critics contend that politicians, instead of choosing a "conservative" central banker, should focus on designing institutions that will induce the central banker to pursue "socially optimal" monetary policies (Fratianni, von Hagen, and Waller 1997; Persson and Tabelinni 1993; Waller and Walsh 1996; Walsh 1995b, 1995c, 1999). Drawing on the principal-agent literature, these economists demonstrate that politicians can exploit a banker's self-interest to achieve desirable outcomes through a performance contract that ties the central banker's compensation to the achievement of preannounced inflation targets. This "contracting" approach to central bank independence formed the basis for central bank reform in New Zealand.[1]

Another group of political economists examines how the legal framework of central bank institutions affects political influence over monetary policy. Lohmann (1997, 1998b), for instance, investigates a situation in which the central bank has multiple principals, each with the power to appoint members to the governing board—a feature of independent central banks in Germany and the United States. She demonstrates that the heterogeneity of appointments can prevent the manipulation of monetary policy surrounding elections or for partisan reasons, even if each central banker is a perfect agent of the political body that appointed him or her—that is, even if central bankers are not conservative. Waller (1989, 1992a) shows how the staggered timing of appointments can help reduce the amplitude of partisan cycles even if board members have partisan policy preferences.

These theoretical arguments and the extensive qualitative literature on central banks (e.g., Goodman 1992; Heisenberg 1999; Kennedy 1991; Kettl 1986; Marsh 1992; Maxfield 1997; Scharpf 1987; Woolley 1984) all point to the important role that the interaction between politicians and bureaucrats plays in the formation of monetary policy, even in countries with an independent central bank. Central bank "independence" does not mean that monetary policy is always dedicated to price stability or that politicians retain no influence over monetary policy. Instead, the central bank's formal rules and legal structure affect how politicians and central bankers interact, shaping both the types of policies that are chosen and how much politicians control policy. Because the legal structure of the central bank shapes this interaction, I define central bank independence on the basis of formal rules and statutes.

Defining Independence

Three formal aspects of central bank institutions make a central bank more or less independent of direct political control. One dimension of independence is the control of monetary-policy instruments (Debelle and Fischer 1994; Fischer 1995; Grilli, Masciandaro, and Tabellini 1991; Havrilesky 1994a, 1994b). Fischer (1995), for instance, distinguishes between "goal" independence and "instrument" independence. Goal independence refers to the capacity of the central bank to choose the "final goals" of monetary policy. Instrument independence, on the other hand, evaluates the central bank's autonomy in choosing the levers of monetary policy, including restrictions on monetary financing of budget deficits. The less influence that politicians can exert on monetary-policy instruments—that is, the greater the instrument independence—the more independent the central bank.

Second, the appointments procedure shapes a central bank's independence. An appointments procedure that limits the cabinet's ability to determine the composition of the bank's entire governing body increases the bank's independence. This may involve a decentralized procedure that allows other bodies—for example, the legislature, states, or commercial banks—to appoint some central bankers. Other limitations on the cabinet's authority over appointments include lengthy terms for central bank directors and an appointments schedule nonconcurrent with the government's electoral cycle.

The third aspect of independence centers on the cabinet's ability to punish the central bank using ex-post sanctions, such as oversight (Lupia and McCubbins 1993; McCubbins and Schwartz 1983), dismissal (Lohmann 1992), policy veto (Ferejohn and Shipan 1990), and budget cuts.[2] Restrictions on the cabinet's ability to punish the central bank increase the bank's independence. Politicians can still punish an independent central bank by changing its charter or altering its institutional structure. But these actions tend to be costly and require the support of politicians outside the cabinet to be implemented. In countries with dependent banks, on the other hand, governments retain the ability to punish central bankers through a policy veto, personnel dismissal, and budget cuts.

Central bank independence therefore reflects the bank's ability to control monetary instruments, restrictions on the cabinet's influence over the appointments procedure, and limitations on the cabinet's ability to punish the central bank. According to this definition, central bank independence is not a dichotomous variable. Instead, it is a continuum. Institutional reforms can make the central bank more or less independent of direct government control.

Measuring Independence

Because relations between governments and central bankers are complex and dynamic, measuring central bank independence is difficult. Political economists have employed a variety of legal characteristics to measure independence, including procedures for the appointment, term duration, and dismissal of central bank directors; government veto over monetary policy; explicit policy goals; budgetary autonomy for the central bank; performance incentives for bank directors; limitations on monetary financing of budget deficits; and control over monetary instruments (Alesina 1988b; Alesina and Summers 1993; Burdekin and Willett 1991; Cukierman 1992; Cukierman, Webb, and Neyapti 1992; Eijffinger and de Haan 1996; Eizenga 1987; Grilli, Masciandaro, and Tabellini 1991; Havrilesky 1994b; Neumann 1991; Swinburne and Castello-Branco 1991; Tavelli, Tullio, and Spinelli 1998).[3] Most indices combine these factors to produce either a one-dimensional or two-dimensional scale of central bank independence (see table 1).

These legal indicators provide an a priori measure of central bank independence.[4] In principle, the availability of central bank statutes should make these measures reliable, although political economists have criticized some indices for misinterpreting the statutes of specific central banks (e.g., Forder 1996; Mangano 1998; Pollard 1993). Although each scale emphasizes slightly different factors, they are in relative agreement about the ranking of central bank independence across systems. Rather than develop my own ranking of central bank independence, I use a variety of these scales for empirical tests.

Central Bank Institutions

Table 1 lists rankings of central bank independence for 18 industrial democracies from 1970 to 1990. The scales generally recognize the German Bundesbank as the most independent bank in the world. Most analysts also agree that the U.S. Federal Reserve and the Swiss National Bank possess a good deal of independence. At the other end of the spectrum, analysts traditionally classify the Bank of England, the Bank of France, and the Bank of Italy as relatively dependent banks. In the following sections, I describe the institutions of the German Bundesbank, the Bank of England, the Bank of Italy, and the Bank of France.

The German Bundesbank

Political economists agree that the Bundesbank is one of the most independent central banks in the world. It retains complete control over all monetary instru-

TABLE 1. Rankings of Central Bank Independence, 1970–90

Country	Grilli, Masciandaro, and Tabellini[a]	Alesina and Summers[b]	Cukierman[c]	Mean Independence[d]
Germany	0.87	1.00	0.66	0.84
Switzerland	0.80	1.00	0.68	0.83
United States	0.80	0.875	0.51	0.73
Canada	0.73	0.625	0.46	0.61
Austria	0.60	0.625	0.58	0.60
Netherlands	0.67	0.625	0.42	0.57
Denmark	0.53	0.625	0.47	0.54
Ireland[e]	0.47	0.625	0.39	0.49
Australia	0.60	0.50	0.31	0.47
France[f]	0.47	0.50	0.28	0.42
Britain[g]	0.40	0.50	0.31	0.42
Japan[h]	0.40	0.625	0.16	0.40
Norway	0.44[m]	0.50	0.14	0.40
Sweden[i]	0.44[m]	0.50	0.27	0.40
Belgium[j]	0.47	0.50	0.19	0.39
Italy	0.33	0.45	0.16	0.33
Spain[k]	0.33	0.375	0.21	0.31
New Zealand[l]	0.20	0.25	0.27	0.24

Note: All rankings normalized from 0 (low independence) to 1 (high independence).

[a]Grilli, Masciandaro, and Tabellini (1991) Total Independence.

[b]Alesina and Summers's (1993) index, computed by averaging the Bade and Parkin/Alesina index and their conversion of the Grilli, Masciandaro, and Tabellini scale.

[c]Cukierman's (1992) index of Legal Independence (LVAU).

[d]Mean independence, computed from Grilli, Masciandaro, and Tabellini (1991), Alesina and Summers (1993), and Cukierman (1992).

[e]Ranking prior to 1998 reform.

[f]Ranking prior to 1993 reform.

[g]Ranking prior to 1997 reform.

[h]Ranking prior to 1998 reform.

[i]Ranking prior to 1998 reform.

[j]Ranking prior to 1993 reform.

[k]Ranking prior to 1994 reform.

[l]Ranking prior to 1989 reform.

[m]Unranked by Grilli, Masciandaro, and Tabellini (1991). The missing values were imputed by regressing the Grilli, Masciandaro, and Tabellini index on the Cukierman and Alesina and Summers indices for all countries. Using the coefficients from the equation and the values of the missing countries on the Cukierman and Alesina and Summers indices, I computed the missing values for the Grilli, Masciandaro, and Tabellini index. The correlation between the Grilli, Masciandaro, and Tabellini index and the Cukierman index is $r = 0.86$. The correlation between the Grilli, Masciandaro, and Tabellini index and the Alesina and Summers index is $r = 0.89$ The correlation between the Cukierman Index and the Alesina and Summers index is $r = 0.85$. All three correlations are significant at the 0.001 level.

ments. A government representative may participate in meetings of the Central Bank Council but cannot vote on policy proposals. The government possesses no veto power over the bank's policy actions, although it has the authority to delay the implementation of a Bundesbank policy decision for two weeks. In practice, however, a government has never exercised this authority.

The government appoints only a minority of the Bundesbank Council, the central bank's governing board. Instead, each Land (state) government was until recently entitled to choose one representative to the board. Although technical expertise played a role, appointees usually reflected the partisan character of the appointing Land government. The central government selects the other part of the council, called the Directorate, composed of the president and vice president of the bank and up to eight other members. The Directorate is responsible for carrying out the daily functions of the bank. Both members of the Directorate and Land central bank presidents are normally appointed for eight-year terms.

In 1993, the statutes of the Bundesbank were modified to incorporate the eastern Lander into the system (chap. 5). The postunification reform reduced the number of Lander appointments by requiring some Lander to appoint their representatives jointly. It also reduced the potential number of members on the Directorate to eight, preserving the minority status of central government appointees on the council.

Finally, although the government lacks ex-post controls over the Bundesbank, the independence of the bank does not have constitutional status.[5] Instead, a simple legislative act can change the bank's institutional structure. Consequently, the bank must ensure that it has enough political support to maintain its autonomy and takes seriously even implied threats to its independence.

The Bank of England

Founded over 300 years ago and nationalized in 1946, the Bank of England regularly ranked near the bottom of the scales of independence. Throughout the postwar period, the government determined monetary policy (Cairncross 1988; Fay 1988; Kynaston 1995). Until recently, the chancellor of the Exchequer controlled monetary instruments directly. The government appointed the central bank governor and the Court of Directors. Finally, unlike many other central banks, the Bank of England was responsible for the supervision and regulation of the banking system. Political economists argue that this supervisory role detracted from the bank's ability to focus on the management of monetary policy.

Nonetheless, the Bank of England possessed a solid reputation for policy expertise. Bank officials regularly participated in the policy-making process, offering opinions and policy evaluations. Bank officials discounted their lack of legal independence, arguing that it was "more than offset by the greater degree of influence we can bring to bear on the whole range of the government's economic and fiscal policies" (*Financial Times,* 2 November 1989). In the early 1990s, the bank became more open in its criticism of the government's monetary policies (*Guardian,* 20 May 1991, 1 November 1991, 17 December 1993). This critical stance became institutionalized in 1993, when the bank no longer cleared its annual inflation report with the government prior to publication.

In May 1997, the newly elected Labour government implemented a number of changes to the legal status of the Bank of England (chap. 7). Under the reform, the bank gained institutional control over interest rates and is charged with using monetary policy to meet the government's inflation target. A Monetary Committee, composed of the governor, two deputy governors, and six other experts, takes policy decisions. The chancellor appoints a majority of the committee, including the governor, deputy governors, and four of the experts. A representative from the Treasury can attend meetings of the committee but does not have a vote in policy. In extreme circumstances, the government, with the Parliament's approval, may issue instructions to the bank concerning interest rates. The reform also limited the bank's role in regulation of the banking system.

The Bank of Italy

For much of the postwar period, international observers classified the Bank of Italy as dependent. The government controlled the appointments procedure, selecting the bank's governor and the other members of its directorate—a director general and two deputy directors general. These individuals possessed responsibility for almost all of the bank's activities. Additionally, the government could until recently influence monetary policy in a number of ways. First, the government had to approve changes in interest rates, reserve requirements, and exchange-rate decisions. In 1992, the bank received control of monetary-policy instruments. Second, the bank had to finance government expenditures. The Treasury can still borrow up to 14 percent of total expenditures in the budget law. Above this limit, the parliament may authorize an "extraordinary advance" to finance spending. Finally, between 1975 and 1981, the bank was obligated to purchase unsold government securities. The so-called divorce ended this requirement (chap. 7).

Despite the Bank of Italy's statutory dependence, its technical expertise and a history of nonpartisan appointments have given it a reputation for competence and impartiality. One oft-quoted businessman stated, "It is quite possible to run the economy without the government provided that . . . the Bank of

Italy, one of the most modern central banks with an excellent research staff, runs credit policy" (Allum 1973, 246). Unlike other government agencies, the bank possessed an outstanding research department. Consequently, during the 1950s and 1960s, the government regularly consulted the bank on major economic decisions (Goodman 1992).

At the same time, however, the bank's legal obligations to finance budget deficits made it subservient to the government's wishes. Bank officials have at times appeared uncomfortable with their position, recognizing the conflict between the bank's legal duties and their desire for economic responsibility. During the early 1970s, as government budget deficits began to explode, Governor Guido Carli expressed this tension publicly:

> [I wonder] whether the Bank could have refused, or could still refuse, to finance the public sector's deficit by abstaining from exercising the faculty, granted by law, to purchase government securities. Refusal would have made it impossible for the Government to pay the salaries of the armed forces, of the judiciary and of civil servants, and the pensions of most citizens. . . . It would be a seditious act, which would be followed by a paralysis of the public administration. One must ensure that the public administration continues to function, even if the economy grinds to a halt. (Goodman 1992, 148)

Bank of France

Since its creation in 1800 under Napoleon, the Bank of France lacked autonomy from the government. Nationalized in 1946, the government appointed 12 of the 13 members of the bank's General Council, the main policy-making body, including the governor and the two deputy governors. The governor and the deputy governors did not have a fixed term and could have been fired by the president at any time. The bank's mandate did not mention price stability but charged the bank with overseeing money and credit. Monetary policy was designed to facilitate industrial and agricultural development, subordinating concerns about inflation to the need for economic growth (Goodman 1992; Loriaux 1991; Zysman 1983).

Politicians placed central bank reform on the agenda in the run up to the 1993 election. In late 1992, Valery Giscard d'Estaing, former French president and leader of the center-right party the Union for French Democracy (UDF), announced his support for an independent central bank. This move reflected in part the need to head off potential intraparty conflicts within the UDF over the goals of French monetary policy (*The Economist,* 16 January 1993; *Guardian,* 25 January 1993). In response, the Socialists also announced their support for immediate reform (*Le Monde,* 4 January 1993).

Shortly after the election, the new Right government under Prime Minister Edouard Balladur announced its plans for a more independent central bank (*Le Monde*, 5 April 1993, 19 April 1993, 20 April 1993, 22 April 1993). Under the reform, a 12-member Monetary Policy Committee, modeled on the U.S. Federal Reserve's Open Market Committee, controls monetary-policy instruments. This committee includes the bank's governor and two deputy governors, each appointed by the central government for a fixed six-year term. They cannot be dismissed for policy reasons. The other nine members of the committee are appointed from a list of nominees drawn up by institutions including the judiciary and the parliament. Members of the committee cannot seek or accept instructions from the government. The bank's mandated policy goal is price stability "within the framework of the government's general economic policy."[6]

Political Control and Central Bank Independence

To many observers, the formal and legal rules of an independent central bank make it appear that politicians have abdicated policy responsibility to the central bank. Indeed, popular accounts of monetary policy often emphasize an independent central bank's political power in economic policy-making. Even some academic accounts imply that an independent central bank autonomously controls policy, free from political influence.

Both theoretical and empirical research into bureaucratic delegation and central banks, however, suggests that such conclusions are unwarranted. Independence does not mean that politicians have abdicated control of monetary policy. Qualitative accounts of monetary policy-making in countries with an independent central bank illustrate the strategic interaction between politicians and central bank bureaucrats in the formulation of monetary policy (e.g., Goodman 1992; Heisenberg 1999; Kennedy 1991; Kettl 1986; Marsh 1992; Scharpf 1987; Sturm 1989; Woolley 1984). Quantitative analyses also demonstrate evidence of political influence on monetary policy (e.g., Beck 1987, 1990a, 1990b; Berger and Woitek 1997b; Granato 1996; Grier 1989; Havrilesky 1993; Lohmann 1997, 1998a; Vaubel 1997). In particular, politicians retain two key channels of influence with an independent central bank: appointments and threats to the bank's institutional status (Lohmann 1998a).

Appointments

Appointments represent perhaps the most effective method of ensuring that bureaucracies pursue policies favored by elected politicians. By carefully choosing individuals to fill vacancies, politicians can obtain preferred outcomes even without significant ex-post authority (Calvert, McCubbins, and Weingast 1989; Hammond, Hill, and Miller 1986; Moe 1987).

For example, research on both the U.S. Federal Reserve and the German Bundesbank demonstrates that appointments procedures influence monetary policy. In the United States, political economists have examined the behavior of appointees to the Federal Open Market Committee (FOMC), the Federal Reserve's main decision-making body. Twelve members compose the FOMC: seven governors appointed by the federal government (i.e., the president with the Senate's approval) and five bank presidents, selected by the regional banks. The FOMC meets about eight times a year to determine the Federal Reserve's open market operations. Studies find that nongovernment appointees dissent more often from Federal Reserve decisions in favor of tight monetary policy than do governors, suggesting that the president's appointees are more willing to accommodate political pressures (Belden 1989; Chappell, Havrilesky, and MacGregor 1993; Havrilesky and Gildea 1992; Gildea 1990; Havrilesky and Schweitzer 1990; McGregor 1996). Further, researchers argue that presidents often choose appointments not only to influence policy (Chang 1997; Morris 2000; Waller 1992a, 1992b) but also to appeal to interest groups (Havrilesky and Gildea 1992). Staggered appointments to the Federal Reserve, however, help prevent the president from stacking the FOMC (Chang 1997; Nokken and Sala 2000; Waller 1989).

In Germany, the majority of the Central Bank Council is composed of Land central bank presidents, each appointed by a Land government. These individuals usually reflect the monetary preferences of the appointing Land government, with Christian Democratic appointees favoring tighter monetary policies than Social Democratic appointees. Lohmann (1997, 1998a) and Vaubal (1997) demonstrate that German monetary policy varies according to which political party has a majority of appointments on the council (see also Berger and Woitek 1997a).

Threats to the Bank's Status

Politicians also use threats to the central bank's institutional status to signal their policy preferences. Research on the U.S. Federal Reserve shows that politicians signal their monetary-policy preferences to the central bank by issuing policy statements to indicate their preferences over the future course of monetary policy or to voice their dissatisfaction with present policy (Havrilesky 1988, 1993; Kane 1980; Morris 2000; Waller 1989, 1991). These policy signals appear to affect policy, especially when accompanied by a credible threat of sanction. Havrilesky (1993), for instance, finds evidence that the Federal Reserve systematically responds to congressional policy signaling, particularly legislative threats to increase its accountability or enlarge political involvement in policy-making. Interestingly, the Federal Reserve reacts to these threats by incorporating demands from the administration into its policy decisions.

In Germany, threats to the Bundesbank's status also affect the bank's behavior, making it more cooperative to the government's policy demands (chap. 4). For instance, Chancellor Helmut Schmidt claimed that he threatened to reform the Bundesbank if it did not go along with plans for German participation in the EMS in 1979.

Empirically, politicians rarely sanction central banks. Indeed, legislative oversight appears to play little role in monetary policy-making, regardless of the central bank's status (LeLoup and Woolley 1991; Munger and Roberts 1990; Woolley and LeLoup 1989). The infrequency of sanctions against central bankers has two plausible interpretations. First, one could argue that politicians have relinquished monetary policy to unaccountable central bankers. The second interpretation, drawn from the delegation literature, suggests that the infrequency of sanctions reflects politicians' satisfaction with central bankers.[7] To avoid punishment, central bankers anticipate the policy preferences of their political principals and incorporate them into their policy decisions. Because the bank has already taken actions desired by its political principals, politicians have no need to punish the bank.

Independence and Political Control

Although politicians retain the ability to influence policy in countries with an independent central bank through the appointments procedure and threats to the bank's status, the central bank's formal characteristics shape the methods of political influence and control. The legal rules of central bank institutions help define the strategic interaction between central bankers and politicians. With a relatively dependent central bank, central bank bureaucrats are accountable to one political principal: the cabinet. The cabinet decides whom to hire and whom to fire. An independent central bank, on the other hand, is responsible to political actors beyond the cabinet—usually the legislature. With a decentralized appointments procedure, each political principal determines a portion of the bank's governing board. Further, punishing an independent central bank through changes to its structure or mandate requires the cooperation of both the cabinet and a legislative majority.

An independent central bank's multiple principals have consequences for the bank's behavior. First, independent central bankers can increase their range of bureaucratic discretion by playing one principal off another (McCubbins, Noll, and Weingast 1989). Because both the cabinet and the legislature need to approve changes to the bank's structure, an independent central bank can protect itself by ensuring that either the cabinet or the legislature—or at least one veto point in the policy process—is satisfied with the bank's performance (Keefer and Stasavage 2000; Morris 2000). Second, an independent central bank's position allows it to publicize policy disputes with its political principals, particularly the cabinet. The bank can point out when the cabinet's policy plans will not have the promised consequences. It can also make other actors aware if the cabinet is trying to influence monetary policy indirectly.

Careful consideration of how the institutional environment influences strategic behavior not only between central bankers and politicians but also between politicians themselves should allow us to make predictions about policymaking strategies and outputs. It will also yield insight into the question of why central bank independence varies across systems and over time.

Approaches to the Choice of Central Bank Institutions

Three literatures address central bank choice and reform: macroeconomic theory, international political economy, and bureaucratic delegation. Although I draw on all three to form my argument, none offers a satisfactory account of the variation of central bank independence across systems and over time.

Macroeconomic Theory

Most political-economy explanations of the choice of central bank institutions focus on the macroeconomic consequences of monetary institutions: an independent central bank secures superior inflation outcomes by insulating monetary policy from short-term political pressures. According to economists, discretionary monetary policy may produce an inflationary bias due to the time-consistency problem (Barro and Gordon 1983; Drazen 2000; Kydland and Prescott 1977).[8] In this perspective, once economic agents commit to nominal wage contracts, policymakers have an incentive to generate short-term improvements in output and unemployment by implementing a surprise expansion of monetary policy. Economic agents, however, recognize these incentives and will build expectations of higher inflation into their wage contracts. As a result, the monetary expansion simply produces higher levels of inflation but not the desired gains in real economic variables.

Rogoff (1985) argues that the appointment of an independent central banker who is more inflation averse than society could help overcome this inflationary bias (but with higher variability in output), providing a theoretical rationale for adopting an independent central bank (see also Alesina and Gatti 1995). Other economists argue that an independent central bank enhances the credibility of monetary-policy goals by shielding policy from competing partisan pressures (Alesina 1989) and because central bankers possess a different time horizon from politicians (Persson and Tabellini 1990). An independent central bank, therefore, would produce more stable and predictable monetary policy, leading to superior inflation outcomes.

Indeed, empirical research has demonstrated that independent central banks are associated with superior inflation performance. Countries with independent central banks enjoyed lower rates of inflation during the 1970s and 1980s than countries with dependent central banks (Alesina 1989; Banaian, Laney, and Willett 1983; Burdekin and Willett 1991; Eijffinger and de Haan 1996; Eijffinger, Schaling, and Hoeberichts 1998; Grilli, Masciandaro, and Tabellini 1991; Havrilesky and Granato 1993). Early research also indicated that central bank independence did not appear to be correlated with other economic variables, suggesting that independent central banks could deliver lower inflation in the long term without hurting growth or employment (Alesina and Summers 1993; Cukierman et al. 1993; Grilli, Masciandaro, and Tabellini 1991).[9] Central bank independence therefore seemed to be a "free lunch," an institutional arrangement that could deliver lower levels of inflation without affecting growth or employment (Grilli, Masciandaro, and Tabellini 1991). Consequently, central bank reform became a ubiquitous policy prescription not just for the industrial democracies but for countries throughout the world.

This research appeared in debates over economic and monetary reform (Dalziel 1993; Havrilesky 1994b). In New Zealand, MPs cited Alesina's research linking central bank independence and inflation performance during parliamentary discussions over the adoption of an independent central bank (*New Zealand Parliamentary Debates* 1989, 14684). In the EU, the final plans for the European Central Bank reflected current economic insights about central bank design (see, for example, the background reports in *One Market, One Money* (Emerson et al. 1991) and *The Economics of EMU* (1991)).

Building on these results, political economists have argued that the anti-inflationary value of an independent central bank depends on the degree of inflationary pressures faced by the government: the higher the inflationary pressure, the more incentive to adopt an independent central bank (de Haan and Van't Hag 1995; Franzese 1999). Political economists have pointed to government turnover (Alesina 1988a; Cukierman 1992) and high public debt (de Haan and Van't Hag 1995) as factors that would create inflationary pressure and thus increase the need for an independent central bank.

Other research suggests that the macroeconomic consequences of central bank independence—both nominal and real—depend on labor market organization (Franzese 1999, 2000; Hall and Franzese 1998; Iversen 1999; Soskice and Iversen 1998). According to Hall and Franzese, an independent central bank reduces inflation most where wage bargaining is least coordinated. Central bank independence tends to increase unemployment, but at a diminishing rate where wage bargaining is more highly coordinated. These arguments suggest that the overall benefits of an independent central bank may be greatest when wage bargaining is moderately coordinated.

Tests of these hypotheses, however, produce mixed results. De Haan and Van't Hag (1995), for instance, employ a data set of 16 to 21 industrial democracies to evaluate a variety of arguments about the choice of central bank institutions. They find no relationship between central bank independence and government turnover, public debt, or the equilibrium unemployment rate.

Arguments that rely solely on macroeconomic consequences of central bank independence cannot account for the variation of central bank institutions because they fail to consider politicians' incentives over central bank institutions. Politicians possess a variety of electoral and policy incentives that affect the choice of central bank institutions, leading them in some cases to adopt economically "inefficient" institutions.

International Political Economy

A second literature addresses the politics of central bank choice from the perspective of international political economy (Broz 1997; Simmons 1994, 1996). According to recent research in this field, international markets—particularly global capital markets—constrain the policy choices available to domestic policymakers. During the 1970s and 1980s, both technological advances and regulatory liberalization of the international financial sector dramatically increased the volume and ease of international capital movement (Simmons 1999). Indeed, some political economists have argued that international and domestic capital markets have become so integrated that capital mobility should be considered a structural component of the international system (Andrews 1994).

According to this literature, the increase in capital mobility pushes policymakers to adopt "market-friendly" policies and institutions, including an independent central bank (Goodman 1992). Maxfield (1997), for instance, argues that when politicians perceive a need to attract foreign capital inflows, they are more likely to respect the central bank's policy authority as a signal of their country's creditworthiness to potential investors. An independent central bank represents "both a sign of government commitment to desirable economic policies and an opportunity for increased creditor influence over government policy" (34). The integration of domestic and international capital markets in the 1980s and 1990s, particularly the development of an international market for government bonds, forced states to compete for capital, giving politicians an incentive to make central banks more independent.

This recent scholarship focuses attention on how the international economy presents constraints and opportunities to states. However, it has had less success explaining cross-national variation in central bank institutions and monetary outcomes. The emphasis on the international economy as an explanatory factor implies a convergence across all states in the choice of central bank institutions. Nevertheless, considerable differences remain across systems, both in the type of central bank institutions and in the timing of reform. These variations require consideration of the role of domestic politics to delineate more clearly how domestic political institutions and processes shape and channel the pressures created by economic internationalization.

Bureaucratic Delegation

According to the literature on bureaucratic delegation, political actors recognize that their choices about bureaucratic structure strongly affect policymaking in the future. The institutional structure can lock in the policy preferences of the enacting coalition (McCubbins, Noll, and Weingast 1989) or benefit particular interest groups (Moe 1989, 1990).

Some political scientists argue that politicians will structure the bureaucracy to protect the policy preferences of the enacting legislative coalition, tying the hands of future politicians (McCubbins, Noll, and Weingast 1989). Lohmann (1994), for instance, argues that political actors were engaged in a "turf battle" during the Bundesbank's founding, trying to choose institutions that would protect their ability to affect policy in the future. Goodman (1991) argues that politicians will choose an independent central bank to insulate policy from future opposition governments. According to his argument, governments that favor price stability and that expect a short tenure in office will choose an independent central bank to prevent future governments from pursuing high-inflation policies.

The "tying-the hands" argument suggests more temporal variation in central bank institutions than is observed empirically, as alternating governments would have changed the central bank for their own policy purposes. Additionally, the argument implies that polarized systems with extremist or highly antagonistic parties will have independent central banks, whereas systems with moderate centrist parties should have dependent banks because politicians can trust the opposition to pursue similar policies. Neither hypothesis predicts the variation of central bank independence correctly.

According to the first hypothesis, both Italy and Britain should have possessed independent central banks in the 1970s and 1980s. In Italy, the right Christian Democrats should have instituted an independent bank to insulate monetary policy from a potential extremist government formed by its main rival, the Communist Party. In Britain during the 1980s, the two main parties had strongly divergent preferences over the proper objectives of economic and monetary policy. The Conservative government could have implemented an independent central bank to prevent a future Labour government from pursuing inflationary policies. In contrast to the predictions, however, both Italy and Britain had dependent central banks during those periods. The second hypothesis implies that the United States and Austria, two countries with a relatively strong, cross-party consensus over monetary policy, should have dependent central banks. In fact, both countries possess independent central banks.

Another set of explanations emphasizes the role of interest groups in the choice of bureaucratic structure (Moe 1989, 1990). Groups that benefit from a policy will try to structure the bureaucracy to maintain the provision of those policies, even when the political balance shifts. Following this line of argument, Posen (1993) maintains that the organization and political influence of a nation's financial sector determine the independence of its central bank.

Central banks often enjoy close links with the financial sector, exchanging ideas and information. It is therefore unsurprising that political economists would search for a correlation between central bank independence and the strength of the financial sector. Indeed, both the United States and Germany, two countries with powerful financial sectors (Zysman 1983), possess independent central banks. But Britain also has a large financial sector, and its central bank was clearly dependent throughout the 1970s and 1980s. Additionally, the causality of the relationship between central bank independence and the financial sector is unclear. Central bank policies and procedures may determine the strength of the financial sector more than the financial sector influences the central bank's institutional status.

The interest-group arguments focus almost solely on the demanders of institutions and policies rather than the suppliers—politicians. Politicians, however, have their own incentives over policy and institutions, independent of group demands.[10] Additionally, politicians may have heterogeneous policy incentives, given their position in the institutional environment and their party affiliation.

Conclusion

The legal structure of an independent central bank limits the government's ex-ante and ex-post authority over central bankers. The central government usually appoints only a portion of the central bank's governing board. Additionally, the government's ability to punish the bank or veto the bank's policy decisions is curtailed. Consequently, independent central banks may constrain the cabinet's policy flexibility or limit the cabinet's ability to react to unforeseen circumstances. Furthermore, these institutions may also prevent government ministers from pursuing policies with strictly partisan benefits. Under what conditions, then, will politicians choose an independent central bank?

The traditional literatures do not offer adequate explanations for the choice of central bank institutions. In particular, they fail to emphasize politicians' incentives over the institutional structure of the central bank. These incentives are important because ultimately, it is politicians who supply the institution. They must decide to choose and remain committed to an independent central bank.

Politicians are interested in attaining and retaining office. They are also interested in ensuring that other members of their political party win office. Politicians understand that the institutional structure of the central bank conditions the policy process, influencing not only patterns of policy outcomes but also the pattern of interaction between politicians and central bankers. One can infer politicians' incentives over the structure of the central bank by examining how those patterns of interaction might affect the ability of parties to hold office. The next chapter develops a general explanation of the choice of central bank institutions based on the relationship between party legislators, coalition partners, and government ministers.

Chapter 3

Monetary Policy, Intraparty Conflict, and Central Bank Independence

The design of central bank institutions represents an explicitly political choice. Therefore, an explanation of the variation of central bank institutions must consider politicians' interests, particularly their desire to attain and hold office. It must take into account how different electoral, legislative, and government institutions affect politicians' incentives over central bank structure. Finally, it must explain why politicians remain committed to a particular central bank institution, even if preferences over policy outcomes change, and describe the conditions under which politicians may alter the institution.

In this chapter, I develop an explanation of the choice of central bank institutions, focusing on the potential for intraparty conflict over monetary policy and the principal-agent relationship between backbench legislators, coalition partners, and the cabinet. At a fundamental level, party legislators and coalition partners delegate policy responsibility to the cabinet, allowing legislators and coalition partners to remain ignorant of issue areas while cabinet ministers develop expertise in their portfolio. Cabinet ministers, however, can exploit their informational advantages over backbench legislators and coalition partners to implement their own preferred policies—policies that may not benefit the party as a whole. The informational asymmetries of the policy process therefore can create potential conflicts between party legislators, coalition partners, and cabinet ministers. I argue that an independent central bank can help alleviate some of these conflicts by supplying credible information about monetary policy.

The nature of this intraparty principal-agent relationship conditions the choice of central bank institutions. In situations where conflict over monetary policy between party legislators and cabinet ministers is likely, politicians will choose an independent central bank. If conflict is unlikely, politicians will opt for a dependent central bank. Consequently, variations in the potential for intraparty conflict can help explain differences in central bank institutions across systems and over time.

This chapter develops the logic of the argument. The first section discusses how the informational asymmetries of the monetary-policy process affect the incentives of legislators, coalition partners, and cabinet ministers over the choice of central bank institutions. The second and third sections explore the institutional conditions under which information from a central bank bureaucrat can solve the potential conflicts created by the informational asymmetries of the policy process. The fourth section lays out the observable implications of the argument.

Monetary Policy, Political Parties, and Delegation

I begin with the assumption that politicians and parties are fundamentally motivated by a desire to retain office. Before any concern with either policy or "pork," politicians and parties must hold office. Politicians' preference for attaining (and retaining) office provides them with policy incentives. Because voters generally use economic outcomes, rather than policy outputs, to evaluate candidates and parties, politicians and parties must pursue policy outcomes that satisfy the preferences of their constituents.

But in a complex issue area such as monetary policy, politicians may have difficulty choosing policies that will produce desired outcomes (Krehbiel 1991). First, changes in monetary policy do not always have expected consequences. Monetary policy has indirect effects throughout the economy, often with uneven and variable lag times (Beck 1987; Friedman 1968). These outcomes are vulnerable to exogenous shocks and international influences. Second, changes in monetary policy may have different effects across economic sectors. Higher interest rates, for instance, may benefit banking and financial interests but hurt firms in the construction industry. Third, monetary policy takes time to affect the economy. Politicians must consider this lag to deliver outcomes in a timely manner. Finally, the relationship between policy and outcomes may itself change as new technology evolves or as individuals modify their behavior in response to current regulations. The advent of electronic banking, for example, significantly altered the conduct of monetary policy, forcing policymakers to reconsider how they estimate the money supply. Successful monetary policy-making therefore requires that politicians invest resources to develop the expertise necessary to predict the consequences of a variety of policy proposals.

Party Legislators

Although individual legislators want policy outcomes to reflect the preferences of their constituents, each legislator must budget his or her limited time and resources toward achieving reelection. These individual electoral incentives create collective dilemmas for the legislative majority in the production and implementation of legislation (Kiewiet and McCubbins 1991).

Legislators face a dilemma in the development of policy expertise (Gilligan and Krehbiel 1989, 1990; Krehbiel 1991). Information about the relationship between policy choices and economic outcomes represents a collective good for legislators; it enhances the quality of legislation and ensures that policy leads to outcomes that accurately reflect the desires of the enacting coalition. Each legislator, however, has high opportunity costs in the development of the expertise necessary to legislate and to oversee policy implementation effectively. They can better spend their time and effort campaigning or focusing on issue areas with specific electoral benefits. As a result of these electoral pressures, no individual legislator may have an incentive to gather information about an issue area, limiting the quality of both initial legislation and legislative oversight of policy implementation.

Although legislators desire policies that enhance their reelectoral fortunes, they may not possess the ability to organize themselves to achieve those policies. To help solve these collective dilemmas, legislators delegate policy responsibility to cabinet ministers.

Coalition Partners

In forming a coalition government, parties make both policy compromises and policy logrolls—trading policies across issue areas. They also divide the cabinet portfolios (Laver and Schofield 1990; Laver and Shepsle 1994). In doing so, parties in a coalition delegate management of monetary policy to one party. Although formally constrained by the coalition agreement, the party controlling that dimension, the portfolio party, has some discretion in developing new policies and in responding to situations unforeseen in the coalition agreement.[1]

The nonportfolio party, which does not control monetary policy (although it may control other issue areas), possesses interests similar to those of the backbenchers in the portfolio party.[2] Because the government's economic-policy performance affects the nonportfolio party's electoral support (even if it does not hold the monetary-policy portfolio), the nonportfolio party wants outcomes to reflect the interests of its constituents as closely as possible. At the same time, however, the nonportfolio party does not want to make costly investments in developing expertise in portfolios it does not control or in monitoring the portfolio party's compliance with the coalition agreement. Instead, it prefers to devote resources to its own portfolios and electoral campaigns.

Cabinet Ministers

To overcome these dilemmas, backbench legislators and coalition partners delegate monetary-policy authority to the cabinet (i.e., the president, prime minister, or cabinet ministers). In parliamentary systems, in which the cabinet "emerges from" and "is responsible to" the legislature, the legislative majority explicitly delegates this responsibility to the cabinet (Lijphart 1984). But even in presidential systems, in which the executive is not responsible to the legislature, legislators still depend on the government. Cabinet ministers acquire policy expertise, allowing them to develop legislative proposals and oversee policy implementation. By gathering information about the relationship between monetary policy and macroeconomic performance, cabinet ministers may help guarantee that policy outcomes reflect the desires of their party's and their coalition partners' constituents.

As an incentive for ministers to develop expertise, legislators and parties grant ministers institutional power over monetary policy, including agenda control and discretionary authority. First, with agenda control powers, the minister can limit the policy proposals considered by the cabinet and by the legislature as a whole (Huber 1996; Laver and Shepsle 1994). The minister may therefore manipulate policy by acting as a gatekeeper.

Second, cabinet ministers also possess some discretion over monetary policy. They may choose policies without explicit approval as long as those choices do not cause backbench legislators or coalition partners to withdraw their support. In a parliamentary system, the cabinet needs the support of party legislators and—in multiparty systems—coalition partners to remain in office. In a presidential system, the government does not need the support of party legislators to remain in office, but it does require their support to achieve its policy goals.

The range of the cabinet's discretion reflects the configuration of policy preferences among the cabinet's legislative and coalition supporters, as well as the expected policy outcome that would result if the legislature vetoed the cabinet (Aldrich 1995; Austen-Smith and Banks 1990; Cox and McCubbins 1993; Laver and Schofield 1990; Laver and Shepsle 1996). If the policy preferences of party (or coalition) legislators lie relatively close to one another—if a consensus over outcomes exists within the government's party or the coalition—the cabinet minister has less discretion. That is, the set of acceptable policies from which the minister can choose policy is relatively small. As the policy preferences of government supporters become more diverse, the minister's discretion generally increases. In some situations, the cabinet can manipulate the agenda to build support for almost any policy.

The expected outcome of a legislative veto of cabinet policy also influences the level of cabinet discretion. In some systems, a veto may result in a simple policy change, bringing it closer to the ideal points of backbench legislators and coalition partners. In other systems, a veto may force a change in the partisan identity of the cabinet (Huber 1996). If the expected outcome of a veto lies close to the preferences of the party legislators and coalition partners, then the cabinet has less discretion. As the cabinet's legislative and coalition supporters find the alternative less and less acceptable, however, the cabinet enjoys greater discretion.

The Cabinet's Informational Advantages

In return for institutional authority over their portfolio, ministers develop the expertise necessary to forecast relatively accurately the relationship between policy outputs and outcomes. Although cabinet ministers must maintain the support of backbench legislators and coalition partners, they may be tempted to exploit their expertise to manipulate monetary policy for their own electoral and policy goals—goals that might differ from those of their legislative and coalition supporters.

In fact, the cabinet possesses a twofold informational advantage over backbench legislators and coalition partners in monetary policy. First, cabinet ministers are in a position to know more about the relationship between policy outputs and outcomes. The complex relationship between monetary policy and economic performance, including the lag between policy choices and results, allows the cabinet to avoid responsibility for bad outcomes they may have caused and to claim credit for good outcomes they did not create. For instance, the cabinet may propose a loosening of monetary policy, lowering interest rates. Legislators and coalition partners do not know whether economic conditions justify lower interest rates—for example, if inflation is under control and continued high rates would stifle potential economic expansion—or if the cabinet has lowered rates to create a short-term economic boom, with negative long-term consequences.

Second, cabinet ministers may conceal their actual monetary-policy choices from party legislators and coalition partners. No single policy indicator captures the direction of monetary policy, allowing the cabinet to obfuscate its intentions. For example, during the early 1980s, British policymakers announced several monetary targets and then emphasized the monetary aggregate that came closest to the announced target (Temperton 1991).

Furthermore, the cabinet has incentives to maintain secrecy surrounding its monetary-policy plans (Cukierman 1992). Secrecy allows the cabinet to generate politically expedient temporary booms in real economic conditions through surprise monetary expansions. Providing information to its legislative and coalition supporters about plans for monetary policy could actually negate the ability of the cabinet to manipulate short-term economic outcomes.

The Potential for Conflict

The delegation of authority to the cabinet solves the policy-information dilemma, but it creates the potential for new conflicts between legislators, coalition partners, and cabinet ministers—conflicts that could threaten the ability of the party to remain in office. First, the cabinet's monetary-policy choices influence the electoral fortunes of party legislators and coalition partners. Although macroeconomic outcomes may not be a decisive factor for an individual legislator or for a nonportfolio party, empirical evidence across systems indicates that inflation negatively affects the incumbent government's electoral fortunes (Lewis-Beck 1988; Powell and Whitten 1993). Moreover, the cabinet's policy choices fundamentally shape the party's social coalition, benefiting some constituents while hurting others. Over time, these policy decisions determine the party's electoral strategy and condition the party's viability. Backbench legislators and coalition partners must therefore decide whether to trust cabinet ministers to pursue policies that will help their electoral fortunes. If the cabinet's incentives over monetary policy differ from those of its legislative supporters or coalition partners, backbenchers and coalition partners will likely decide that they cannot trust the cabinet.

Second, these information asymmetries can threaten the party's position in office. Despite government ministers' expertise, policy outputs may have unintended consequences, producing outcomes unacceptable to the cabinet's legislative and coalition supporters. Without the technical expertise and oversight capability to evaluate monetary policy, party legislators and coalition partners may blame the cabinet for outcomes that the cabinet could not control, withdrawing their support even after ministers had attempted to pursue policies in the party's (or coalition's) overall interest. If the cabinet's supporters can credibly threaten to punish the cabinet for negative policy outcomes—for instance, if a policy consensus exists in favor of low inflation—then the cabinet has an incentive to find ways to reassure party legislators and coalition partners about its policy behavior.

Accurate information about the cabinet's monetary-policy choices and the consequences of those choices can help alleviate these potential conflicts.[3] With this information, backbench legislators and coalition partners can implicitly threaten to punish the cabinet if it does not pursue policies that benefit them. At the same time, cabinet ministers can use this information to maintain the support of their legislative and coalition principals—and keep the party in office for a longer time.

Informational Checks on Cabinet Discretion

The cabinet's principals can monitor the cabinet's policy behavior in three ways: by gathering information themselves, by observing the cabinet's compliance with policy rules, and by relying on endorsements from outside actors. First, backbench legislators and coalition partners can monitor the cabinet's policy choices themselves. Legislators can institute strong committee systems, allowing MPs to develop expertise in particular issue areas (Krehbiel 1991). In a coalition government, nonportfolio parties may demand deputy-level cabinet positions, which permit them to participate in the ministry's policy-making process. These institutions, however, require costly investments in time and resources—resources that may be better employed in electoral campaigns or directed toward particularly salient issues for the party. The responsibility of cabinet oversight may also create new collective dilemmas for legislators. Individual legislators may lack incentives to gather information in a particular issue area, hurting the ability of party legislators to monitor cabinet activity. Finally, the cabinet's control of the legislative agenda in some systems (and the existence of party discipline) may make it difficult for legislators to propose bills that challenge the cabinet's position, limiting the incentive for legislators to gather information.

Easily observable policy rules represent a second way to monitor the cabinet's policy choices. Policy rules provide ex-ante information about the cabinet's responses to different circumstances.[4] These policy rules not only make outputs more predictable, but they also allow backbench legislators and coalition partners to evaluate the cabinet's policy performance against clear standards. Rules are an attractive option to monitor the cabinet when compliance usually leads to satisfactory outcomes. Strict adherence to policy rules, however, may not give the cabinet enough flexibility to respond satisfactorily to unforeseen or ambiguous circumstances. Additionally, the relationship between the policy rule and outcomes may change over time, so that compliance produces undesirable consequences.

Despite these limitations, European Community member states successfully employed a policy rule during the 1980s: exchange rate stability in the EMS. The EMS established clear policy guidelines for governments based on changes in the value of the country's currency. These rules allowed each government's legislative and coalition supporters, financial markets, and the public to easily monitor their cabinet's policy actions (Bernhard 1998).

A third method to monitor the cabinet is to rely on information from actors affected by or involved in the policy process. These actors often possess policy expertise. Their endorsement or criticism of policy may allow the cabinet's principals to infer the consequences of the cabinet's policy choices (Calvert 1985; Lupia 1992). Additionally, these actors can help party legislators interpret cabinet behavior in the event of unanticipated situations.

Interest groups, for example, often provide information about the consequences of government policy in their issue area. They serve as "fire alarms" for party legislators, notifying them if policy choices adversely affect their constituents (Banks and Weingast 1992; Lupia and McCubbins 1993; McCubbins and Schwartz 1983). If the interest group has a known policy position or possesses strong ties with a political party—for instance, as unions and social democratic parties do in many European countries—then party MPs can rely on the interest group's evaluation of the government's policy choices.[5]

Backbench legislators and coalition partners may also use central bank bureaucrats to help them monitor the cabinet. Central bankers possess information about the cabinet's policy choices and their economic effects. The cabinet relies on the central bank to implement its policy choices, ensuring that bureaucrats will be informed of policy changes. Moreover, as experts in the policy area, central bankers can forecast and evaluate the consequences of the cabinet's policy.

But how can politicians ensure that central bankers will provide the information that they need to prevent potential intraparty conflicts? Under what conditions will backbench legislators and coalition partners find the central bank's policy evaluations credible and informative? To answer these questions, I develop a game-theoretic model of the monetary-policy process to determine the conditions under which legislators and coalition partners can infer consequences of the cabinet's policy choices. The results of the model have implications for the choice of central bank institutions and for the behavior of cabinet ministers, central bankers, and legislators in the policy process.

Central Bank Institutions, Information, and the Policy Process

In this section, I informally sketch the logic of my model of the monetary-policy process. The appendix contains the formal model. The next section discusses, again informally, the results of the model.

The game has three players: the government (i.e., the president, the prime minister, the minister of finance), the central bank bureaucrat, and the legislator. The legislator represents the cabinet minister's principals—either party legislators, coalition partners, or both. It may be useful to think of the legislator as a set of party MPs (or a coalition partner) who can act as a veto point to block legislation.

The model is one of asymmetric information. The information asymmetry stems from the ignorance of backbench legislators and coalition partners about the relationship between policy outputs and economic outcomes (Gilligan and Krehbiel 1989, 1990; Krehbiel 1991). The legislator knows the location of the status quo but does not know the outcomes associated with a policy change. A policy change could result in an outcome that backbench legislators and coalition partners prefer to the status quo, p_1, or in an outcome that is worse for them than the status quo, p_2 (see fig. 1).

Cabinet ministers and central bankers, on the other hand, have expertise in monetary policy. They have access to a variety of economic indicators, forecasts, and analyses, allowing them to predict the consequence of a policy change more accurately than backbench legislators or coalition partners. As a result, cabinet ministers and central bankers have full knowledge of both the location of the status quo and the consequences of a policy change.

The sequence of play is as follows. Nature first determines whether a policy change will lead to an outcome that benefits the legislator (with probability d) or hurts the legislator (with probablility $1-d$). The government makes a proposal to either enact a new policy (M) or to retain the status quo (Q). The central bank then offers an explicity endorsement (E) or rejection (C) of the government's proposal.[6] In effect, the central bank says to the legislator, "Based on what I know about the consequences of a policy change, you should or should not approve the policy." In practice, central bankers are not usually so blunt (although they can be). More often, central bankers provide a forecast and analysis of policy out-

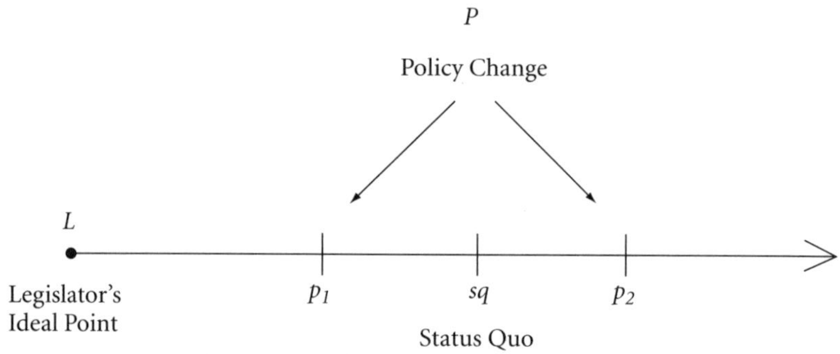

Fig. 1. Potential outcomes of a policy change

comes, signaling whether good or bad news is on the economic horizon. They may also provide some policy prescriptions based on their analysis. From these pronouncements, backbench legislators, coalition partners, and the public can determine the bank's opinion on the government's choice. Finally, after observing the government and the bureaucrat, the legislator votes to accept or reject a policy change. Figure 2 presents a game tree for the sequence of moves.

The three players receive payoffs from the policy outcomes: the closer the outcome to the player's preferences, the higher the payoff. The preferences of the legislator are the baseline, ranking the outcomes as follows: a policy change, p_1, that would hurt them < status quo (sq) < a policy change, p_2, that would help them. I evaluated the game based on different preference configurations for the government and bureaucrat, where each had preferences over the policy outcomes that (1) were the same as those of the legislature, (2) were opposed to those of the legislature, or (3) were in partial agreement with those of the legislature (e.g., $sq < p_2 < p_1$). This created a possible total of 36 different preference configurations (see appendix for details).

In addition to receiving payoffs from the policy outcomes, the government and the bureaucrat receive a payoff from the legislator's action. If the legislator vetoes a government proposal, the government receives a penalty larger than any possible gain in utility from achieving his or her preferred policy outcome. A veto represents a challenge to the policy on the legislative floor or, in a multiparty government, when a coalition partner chooses to withdraw from the government. No government likes to suffer the loss in political reputation resulting from a legislative veto. In a parliamentary system, a legislative veto might also precipitate a vote of no confidence. In a coalition government, the withdrawal of the nonportfolio party could cause the government to collapse.

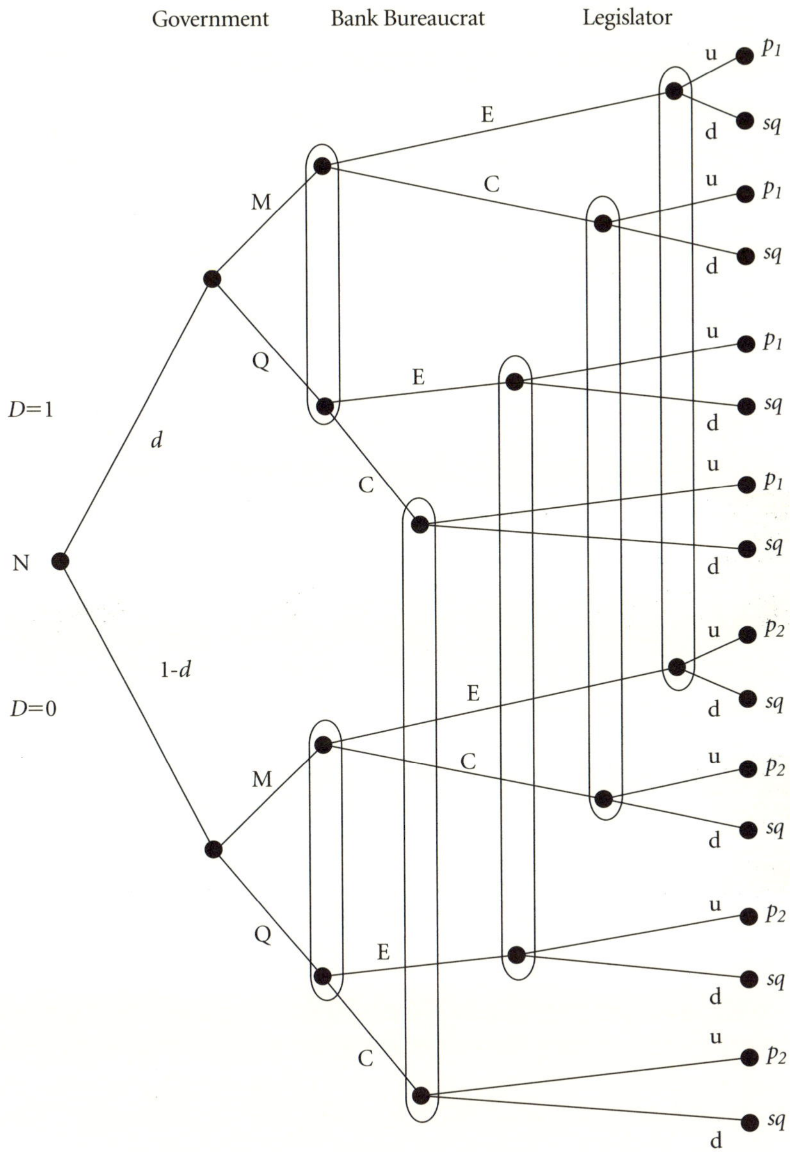

Fig. 2. Game tree and outcomes

Similarly, if the legislator votes against the central bank's advice, the central bank receives a penalty larger than any possible gain from achieving the bureaucrat's preferred policy outcome. Bureaucrats do not like to have their decisions vetoed (Ferejohn and Shipan 1990). A veto could hurt the central bank's reputation or demonstrate its irrelevance to the policy process. A legislative veto could also represent an attempt to alter the bank's institutional structure.

I evaluated two possible scenarios based on the central bank's institutional status. In the first, the government has no ex-post power over the bank; that is, the government does not have the authority to dismiss central bankers or veto the bank's policy decisions. In the second scenario, the government has ex-post power over the central bank: the authority to dismiss central bank directors, cut the bank's budget, or veto the bank's decisions. After the legislature votes on the policy, the government imposes a cost on the central bank if the bank's comment contradicts the government's proposal.[7] This penalty is larger than any possible payoff that the bureaucrat could receive from achieving the preferred policy outcome.

The structure of the game has strong empirical analogues. The legal statutes of the Dutch central bank, for example, contain formal procedures to resolve conflicts between the government and the central bank, with the parliament as the final arbiter (*The Economist,* 10 February 1990; Eizenga 1987). If the government and the bank disagree over the proper course of monetary policy, each submits a report to the parliament to explain its position. Once MPs have considered the two positions, the parliament chooses which policy to support. Interestingly, the parliament has never been called upon to resolve a dispute. Rather than risk a parliamentary vote—which would almost inevitably result in the resignation of the defeated actor—the government and the bank have resolved their differences behind closed doors.

Results

I solved the model to determine the conditions under which legislators and coalition partners can infer the consequences of the government's policy choices. These conditions reflect (1) the amount of preference agreement between the government, the central bank, and the legislator and (2) the bank's formal structure—in particular, whether the government has the authority to punish the central bank. The following two results are particularly relevant.

The Legislator Trusts the Government's Proposal

In the model, the legislator trusts the government's recommendation if the government shares its preference ordering over policy outcomes. The government's ex-post authority over the central bank does not affect the result. In other words, if party legislators and coalition partners share the government's policy objectives, they accept its policy evaluation regardless of the central bank's structure.

The Legislator Trusts the Central Bank's Evaluation

According to the results, the legislator finds the central bank's policy evaluation informative under two conditions: (1) the central bank and the legislator share the same policy objectives and (2) the government does not have ex-post authority over the central bank. These conditions, I contend, describe facets of an independent central bank.

The Political Credibility of an Independent Central Bank

The model implies that the institutional features of central bank independence provide central bank bureaucrats with credibility among party legislators, coalition partners, and the public. In particular, the appointments procedure and lack of ex-post authority enhance the bank's trustworthiness. Consequently, an independent central bank may act as a check on the cabinet's discretion and help prevent intraparty conflicts over monetary policy. In turn, political parties may grant central banks more independence in order to capitalize on the bank's political credibility.

Policy Preference Agreement and the Appointments Procedure

According to the results, the central bank's policy preferences determine the possibility of information transmission. If the cabinet cannot punish the central bank, preference agreement between the legislator and the central bank is sufficient to ensure that the legislator will be informed about the consequences of a policy change. If the central bank's (and the cabinet's) preferences differ from those of the legislator, then the legislator has at best only the possibility of knowing the effects of a policy proposal.

The model also implies that the legislator and the cabinet rarely agree about the type of central banker to appoint. If the cabinet cannot punish the central bank, the legislator naturally prefers a central bank that mirrors its own preferences. The cabinet, on the other hand, prefers to increase its discretion and will want a central bank that does not share the legislator's preferences. In contrast, if the cabinet and the legislator share the same preferences or if the cabinet can dismiss the bureaucrat, the legislator is indifferent to the bureaucrat's preferences. Institutional control over the appointments procedure therefore critically shapes the central bank's ability to influence the policy process.

Institutional control of the appointments procedure distinguishes dependent and independent central banks. In dependent central banks, the cabinet controls all appointments to the bank's governing board. Independent central banks, in contrast, have only a limited number of cabinet appointees on the bank's board, which instead includes a variety of political, regional, or sectoral representatives. These appointment procedures produce central bank councils that reflect the major divisions over monetary policy within the society, enhancing the central bank's credibility across constituents with a variety of economic policy demands. Because of these appointments procedures, the preferences of an independent central bank roughly mirror the preferences of the legislature (except that the bank does not have a short-term electoral imperative).

In Germany, for example, differences in monetary-policy preferences usually follow party lines. Until recently, each Land government appointed a representative to the central bank council, ensuring that the political composition of the Bundesbank's central council echoed the balance of political representation in the country as a whole. In the United States, differences over monetary policy are traditionally regional rather than partisan, pitting conservative easterners against southern and western monetary populists. Placing Reserve Bank governors, elected by regional stockholders, on the FOMC ensures that it has a balance of regional interests over monetary policy similar to those found in Congress. In Austria, representatives of the employers' associations and the labor unions sit on the bank's governing board, reflecting the corporatist structure of Austrian society. These appointments procedures ensure that the central bank will possess preferences similar to those found within the legislature, allowing the bank to provide credible information to the legislature and to the public about the cabinet's monetary-policy choices.

Ex-Post Authority

The cabinet's ex-post power also affects the central bank's ability to provide information about the consequences of the cabinet's policy choices. According to the model, unless the cabinet and the legislator fully agree, the legislature has a possibility of receiving new information during the policy process only if the cabinet can impose a penalty on the central bank. Therefore, when the central bank shares the legislator's preferences, the legislator loses information by granting ex-post power to the cabinet. If the central bank does not share the legislator's preferences, however, the legislator is indifferent about granting ex-post authority to the cabinet or in some cases may actually prefer the cabinet to have that authority.

The cabinet's lack of ability to punish the central bank is another characteristic of an independent central bank. The formal rules of an independent central bank prevent the government from vetoing the bank's policy decision, dismissing central bankers, or cutting the bank's budget. In contrast, the cabinet can punish a dependent central bank, severely limiting central bankers' ability to reveal information about the cabinet's policies; criticism of cabinet policy may result in retaliation through dismissal or budget cuts. Consequently, backbench legislators and coalition partners place less weight on the bank's policy evaluation because they know that the bank must tailor its statements to ensure the cabinet's approval. Without a credible alternative source of information, legislators and coalition partners must instead rely on the cabinet's policy recommendations. Consequently, the cabinet has more discretion over policy.

A Check on the Cabinet's Discretion

The conditions under which the legislator trusts the central bank's policy evaluation depict the institutional structure of an independent central bank. Party legislators and coalition partners will rely on an independent central bank's credibility to remain informed about monetary policy. In turn, this information can help prevent potential intraparty conflicts over monetary policy.

If independent central bankers send approving signals about the cabinet's policy, the cabinet's legislative supporters and coalition partners can have confidence that policy reflects their interests. If the bank criticizes the cabinet's monetary policy, party legislators can infer that the cabinet's policy has consequences that may hurt them. Armed with better information, the cabinet's legislative and coalition supporters can then accept or veto the cabinet's choices.

The policy information can also enhance the cabinet's credibility with its legislative and coalition principals. An independent central bank can reassure legislators that the cabinet had attempted to pursue policies in their interests, even if outcomes are less than satisfactory. Consequently, party legislators and coalition partners will be less likely to withdraw their support from the cabinet.

Implications

The argument yields three sets of observable implications concerning the patterns of policy disputes between governments and independent central bankers, the cross-national variation of central bank independence, and the durability of cabinets in systems with an independent central bank.

The Threat of Legislative Punishment and Monetary-Policy Disputes

The model emphasizes the role of the legislature in the policy process. Indeed, the results indicate that the legislature strongly shapes monetary-policy choices. Nevertheless, analysts have noted the relative lack of legislative involvement in monetary policy throughout the industrial countries (LeLoup and Woolley 1991; Woolley and LeLoup 1989). In fact, the model suggests that legislators will not act on monetary policy. In equilibrium, both the cabinet and the central bank make the same policy recommendation. The costs associated with a veto provide an incentive for both the cabinet and the central bank to appear united about the potential consequences of a policy change. As a result, the legislature does not need to decide between the alternative recommendations. Instead, it takes only a passive action, simply supporting the cabinet's proposal.

The threat of a legislative veto, however, shapes the cabinet's and the central bank's incentives. Both cabinet ministers and central bankers recognize that the legislature ultimately determines policy in the event of a dispute. Each anticipates the legislature's reaction before making a recommendation. If either the cabinet or the central bank recognizes that it will lose a dispute in the legislature, it will accept the other's recommendation rather than suffer a legislative veto.

An independent central bank's political credibility, therefore, changes the cabinet's strategic incentives. If the cabinet announces a policy change that earns a negative evaluation from an independent bank, it risks punishment from party legislators and coalition partners. Rather than chance a legislative veto, cabinets will choose policies that the independent central bank will not criticize. Although the cabinet retains control over policy goals, the bank forces cabinet ministers to be more truthful about economic and monetary policy, checking the cabinet's ability to manipulate policy for its own purposes. As a result, the bank may appear to control monetary policy.

The possibility that party legislators and coalition partners may support the cabinet's policy position also affects the central bank's incentives. If backbench legislators and coalition partners support the cabinet, the central bank must make the same recommendation as the cabinet or suffer the costs of a policy veto, even if the central bank disagrees about the desirability of the policy. Therefore, independent central banks are constrained when the cabinet and a legislative majority agree about policy. Independent central bankers anticipate the cabinet's level of support in the legislature. If that support is strong, then they are likely to temper their comments in order to avoid the costs of a policy veto. On the other hand, if the cabinet cannot muster a legislative majority to punish an independent central bank, then the bank can criticize cabinet policy.

This strategic interaction in the formulation of monetary policy therefore implies a discernable pattern to disputes between governments and independent central bankers. First, public disagreements between the cabinet and an independent central bank will be relatively rare. Each actor would rather work out a solution privately rather than risk a legislative veto. Second, independent central bankers will be critical of cabinet policy only when they anticipate that the cabinet will be unable to secure a legislative majority to support its position. Third, independent central bankers will not criticize the cabinet, even if they disagree with its policy prescription, when it is clear that the cabinet's position enjoys widespread support among politicians in the governing party(ies).

The Choice of Central Bank Institutions

The model's results indicate that politicians can structure the central bank to help them overcome the conflicts created by the informational asymmetries of the policy process. Under what conditions, then, will party legislators, coalition partners, and the cabinet be willing to limit the cabinet's control over the central bank?

Party legislators and coalition partners will prefer an independent central bank if they cannot trust the cabinet—that is, if the cabinet possesses monetary-policy incentives that differ from their legislative supporters and coalition partners. In this situation, backbench legislators and coalition partners recognize that the cabinet will likely exploit its informational advantages to pursue policies that do not reflect their interests. On the other hand, if party legislators and coalition partners have confidence that the cabinet shares their monetary-policy goals, then they can trust cabinet ministers. They have no incentive to check the cabinet's discretion with an independent central bank. Instead, they will support a dependent bank.

The cabinet must also support the choice of bureaucratic structure. The priority of government ministers is to maintain their positions in office. If party legislators and coalition partners can credibly threaten to punish the cabinet for its monetary-policy performance, then the cabinet will want them to have information that demonstrates the cabinet's policy choices were intended to benefit the party. In this situation, the cabinet has an incentive to support an independent central bank. If party legislators and coalition partners cannot credibly threaten to punish the cabinet, however, then the cabinet has little incentive to restrict its monetary-policy discretion with an independent central bank.

The choice of central bank institutions therefore reflects (1) the divergence of policy incentives between the cabinet and its legislative and coalition supporters and (2) the credibility of legislators' and coalition partners' threat to punish cabinet ministers. In situations where the cabinet faces policy incentives that differ from party legislators and coalition partners and where those backbench legislators or coalition partners can punish the cabinet, politicians will agree to an independent central bank. If one of those conditions is not present, the bank will be less independent of cabinet control. Differences in these two variables across systems should account for the cross-national variation of central bank institutions.

Political Conflict and Central Bank Independence

The informational asymmetries of the monetary-policy process are likely to lead to intraparty conflicts, especially where party politicians face different incentives over monetary policy. Without the information necessary to evaluate the cabinet's monetary-policy choices, backbench legislators and coalition partners will suspect that the cabinet is manipulating monetary policy away from their ideal points, hurting their electoral fortunes and the party's long-term viability. Consequently, backbench legislators and coalition partners may be quick to withdraw their support from the cabinet over a monetary-policy dispute.

The credibility of an independent central bank helps prevent some of these potential conflicts. The bank can provide information about the cabinet's policy behavior to reassure party legislators and coalition partners. Further, the bank can help government ministers justify monetary policy to legislators, coalition partners, and the public.

Therefore, in systems with an independent central bank, one should expect fewer political disputes over monetary policy between party legislators, coalition partners, and government ministers. One way to measure these conflicts is to examine cabinet durability in parliamentary systems. If an independent central bank does prevent conflict over monetary policy, cabinets in parliamentary systems with an independent central bank should have a higher expected duration than cabinets in systems with a dependent central bank, holding all other influences on cabinet durability constant.

Linking central bank independence and cabinet durability can also help explain patterns of central bank reform. Politicians will reform the central bank when it is in their interest to do so—that is, when central bank reform is likely to prolong the tenure of incumbent politicians. Over time, changes in constituent preferences and decreased policy effectiveness may increase the possibility of conflict over monetary policy within the governing party(ies). Where these intraparty conflicts threaten the ability of these parties to stay in office, politicians will adopt an independent central bank to prevent the conflicts from hurting the party's political fortunes.

The following four chapters explore these implications more fully. The next chapter examines patterns of conflict between the Bundesbank and the government in Germany. Chapter 5 shows how the divergence of policy incentives and the threat of punishment condition the choice of central bank institutions across systems. Chapter 6 demonstrates that an independent central bank increases cabinet durability under conditions of economic openness—precisely where we would expect intraparty conflict over monetary policy to be prominent. Chapter 7 explores central bank reform in Italy and Britain, illustrating how political and economic developments increased the political value of an independent central bank.

Chapter 4

Central Bank Independence and the Politics of Monetary Policy: The German Bundesbank in the Policy Process

Monetary policy reflects the strategic interaction of cabinet ministers, legislators, and central bankers in the policy process—strategic interaction that is conditioned by the formal and legal structure of the central bank. With an independent central bank, the cabinet has few direct controls over the central bank. The bank's governing board typically includes individuals appointed by a variety of political actors. Additionally, the cabinet can sanction the central bank only with the cooperation of the legislature. These institutions give central bankers more room to maneuver in the policy process (McCubbins, Noll, and Weingast 1989). As long as the central bank has the support of actors in the legislature who can veto any potential punishment, it does not have to respond to the cabinet's policy demands. Moreover, the bank can even challenge the cabinet's policy choices. This allows other political actors—backbench legislators, coalition partners, upper house legislators, voters, and interest groups—to learn about monetary policy by the interaction between the cabinet and the central bank in the policy process.

An independent central bank therefore provides a check on the cabinet's discretion. This function in turn provides an important incentive in the choice of central bank institutions. In situations where cabinet ministers, party politicians, and potential coalition partners have different incentives over monetary policy, an independent central bank can help prevent political conflicts that could hurt their ability to remain in office.

In this chapter, I examine the process of strategic interaction between the cabinet, legislators, and an independent central bank more fully. I first discuss the behavior to expect in the policy process. Second, I explore cases of strategic interaction between German politicians and the Bundesbank. In the conclusion, I show that politicians and central bankers from a number of countries recognize that an independent central bank can make cabinets more accountable for their policy behavior.

The Political Strategy of Independent Central Banks

As noted in chapter 3, politicians can influence the behavior of an independent central bank through two mechanisms: appointments and threats to reduce the bank's independent status (Lohmann 1998a). With an independent central bank, however, the cabinet does not possess sole control over either mechanism. The appointments procedures of an independent central bank typically limit the number of central government appointees to the bank's governing board. Instead, other institutions possess the authority to determine parts of the bank's board. In Germany, for example, Land governments appoint individuals to the Bundesbank's governing council. In the United States, district bank presidents, selected by regional commercial banks and business interests, form a portion of the Federal Reserve's main governing board.

Furthermore, the formal institutions of an independent central bank drastically curtail the cabinet's authority to sanction the bank unilaterally. Typically, the bank can be punished only by a legislative act, requiring cooperation between the cabinet and the legislature. Threats to the bank's institutional status therefore carry more weight when the cabinet and a legislative majority share similar policy demands. Because central bankers recognize that the cabinet and the legislature are more likely to cooperate to punish the bank under these conditions, it will be more responsive to political demands. If the cabinet and the legislature are divided, however, the threat to sanction the bank is less credible.

These institutional arrangements make an independent central bank accountable to multiple principals. Instead of being responsible only to the cabinet, an independent central bank is also answerable to other political actors, usually the legislature. The existence of multiple principals allows the bank to increase its room for discretionary behavior vis-à-vis the cabinet. Because both the legislature and the cabinet must cooperate to sanction the central bank, central bankers can play one principal off the other, protecting their institutional status by pleasing either the cabinet or the legislature (Morris 2000). In the U.S. context, for example, Havrilesky (1993) shows that the Federal Reserve responds to congressional threats by implementing the president's policy demands. As long as the president is satisfied with the Federal Reserve's policy behavior, any bill to change the bank's institutional status will be vetoed.

The existence of multiple veto points in the legislative process can dilute even further the ability of politicians to threaten the central bank (Lohmann 1998a; Morris 2000). If the bank can satisfy one veto point, any attempt to sanction the bank will be blocked. For instance, central bankers may cultivate a legislative committee with gatekeeping power that can prevent a bill challenging the bank's authority from reaching the legislative floor. In a parliamentary system with a multiparty government, the bank may attempt to appease only one party, as long as that party is pivotal to the coalition.

Central bankers are strategic actors. They carefully consider the consequences of their actions not just for markets but also for politics. They recognize the political environment and anticipate the reaction to their policy actions. They will seek to protect or even enhance their independent status. This strategic behavior is evident in two areas.

First, independent central bankers recognize that to maintain their policy discretion and even their independence, key political players—especially actors in charge of veto points—must understand the reasons behind the bank's behavior. Consequently, central bankers will try to build support for their position, both appealing to society for approval and cultivating specific political actors (Berger 1997; Berger and de Haan 1999; Forder 1996; Goodhart 1994; Goodman 1992). In order to obtain this support, the central bank will selectively provide information and expertise about the available policy options and the consequences of those policy options.

Second, an independent central bank will not pick a fight with the cabinet that it cannot win. An independent central bank will openly criticize the government's policy choices only when it appears that the government will be unable to craft a legislative majority to punish the bank. Likewise, an independent central bank will not challenge government policy, even if it disagrees with the cabinet's proposal, when the government has solid legislative support.

Cabinet ministers are also strategic actors in the policy process, sensitive to the political context. Each actor anticipates the legislature's policy preferences, calculating whether legislative support exists for either the cabinet's or the central bank's position. Because neither wants to suffer a legislative veto, each will defer to the other if it anticipates that it will lose a showdown. In equilibrium, therefore, both the government and an independent central bank will make the same policy recommendation to the legislature. As a consequence, the legislature will not often need to resolve policy disputes between the government and the bank.

The next section examines policy conflicts between the government and the central bank in Germany to illustrate the strategic interaction between politicians and independent central bankers.

Information, Policy Conflict, and the Bundesbank

The Bundesbank's independence creates the potential for conflict over monetary policy with the government.[1] Because the government possesses few controls over the central bank, Bundesbank officials can publicize any policy disputes. In many cases, the bank has "won" the policy dispute, either forcing the resignation of the defeated government minister or touching off controversy between the government and its legislative and coalition supporters (Berger 1997; Berger and de Haan 1999). In 1972, for example, Karl Schiller, the minister of economics, disagreed with the Bundesbank president, Karl Klasen, over the best response to changing international monetary conditions. Schiller favored floating the mark, while Klasen pressed for capital controls to stem the inflow of funds. Trusting the Bundesbank, the cabinet, with the legislature's backing, voted to adopt the bank's position, forcing Schiller to resign (Goodman 1992). In at least three cases, the Bundesbank's policy actions have contributed to the resignation of the government or collapse of the governing coalition (Marsh 1992).[2]

The Bundesbank's success in challenging the government's policy choices reflects its institutional structure, its reputation, and its own strategic action. First, the appointments procedure to the Bundesbank ensures that the Central Bank Council includes representatives of both the Christian Democratic and Social Democratic parties, making the bank's policy analysis more credible to legislators, coalition partners, members of the upper legislative chamber (the Bundesrat), and the public. Second, the Bundesbank's unparalleled reputation for technical competence and inflation aversion gives the bank's policy analyses added weight. Finally, the Bundesbank carefully developed political support both by cultivating specific interests in German society and by choosing its fights with the government carefully (Berger 1997; Berger and de Haan 1999; Goodman 1992). Because a simple legislative act could have overturned the Bundesbank's independence, bank officials had to evaluate the balance of policy preferences in both houses of the legislature, gauging the level of its potential support, before criticizing the government. If the bank could not carry the day, especially if the government enjoyed majority support in the Bundesrat, the bank acquiesced to the government's policy choices. If the government's support in the legislature was divided or if the government did not enjoy majority support in the Bundesrat, however, the Bundesbank was in a better position to publicize its disputes with the government (Lohmann 1998a).

Several episodes of potential conflict between the government and the Bundesbank from 1970 to 1990 demonstrate the Bundesbank's strategic behavior in the policy process. First, during the late 1970s and early 1980s, the Bundesbank used the political cover provided by divisions in the Social Democratic–led government coalition to criticize the government's policy. Because the divisions between the left wing of the Social Democrats and the liberal Free Democrats prevented Chancellor Schmidt from threatening the Bundesbank, the bank could attack the government's policy choices. The bank's criticism exacerbated tensions in the governing coalition and helped precipitate its collapse.

Second, the Bundesbank had only muted responses to Germany's European monetary commitments—participation in the EMS and in EMU. In both instances, one might have expected the Bundesbank to be critical of the government's decisions. Indeed, the decisions to join both arrangements threatened domestic price stability and Germany's policy autonomy. Yet in both situations, a majority of the legislature was likely to support the government's plans to participate in both institutions. Consequently, the Bundesbank made only restrained public comments on these proposals.

Finally, the Bundesbank miscalculated its level of legislative support during Germany's monetary unification. The Bundesbank opposed the generous exchange rate proffered to the East Germans by Chancellor Kohl. Kohl's Christian Democrats, however, supported his move, recognizing the potential to capture new support from eastern voters. Consequently, the Bundesbank was largely excluded from any meaningful role in the process. Indeed, the Bundesbank president, Karl Otto Pohl, resigned because he recognized that he no longer commanded enough legislative support to serve as a counterweight to the government.

The following sections examine each of these episodes in more detail.

The Social Democratic–Free Democratic Coalition and the Bundesbank

Beginning in 1969, the Social Democratic Party became the senior party in government for the first time in the postwar period, forming a coalition with the liberal Free Democratic Party. The two parties favored a more open foreign policy and more secular social policy than did the Christian Democrats. But on the economic-policy dimension, the two parties were unlikely coalition partners. The Social Democrats relied heavily on Germany's trade unions for support. Their policy platform emphasized full employment and an expansionary welfare state. The Free Democrats, in contrast, appealed to middle-class and business interests and favored macroeconomic discipline.

Nonetheless, the coalition survived throughout the 1970s. Part of its longevity was due to the Bundesbank. The bank's independence allowed it to criticize the policy actions of the Social Democratic–led government, alerting the Free Democrats if the Social Democratic Party attempted to cheat on the coalition agreement in the area of monetary policy. The credibility of the bank's policy information, therefore allowed the Free Democrats to join the coalition despite their differences with the Social Democrats on economic policy.

Given the Social Democrats' policy goals and constituents, one would have expected controversies with the Bundesbank over monetary policy. Although the government and the bank did disagree over policy a number of times during the 1970s, these conflicts came to a head only when changes in the composition of the governing coalition made it unlikely that the Bundesbank would lose a policy showdown.

The bank's policy response after the first oil crisis created tension between the bank and the Social Democratic Party. Unlike other industrialized economies, Germany maintained a restrictive monetary policy following the oil-price shock, keeping inflation below the international average but contributing to sharp increases in unemployment. The restrictive monetary policies drew criticism from the trade unions, a key constituent of the Social Democrats. Herbert Ehrenberg, a Social Democratic Bundestag member, introduced a bill to change the Bundesbank's official policy goals to include full employment and economic growth. The Social Democrats' 1975 party program even included these proposals (Goodman 1992; Scharpf 1987).

Because of this threat to its independence, the bank was less willing to question the Social Democrats' policies. Instead, the bank and the government agreed on a new role for monetary policy in 1974–75. Prior to wage negotiations, the bank would announce monetary targets for the upcoming year. These targets could then serve as a guideline for wage negotiations between unions and employers. Schmidt supported the monetary targets, hoping that they would help avoid conflict between the bank and the unions. Additionally, these targets were another way for the government to influence wage negotiations and as a result, maintain the competitiveness of German exports (Franzese 2000; Goodman 1992; Marsh 1992; Scharpf 1987).

The bank also became more accommodative toward the government's economic policies. It eased monetary policy beginning in late 1974, lowering key interest rates. Additionally, it allowed monetary growth to overshoot its 1975 target (Goodman 1992; Scharpf 1987). In 1977, a relatively loose monetary policy complemented the government's expansionary fiscal policy, a policy that increased spending on public investment and provided tax relief for business and families (Scharpf 1987).

The international economic situation, however, continued to deteriorate. In the United States, President Jimmy Carter entered office in 1977 and initiated a series of tax cuts to fuel economic expansion. The Carter administration pressured Germany and Japan to follow suit. When they did not, the U.S. dollar began to depreciate rapidly against the mark and the yen (Henning 1994). Nevertheless, Germany's current account remained in surplus, drawing even more criticism from the United States.

At the 1978 Bonn Summit of the Group of Seven (G-7) countries, Chancellor Schmidt relented to U.S. pressure, agreeing to an immediate increase in aggregate demand of at least 1 percent of gross domestic product (GDP). To ensure the Bundesbank's cooperation, Schmidt carefully gathered support for the program, particularly from the Free Democrats, prior to presenting it to the Bundesbank. Disagreeing with Schmidt's policies would have left the Bundesbank isolated at home and abroad. Consequently, the Bundesbank consented to an increase in the public-sector borrowing requirement, implying it would not raise interest rates to counter higher government spending.

Only a few months later, however, the second oil crisis hit, nearly tripling oil prices between 1978 and 1980. Unlike the first oil crisis, however, the German economy was in a vulnerable position. Other countries decided to deflate their economies in response to the crisis. Consequently, the market for German exports, the traditional engine of economic growth, dried up. At the same time, the German economy was expanding, spurred by higher government spending. The domestic expansion fueled a greater demand for imports. As a result, the current account quickly swung into deficit and inflationary pressures began to build. The D-mark also began to depreciate against the U.S. dollar.

To counter these pressures, the Bundesbank began a gradual tightening of monetary policy in January 1979. The government, however, thought a more restrictive monetary policy would jeopardize the economic recovery—and possibly, its fortunes in the upcoming elections—and argued against interest-rate increases. The Bundesbank ignored the government and increased the Lombard rate by a half point. In response, Social Democratic government ministers openly criticized the bank's policy actions, although Schmidt himself was careful to avoid public debate. Major newspapers and the Free Democratic economics minister, Count Graf Lambsdorff, rallied to the bank's defense, insulating the

Bundesbank from the government's criticisms (Goodman 1992). Consequently, the discount rate increased steadily from early 1979, from a low of 3 percent to a high of 7.5 percent in the summer of 1980 (Henning 1994; Scharpf 1987).

The 1980 elections increased the strength of both the Free Democrats and the left wing of the Social Democrats, accentuating conflicts over the best response to the growing economic crisis (Goodman 1992; Scharpf 1987). Hoping to appeal to business, the Free Democrats argued for tax cuts as a way to stimulate growth and investment. The left wing of the Social Democrats and the trade unions pushed for increased spending to reward the unions' wage moderation in the late 1970s and to combat rising unemployment. Caught in between, Social Democratic cabinet ministers countered with an economically responsible but politically infeasible tax on oil imports to lower the budget deficit (Goodman 1992).

Faced with a dwindling supply of foreign reserves in early 1981, the Bundesbank decided to tighten monetary policy dramatically to stabilize confidence in the mark. The bank suspended the regular Lombard facility, replacing it with an unprecedented special Lombard rate at 12 percent. Money market interest rates soared to over 30 percent. These actions helped to maintain the D-mark's value against the dollar, but they also worsened the recession.

Although Schmidt recognized that U.S. monetary policy constrained German policy options, he pressured the Bundesbank to cut interest rates. Bundesbank officials responded unsympathetically, suggesting that the fiscal crisis needed to be solved before interest-rate reductions could occur. The Bundesbank's policy actions, however, exacerbated tensions within the ruling coalition. Although lower U.S. interest rates brought some relief in mid-1982, the conflict between the Social Democrats and the Free Democrats had become irreconcilable. The Free Democrats left the coalition and formed a new government with the Christian Democrats. The new government immediately undertook a program of deficit reduction. In response, the Bundesbank quickly lowered interest rates (Goodman 1992).

The bank's ability to challenge the cabinet reflected the policy divisions within the Social Democrat–Free Democrat coalition. Because the coalition's priorities were divided between the probusiness Free Democrats, the proworker left wing of the Social Democrats, and moderates in the cabinet, it was unlikely that the governing parties would cooperate to punish the Bundesbank. As a consequence, the bank could act against the government's demands, secure that it had a legislative majority (i.e., the Christian Democrats and the Free Democrats) that generally supported the bank's policy stance and would not overturn its independence.

The Bundesbank and European Monetary Commitments

In contrast to the conflict between the Bundesbank and the Schmidt government, the Bundesbank's criticisms of Germany's commitment to European-level monetary institutions have been muted, even though these commitments threatened both domestic price stability and the Bundesbank's own policy authority. Bundesbank attacks on European commitments were not likely to find support among Germany's politicians. Not only does Germany's role in Europe generally enjoy cross-partisan support, but such criticism might also be viewed as a challenge to the government's authority to make foreign policy.

The Bundesbank was skeptical of plans for the EMS, fearing that participation in the system could compromise domestic price stability (Goodman 1992; Heisenberg 1999; Henning 1994; Kennedy 1991; Marsh 1992). Bank officials also realized that a formal exchange-rate commitment would limit their own policy discretion and make monetary policy more susceptible to political influence through the determination of currency parities. Bank officials were also upset that they had been excluded from the initial negotiations over the system. Indeed, Schmidt and his French counterpart, President Valéry Giscard d'Estaing, had specifically excluded all other actors from their negotiations to limit opposition to the proposal.

Schmidt recognized the Bundesbank's concerns—and its ability to foment opposition to his plans. He traveled to Frankfurt to persuade the Bundesbank Council to support the initiative. His argument in favor of the EMS went beyond the technical merits of the plan, touching on Germany's role in Europe and the historical legacy of World War II (Henning 1994; Kennedy 1991; Marsh 1992). Schmidt suggests that he threatened in a "cautious" and "diplomatic" manner to change the Bundesbank law, although no one corroborates his claim (Marsh 1992). Despite their reservations, Bundesbank officials did not criticize the plan publicly, although they did press the government to make some technical modifications to the agreement concerning the requirements for intervention. Additionally, government officials pledged that they would leave the system if participation threatened domestic price stability.

The Bundesbank's response to EMU was also subdued, considering that the plans for EMU would effectively destroy the Bundesbank's authority. In the late 1980s, the Bundesbank recognized that monetary union would receive serious consideration on the European agenda. Indeed, German foreign minister Hans-Dietrich Genscher had stirred renewed interest in monetary union in 1987. The fall of Communism and German unification also provided fresh impetus to the idea of a single currency. Within Germany, politicians across the political spectrum recognized the importance of reaffirming Germany's commitment to Europe. Consequently, the Bundesbank accepted its inability to stop the process.

Instead of opposing the concept outright, the Bundesbank decided to influence the negotiations, putting forward conditions it would find acceptable (Heisenberg 1999; Henning 1994; Marsh 1992). The bank argued that the final transition to a single currency should be determined by convergence of member-state economies, rather than by fixed deadlines. Additionally, the bank called for a fully independent European Central Bank, dedicated to the goal of price stability. Finally, it maintained that monetary union could succeed only with greater political integration, especially in disputes over the allocation of fiscal resources. These requirements represented a "no-lose" gamble for Germany and the Bundesbank. On the one hand, the conditions would create a monetary union dedicated to price stability. On the other hand, the conditions were so stringent that it was possible that other European member states would not accept them or fail to comply with the convergence criteria, leaving the status quo in place.

The Maastricht Treaty requirements for EMU look similar to the Bundesbank's demands, although the final agreement contained some differences, including deadlines for the transition to the final stage and political control over European participation in exchange-rate agreements. In general, the Bundesbank has faithfully supported the agreement, recognizing the treaty's cross-partisan support at the elite level and foreign-policy implications. At times, Bundesbank officials complained about the terms of the treaty, but these complaints were restrained (March 1992). Indeed, given the German public's potential hostility to the loss of the D-mark, the Bundesbank behaved responsibly by refusing to stir up anti-EMU sentiment.

The Bundesbank and German Monetary Unification

German monetary unification demonstrates that even independent central bankers must gauge the policy preferences of the legislative majority before challenging the government's policy. During monetary unification, the Bundesbank failed to realize the popularity of Chancellor Helmut Kohl's plans among his legislative followers. Consequently, it lost a policy showdown with the government (Henning 1994; Kaltenthaler 1996; Lohmann 1994; Marsh 1992).

After the fall of the Berlin Wall in November 1989, the Bundesbank approached the prospect of monetary unification with a cautious pragmatism, guided by the desire to maintain domestic price stability in the West. Bundesbank president Karl Otto Pohl recognized that monetary unification would require drastic adjustments to the East German economy to be successful. As late as January 1990, Bundesbank representatives characterized a rapid monetary unification as "fantastic" and "very unrealistic" (Marsh 1992, 208). Nevertheless, in early February 1990, Pohl traveled to Berlin to meet with Horst Kaminsky, the head of the Staatsbank—the East German central bank. At their press conference, Pohl suggested that talk of monetary union was "premature." In private meetings with East German officials, the Bundesbank leadership expressed strong opposition to the possibility of a one-to-one exchange of East German marks (Marsh 1992).

Chancellor Kohl, however, had different incentives over monetary unification. He understood that the unification of Germany represented not only an historic opportunity but also a political one. Just as Pohl was traveling to Berlin, Kohl was meeting with his advisors concerning monetary unification. Although most counseled a gradual approach, leaders of the Christian Democratic Party in East Germany persuaded Kohl that a quick move to monetary unification was the only way to stem the tide of westward migration and restore hope to the East. Moreover, by moving quickly to integrate the East, Kohl could ensure that his fellow Christian Democrats would benefit in the upcoming East German elections scheduled for March. The following day, shortly after Pohl's Berlin press conference, Kohl went on television to propose a speedy monetary union.

Pohl and the Bundesbank were caught off guard. Pohl had talked briefly with Kohl and government ministers prior to his trip to Berlin, but they had given no indication of the potential for such an announcement. A few days later, Pohl organized a highly unusual press conference to discuss the difficulties associated with the government's proposal, including the need for structural adjustment in the East and higher taxes in the West. He reacted to the surprise of Kohl's announcements, stating "I always advise the government to consult the Bundesbank first" (Marsh 1992, 214).

Pohl's statements worsened the relationship between Bonn and the Bundesbank. Consequently, the Bundesbank found itself increasingly excluded from the policy choices surrounding unification. As the negotiations for monetary unification commenced, the government requested the Bundesbank to recommend a conversion rate. After internal debate, the Bundesbank settled on a two-to-one ratio—a rate they believed economically and politically feasible. The government, however, overrruled the bank's proposal, instead offering generous terms for monetary conversion, including a one-to-one exchange for smaller savings deposits. In May, without consulting the Bundesbank, the government created the German Unity Fund to transfer funds to the East (Marsh 1992).

Excluding the Bundesbank from the policy process exacerbated tensions between the government and the bank. In May 1990, just as the Monetary Unification Treaty was signed, two Land Central Bank presidents made public statements challenging the government's actions. One complained publicly, "The government has to stop acting as if the autonomy of the Bundesbank has been put aside for the process of reunification" (Marsh 1992, 218). The other warned of the inflationary pressures of the government's plans. Perhaps sensing that the Bundesbank had already lost the fight with the government and that further criticism could result in a change of the bank's independent status, Pohl ordered his fellow council members to soften their public comments (Marsh 1992).

The Bundesbank's predictions for the government's plan—unemployment and loss of competitiveness in the East and deficits and potential inflation in the West—turned out to be largely correct. The Bundesbank's alarms, however, fell on deaf ears. The popularity of monetary unification among Kohl's legislative supporters allowed him to move forward with the generous plan, despite the Bundesbank's position. The Christian Democrats stood to make significant electoral gains by positioning themselves as the party of German unity. Indeed, they had the most votes both in the March 1990 elections in East Germany and in the December 1990 national elections—the first after unification. Unlike previous policy disputes between the bank and the government, the legislature had more to gain from Kohl's plan than from the Bundesbank's caution. Instead of the government losing the policy showdown, the Bundesbank was forced to back down.

Pohl resigned the following year in May 1991. The resignation was triggered in part by some of Pohl's public statements on EMU. He argued that monetary union without convergence would be a "disaster," just as it had been for East Germany. This comment touched off a small run on the D-mark and drew criticism from Kohl (Marsh 1992). More importantly, Pohl stepped down because he had become increasingly marginalized in the policy process following the Bundesbank's political miscalculation over monetary unification. In August 1991, he complained, "I have been talking myself blue in the face for eighteen months. . . . Everything I said was ignored. . . . If I had the feeling I could have prevented it [the deterioration of the budgetary position], I would not have quit" (Marsh 1992, 41).

Conclusion

The Bundesbank's independence creates potential problems for German governments. The history of the bank illustrates that its policy statements carry serious political consequences, potentially causing the government to lose support or preventing the government from satisfying some of its constituents. One might expect that German politicians would attempt to rein in the independent bank by altering its institutional structure. Why do German politicians tolerate the independence of the Bundesbank? What explains their commitment to this institution, despite the bank's ability to challenge the government's policy?

Part of the answer comes from the Bundesbank's strategic action in the policy process. Helmut Schlesinger, Bundesbank president in the 1990s, recognized the bank's situation, stating, "Our independence depends on our ability not to overstep our limits" (Marsh 1992, 256). Independent central bankers must recognize and respond to the policy incentives of the government and its legislative and coalition principals. Before criticizing the government, independent central bankers must gauge whether backbench legislators and coalition partners will follow the bank's advice and reject the government's policies or whether the government's principals stand to gain more from accepting the government's policy choice. Too much or too little criticism can threaten the bank's independence. For most of its existence, the Bundesbank has successfully played this political balancing game (Berger 1997). Indeed, one European central banker noted, "It is ironic that the Bundesbank, the world's most politically independent bank, is also the world's most politically active central bank."[3]

The commitment of Germany's politicians to an independent Bundesbank also reflects the political benefits of an independent central bank. The Bundesbank has a political function—to provide information about the government's monetary policy choices and the consequences of those choices. The Bundesbank's institutional structure and reputation endow its policy evaluations with credibility in the eyes of backbench legislators, coalition partners, and ultimately, voters. The credibility of that information helps politicians in the governing parties—politicians who are likely to have different incentives over monetary policy and different information sets—trust one another. Consequently, the Bundesbank can help prevent monetary policy conflicts from happening and help political parties remain in office.

Indeed, officials at the Bundesbank and the European Commission pointed to the informativeness of the Bundesbank to justify the existence of independent central banks in democratic societies. They argued that the Bundesbank had the responsibility to comment on the direction and consequences of government economic policies. Together with private economic institutes, the Bundesbank's opinions and forecasts provided counterweights to the government's "politically watered-down" statements on economic policy.

Survey evidence indicates that the legislators value the Bundesbank's policy analysis more than the government's policy pronouncements or other sources of economic information. In anticipation of an April 1998 vote on whether to participate in the single currency, Heisenberg (1998) polled Bundestag members about their attitudes toward EMU. She found that Bundestag members relied on the Bundesbank for information about the euro. Over 79 percent indicated that the Bundesbank's opinion on participation in EMU was an "important" factor in their decision—a higher percentage than any other source,[4] including recommendations by the European Commission, a vote of the European Council, party instructions, or public opinion surveys. Interestingly, this result held across the four major parties. Even Social Democratic and Green legislators were very likely to trust the Bundesbank's policy recommendation. The Bundesbank's credibility crosses party lines.

Evidence from a number of other countries indicates that central bankers and politicians recognize the political importance of an independent central bank's credibility in the policy process.[5] Parliamentary debates in New Zealand over the 1989 Reserve Bank Bill echoed this informational justification for reforming their central bank. Proponents argued that an independent central bank would actually increase the transparency of the policy process and as a result increase government accountability. While the government would determine the ultimate objectives of monetary policy, the central bank would report to the parliament about the economic consequences of the government's policy choices and the perseverance with which the government pursued those objectives. Consequently, the bill would improve the cabinet's accountability: "The Bill will help to eliminate . . . uncertainty by enhancing the accountability of both the Reserve Bank and politicians. It will force Ministers of Finance to be open about adopting alternative policies and their inflationary effects, and will make the Reserve Bank more independent by placing the implementation of monetary policy outside day to day ministerial manipulation" (*New Zealand Parliamentary Debates* 1989, 10425). Another proponent argued: "[W]hile it [the bill] provides a means for the Government to change the objective of monetary policy, that will have to be done in a way that is transparent. This should enhance public scrutiny of Government actions" (*New Zealand Parliamentary Debates* 1989, 14501). Some legislators even claimed that the bill did not do enough to encourage the governor to issue evaluations of government policy: "[I]t is essential that . . . the Governor of the Reserve Bank have the capacity to comment on the complete spectrum of economic management," rather than just monetary policy (*New Zealand Parliamentary Debates* 1989, 14698).

In the United States, Congress requires the Federal Reserve chairman to report semiannually on monetary policy. These appearances and the Federal Reserve's regular economic reports give legislators a better understanding of both the central bank's specific activities and the president's monetary policy choices. Additionally, the chairman's appearances have become media events, focusing public attention on the government's economic policy and providing an opportunity for legislators to declare their preferences over the course of monetary policy (Havrilesky 1993).

Although most academic accounts of central bank independence do not emphasize this informational role in the policy process, a number of political economists recognize it. Fair (1979) argues that a central bank's independence should be measured by its ability to publicize policy disputes with the government. Havrilesky (1994b) suggests that independent central banks function as "sound money oracles," making regular anti-inflationary public pronouncements. Goodman (1992) argues that independent central banks build social and political constituencies, presumably by supplying expertise and information about monetary policy.

Providing information about the government's monetary policy therefore represents one of an independent central bank's most critical political functions. Party leaders can use the bank's credibility to help build and maintain diverse social coalitions. An independent central bank can also help prevent intraparty conflicts over monetary policy and consequently help parties stay in office longer. That political function helps to explain the variation of central bank institutions across systems and over time.

Chapter 5

Federalism and Central Bank Independence

Political economists have long noted the association between federalism and central bank independence (e.g., Banaian, Laney, and Willett 1983; Lohmann 1998a; Posen 1995). Federal systems, in which political authority is divided between the central government and constituent units, tend to have independent central banks. Germany, Switzerland, and the United States—all federal systems—have independent central banks. Unitary countries, in which political power is centralized in the national government, were more likely to have dependent central banks during the 1970s and 1980s. Although the association between federalism and central bank independence appears to be strong, the mechanism linking the two institutions remains unclear. Why do we observe a correlation between federalism and independence? How does federalism affect the choice of central bank institutions?

I contend that the association between federalism and central bank independence reflects the potential for intraparty conflicts over monetary policy. Federal systems increase the potential for intraparty conflict over monetary policy, giving politicians incentives to choose an independent central bank. In federal systems, party politicians are likely to face different monetary-policy pressures. Constituents will make a variety of economic policy demands, reflecting regional differences in economic activity. Additionally, the political institutions of federalism—powerful regional offices, bicameral legislatures, and so on—force party politicians to appeal to different sets of constituents and to run for office at different times. Because the possibility of intraparty conflict over monetary policy is high in federal systems, the political benefits of an independent central bank are higher as well.

In this chapter, I provide empirical support for this argument. The first section identifies factors that condition the nature of the relationship between backbench legislators, coalition partners, and cabinet ministers in the area of monetary policy. The second section examines episodes of central bank choice and reform in Germany and Britain to illustrate how federalism shaped the potential for intraparty conflict and, in turn, the choice of central bank institutions. The third section tests the argument statistically against the cross-national variation of central bank independence in the 1970s and 1980s.

Backbench Legislators, Coalition Partners, and Government Ministers

The choice of central bank institutions reflects the potential for intraparty conflict over monetary policy. An independent central bank can prevent some of these potential conflicts by acting as a check on the cabinet's discretion over policy. An independent central bank not only insulates monetary policy from day-to-day political manipulation, but it can also publicize its policy conflicts with the government, providing backbench legislators and coalition partners with information about the cabinet's policy choices and the consequences of those choices. In systems where conflicts over monetary policy are likely, therefore, politicians will choose an independent central bank. In systems where conflict between backbenchers, coalition partners, and government ministers is less likely, politicians will opt for a dependent central bank.

What factors contribute to the potential for conflict over monetary policy? First, party legislators and coalition partners will be more suspicious of the cabinet if cabinet ministers possess policy incentives that differ from their legislative supporters and coalition partners. In this situation, backbench legislators and coalition partners recognize that the government is likely to pursue policies that do not reflect their interests. Second, political conflict is likely where backbench legislators and coalition partners can credibly threaten to punish the government for its monetary-policy performance.

The factors that shape the relationship between backbench legislators, coalition partners, and government ministers reflect the configuration of electoral, legislative, and government institutions, as well as the distribution of constituent preferences between and across political parties. In particular, many of the institutions of federalism increase the possibility of conflict over monetary policy.

Incentive Divergence

The divergence of monetary-policy incentives between legislators, parties, and ministers contributes to the potential for conflict. As policy incentives increasingly diverge, backbench legislators and coalition partners become less trustful that government ministers will pursue policies in their interests. Consequently, they will prefer an independent central bank. If legislators, coalition partners, and government ministers face similar policy incentives, however, conflict over monetary policy is less likely. Backbench legislators and coalition partners will trust the cabinet and consequently will see no need for an independent central bank to check the government's policy discretion.

In the area of monetary policy, the distribution of constituent preferences and electoral institutions conditions the degree of incentive divergence between legislators, parties, and ministers.

Constituent Preferences

The distribution of monetary-policy preferences among party supporters may force candidates from the same party to make different appeals to win votes. Manipulating monetary policy can help some politicians in the party. But if the governing party(ies) has constituents with diverse preferences over monetary policy, changes in monetary policy may generate externalities among other constituents (e.g., an interest-rate increase may help creditors but hurt debtors), damaging the electoral fortunes of other candidates within the party. This problem may be particularly acute for large catch-all parties or parties not based on economic appeals (Budge and Farlie 1983; Kirchheimer 1966).

For example, higher interest rates help exporters and net creditors by keeping inflation low but increase the load on net debtors. If the governing party appeals to both exporters and net debtors, raising interest rates may improve the party's popularity in some areas but hurt its electoral chances in others. This tension occurred in Britain during the early 1990s, damaging the popularity of the incumbent Conservative government. During the 1980s, Prime Minister Thatcher sold public housing to the current occupants, creating a new class of home owners and potential Conservative voters (Garrett 1992). Most of these mortgages were variable rate; that is, the interest payments fluctuated according to the current interest rate. During the early 1990s, the Conservative government increased interest rates in order to preserve the pound's position in the EMS. These increases squeezed private debtors, particularly working-class individuals who had recently purchased their own homes. These new home owners, once grateful to the Conservatives, soon turned hostile as the government's monetary policy saddled them with exorbitant mortgage payments.

Electoral Institutions

Electoral institutions may also provide politicians from the same party with divergent monetary-policy incentives. Parties that compete across differently sized electoral districts are likely to have conflicts over monetary policy. Candidates in smaller districts may want to use monetary policy to appeal to particular interests, while candidates in larger districts must balance demands from a variety of constituents (Rogowski 1987).

Additionally, nonconcurrent elections for the government and part of the legislature provide politicians within the governing party(ies) with different incentives over the sequencing of monetary policy. For instance, the government may manipulate monetary policy in order to engineer an economic boom for its election period. The eventual increase in inflation resulting from a monetary surprise, however, may adversely affect legislative elections in the next period (Alesina and Rosenthal 1995).

Finally, electoral institutions may encourage the formation of coalition governments. The existence of coalition governments creates a higher potential for monetary-policy conflicts within the governing parties. If coalition partners face constituents with different preferences over monetary policy, they will disagree about the proper course for policy. Cabinet ministers must therefore make policy choices that will not alienate either their own legislative party or their coalition partner.

The Threat of Punishment

If the government's legislative and coalition supporters can punish the government—if, for example, a policy consensus exists within the governing party(ies)—then the government has an incentive to demonstrate that its policy choices reflect the interests of its party legislators and coalition partners. It does not want backbench legislators or coalition partners to withdraw their support even if its policy choices unexpectedly lead to unfavorable outcomes. In this situation, the government has incentives to support an independent central bank.

If the government's principals cannot levy a punishment on the government, however, the government has little incentive to support institutions that enhance the transparency of its policy choices. Legislators and coalition partners, for instance, may lack the capacity to organize themselves to punish the government. Or they may accept the government's policy choices because the expected outcome of challenging the government is worse than the current policy. Finally, government ministers may possess the (institutional and persuasive) ability to build new majorities in favor of the outcomes they produced (McCubbins, Noll, and Weingast 1989). At the very least, they may have the capability to prevent their legislative and coalition supporters from organizing themselves to punish the government. If the government's principals cannot punish the government, the government will not want to limit its policy flexibility by supporting institutions that supply information to its legislative and coalition supporters. Instead, the government will support a dependent central bank.

The credibility of backbench legislators' and coalition partners' threats to punish the government reflects the polarization of the political system, the organization of legislative institutions, and the existence of coalition and minority governments.

Polarization

The polarization of the system affects the ability of backbench legislators and coalition partners to punish the government over a policy dispute. Dissatisfied backbenchers and coalition partners must cooperate with at least part of the opposition to challenge the government's policy. Highly polarized systems present few opportunities to cooperate with the opposition because of the large policy distance between parties (Sartori 1976). Consequently, backbench legislators and coalition partners will be less likely to challenge the government's policy. In systems with low polarization, however, backbenchers and coalition partners will be more willing to craft a temporary legislative coalition with the opposition to defeat the government.

Legislative Institutions

Legislative institutions influence the possibility of punishment by affecting the cost to backbench legislators and coalition partners of challenging the government's policy. In systems with endogenous electoral timing, dissatisfied party legislators and coalition partners must consider the possibility that a challenge to the government's policy could precipitate early elections (Huber 1996). The possibility of losing their seats in a general election may provide them with an incentive not to challenge the government. In systems with strict party discipline, backbenchers face another disincentive to challenge the government because party leaders possess the institutional authority to punish legislators who fail to support the government. Finally, if the political fortunes of legislators are closely tied to their party's participation in the government, party legislators may be reluctant to risk their status by challenging government policy. In contrast, in systems where the benefits of serving in the governing party are low—if, for example, opposition legislators can still influence policy through a strong committee system—then party legislators may be more willing to veto government policy (Strom 1990a, 1990b).

Coalition and Minority Governments

In multiparty parliamentary systems, the government faces the threat of punishment not only from party legislators but also from coalition partners. The existence of coalition or minority governments increases the potential for punishment. Multiparty coalition governments are more likely to fall over a policy dispute than are single-party majority governments.

Political Systems and the Choice of Central Bank Institutions

The political systems of Germany and Britain illustrate how legislative-cabinet relations and the potential for intraparty conflict over monetary policy shape the choice of central bank institutions. Although specific events may precipitate an episode of central bank reform, the relationship between legislators, coalition partners, and government ministers provides the underlying conditions that shape the choice and stability of central bank institutions.

Germany

The divergence of policy incentives among German politicians and the possibility that the government will be punished over a policy dispute help ensure the commitment to an independent Bundesbank. The government's legislative and coalition supporters depend on the bank to help them check the government's informational advantages in monetary policy. The government relies on the bank to help soothe potential conflicts with its principals—backbench legislators, coalition partners, and voters—allowing the government to retain its position in office.

Backbench legislators and coalition partners possess monetary-policy incentives that differ from those of the government, due in part to Germany's federal system. As a consequence, the government's legislative and coalition principals cannot trust the government to pursue the monetary policies they desire. First, each party's constituents possess a range of interests over monetary policy, reflecting the regionalization of the German economy. Because Land party organizations control the party list for elections to the lower house, members of parliament must balance Land interests with the demands of the government to ensure their renomination.

Second, the bicameral legislature creates the potential for conflict between the government, selected in the lower house (Bundestag), and party legislators in the upper house, the Bundesrat. Legislators in the Bundesrat are appointed representatives of the Land governments. Under certain circumstances, the

Bundesrat may veto legislation (Conradt 1989; Lohmann 1998a).[1] These veto powers prevent the government from proposing legislation that will enhance its own authority at the expense of the Lander. Because the government needs a majority in the Bundesrat to pass partisan legislation, it cannot enact policies that could damage the party's electoral fortunes at the Land level. In particular, nonconcurrent elections for the Bundestag and Land governments provide party politicians with different incentives over monetary-policy sequencing. If the government attempts to manipulate monetary policy to engineer an economic boom for its own election, it may produce outcomes that hurt the party's electoral fortunes at subsequent Lander elections.

Finally, the proportional representation electoral system strongly discourages the formation of single-party majority governments. Throughout the postwar period, Germany has been governed by a coalition government. Coalition partners often have constituents with different and sometimes conflicting preferences, as illustrated by the tension between the Social Democrats and the Free Democrats in the late 1970s and early 1980s (Goodman 1992; Scharpf 1987). An independent Bundesbank helps prevent the government from pursuing policies that will hurt their party legislators and coalition partners.

An independent Bundesbank can also help the government stay in office by bolstering the credibility of its economic policies. Because monetary policy remains a high-salience issue in Germany, the government's principals—backbench legislators, coalition partners, and ultimately, voters—use it to gauge the government's competence. The nature of the political system enhances the government's vulnerability on this dimension. First, the relative proximity of the major parties on the economic and monetary-policy dimension contributes to the possibility of punishment. Although each party espouses different policy priorities, their economic programs reflect a German consensus about the proper balance between market and state. The Christian Democrats and the Free Democrats share a procapitalist orientation. But the Christian Democrats also implemented the "social market" economy, designed to ameliorate the less-desirable aspects of capitalism. Unlike other Socialist parties in Europe, the Social Democrats moderated their economic policies relatively early after World War II. Frozen out of national office for over a decade, the Social Democrats rejected radical Marxism in the Bad Godesberg program of 1959, attempting to make themselves a more palatable alternative to Christian Democratic rule. Participation in the Grand Coalition in the late 1960s gave the Social Democrats a reputation as a stable center-left party capable of governing Germany.

Second, the coalition dynamics of the German party system also increase the possibility that the government will lose office over a policy dispute. As the pivot party in the party system for much of the postwar period, the small Free Democrats have participated in coalitions with both the Christian Democrats and the Social Democrats. Consequently, the Free Democrats could threaten to leave the government if their senior partner did not comply with the coalition agreement.

The Bundesbank's independence can prevent party legislators, the Free Democrats, and voters from defecting from the governing coalition. During the 1970s, the Social Democrats relied on the policy credibility of the Bundesbank to forge a coalition with the Free Democrats, despite their differences on economic policy. Although many blame the Bundesbank for exacerbating tensions between the two parties in the early 1980s (e.g., Scharpf 1987), the bank contributed to the coalition's longevity by helping assuage the Free Democrats' concerns about the influence of the Social Democrats' left wing. Social Democratic ministers therefore had an incentive to tolerate an independent central bank in the 1970s. In contrast, Christian Democratic governments have less incentive to support an independent central bank. Because they share similar economic priorities with the Free Democrats, the Free Democrats are less likely to withdraw their support over an economic policy dispute. Consequently, the Christian Democratic governments have less need to rely on an independent central bank to verify their policy performance.

Indeed, Christian Democratic governments have twice attempted to increase the central government's authority over the Bundesbank. During the founding of the Bundesbank in the 1950s and the reorganization of the Bundesbank in the 1990s, the Christian Democratic–led government tried to enhance its influence over the composition of the central bank's main decision-making body. In both instances, mistrust between the government and its party supporters in the Bundesrat helped ensure the Bundesbank's independence.

The Founding of the Bundesbank

After World War II, the Allies created a decentralized central banking structure consisting of legally autonomous Land central banks coordinated by the Bank deutscher Lander (BdL). Article 88 of the 1949 German Basic Law required the new German government to reorganize this central bank system, touching off a prolonged debate about its institutional design. The appointments procedure to the new central bank emerged as a key issue (Berger 1997; Goodman 1992; Lohmann 1994). One side called for a centralized system, where a directorate composed only of central government appointees would determine monetary policy. Proposals for a more decentralized system sought to retain the BdL's federal structure and increase the influence of the Land central bank presidents, appointed by the Land governments, in the policy process.

The issue divided the Christian Democratic–led coalition government. After heated internal debate, the cabinet eventually agreed to a decentralized plan, sending it to the legislature (Lohmann 1994). The Bundesrat, composed of Land representatives, easily endorsed this decentralized proposal, with support from both Christian Democratic representatives and the Social Democratic opposition. The Social Democrats' support for the plan reflected in part their lack of strength at the national level. Frozen out of power at the national level but with significant representation in the state governments, the Social Democrats perceived a decentralized structure as the best way for them to influence monetary policy (Goodman 1992). Opposition to the bill, however, came from the Free Democrats, who had weak support at the state level. They believed that a centralized structure would afford them the best opportunity to affect policy. Consequently, the Free Democrats introduced a counterproposal for a centralized bank to the Bundestag. Legislators referred the competing bills to committee, where the legislation stalled (Lohmann 1994).

In 1955–56, the BdL pursued a restrictive monetary policy, initiating a conflict with the government (Berger 1997). Upset with the BdL's policies, Chancellor Adenauer publicly criticized the bank. The government called for a new centralized structure, which would integrate the bank with other policy-making institutions. The Bundestag passed the government's motion, but the Bundesrat rejected it and reintroduced the proposal for a decentralized structure. With a majority in the Bundesrat, the Christian Democrats may have been expected to support a centralized plan that would increase the influence of the national party over monetary policy. Christian Democratic representatives in the Bundesrat, however, were motivated both by the desire to maintain state influence over monetary policy and by the need to place an institutional check on their own party's government because they had different incentives over monetary policy.

The competing proposals went again to a Bundestag committee. This time, the committee produced a compromise, outlining a Central Bank Council composed of up to 10 central government appointees and 11 Land central bank presidents, chosen by their respective state governments. Proponents argued that the majority status of Land central bank presidents on the council provided a vital safeguard against the ability of the central government to manipulate policy. The proposal unanimously passed the Bundestag and overwhelmingly passed the Bundesrat, with support from states dominated by both the Christian Democrats and the Social Democrats (Lohmann 1994). The divergence of policy incentives between the government and party legislators in the Bundesrat therefore helped to guarantee the Bundesbank's independence.

The Reorganization of the Bundesbank

In the early 1990s, the Bundesbank was reorganized to incorporate the eastern Lander into the system. Again, the composition of the Central Bank Council surfaced as one of the central issues. Advocates of centralization, including the Christian Democratic–led government and central government appointees to the Bundesbank, argued that the addition of new Land central bank presidents would render decision making cumbersome and unwieldy. Opponents of centralization, including most Land central bank presidents, argued that the majority status of Land central bank presidents on the council ensured the Bundesbank's independence (Henning 1994; Kaltenthaler 1996; Lohmann 1994, 1998a).

The Bundesbank president, Karl Otto Pohl, originally proposed a Central Bank Council composed of seven government appointees and seven Land central bank presidents, with the president (appointed by the central government) as a tiebreaker. The Bundesbank Council rejected this proposal as too centralized. Pohl next proposed reducing the number of Land central banks to eight, with no change in the number of central government appointees (up to 10). By specifying which states would maintain representation on the council, Pohl was able to buy off some Land central bank presidents and forge a winning coalition within the council. In an unusual move, Land central bank presidents who voted against the proposal protested by sending a letter to Chancellor Kohl requesting that each Land retain a seat on the Central Bank Council. This opposition included Land central bank presidents who had been nominated by both Social Democratic and Christian Democratic state governments.

Anticipating opposition from the Bundesrat, the government proposed a Central Bank Council composed of nine Land central bank presidents and eight government appointees, increasing the relative influence of central government appointees but preserving the majority status of the Land central bank presidents. The Bundesrat, however, rejected that proposal by a two-thirds majority, which included some representatives from Christian Democratic states, and reiterated its preference for the "one Land, one Land Central Bank" principle. The government countered by promising key states that they would retain a Land central bank, eventually reducing the opposition in the Bundesrat to a simple majority. Under German law, this simple majority could not block the Bundestag's passage of the bill. Although the reform increased the relative influence of central government appointees, the opposition from party legislators in the Bundesrat forced compromises that preserved the Bundesbank's independence.

Germany's federal institutions therefore strongly shaped the Bundesbank's independence. In particular, the Bundesrat has consistently opposed any increase in the central government's control over the central bank. Although Bundesrat legislators may come from the same party as the cabinet, they have different monetary-policy incentives than their lower house counterparts. Consequently, they cannot trust the cabinet to pursue policies in their interests. As a result, they supported an independent central bank to act as a check on the government's discretion.

Britain

Throughout the postwar period, Britain possessed a dependent central bank, firmly under government control. The Bank of England's dependent status reflected the similarity of monetary-policy incentives between party legislators and government ministers. That similarity in turn stems from the relative homogeneity of intraparty constituent demands and Britain's majoritarian institutions.

Until the 1970s, the Conservative and Labour parties each appealed to constituents with fairly homogenous preferences over monetary policy (Hall 1986). The Conservatives represented business and middle-class interests. Labour's main constituents included the trade unions and the working class. Although for much of the postwar period British economic policy reflected a consensus of the two parties, each party had different economic priorities. The Conservatives stressed controlling inflation. Labour emphasized unemployment.

The Westminster political system reinforced the ideological coherence between party legislators and the government (Lijphart 1984). The majoritarian electoral system helps to ensure single-party majority governments, preventing coalition governments. Because Parliament is essentially a unicameral legislature, party politicians do not face nonconcurrent elections, giving them similar incentives over policy sequencing. Additionally, the unitary nature of the British system meant that the governing party did not have to win regional and local elections to implement its legislative agenda. Backbench legislators and government ministers, therefore, had similar incentives over monetary policy. Consequently, backbenchers had no reason to support an independent central bank. Instead, they could trust their government ministers to pursue policies that reflected their interests.

Government ministers also had little incentive to support a more independent central bank. The legislative and electoral institutions of a Westminster system make it highly unlikely that party legislators would withdraw their support over a policy dispute. Although party legislators possess the formal authority to dismiss the government over policy disputes and conflicts, backbenchers face a number of institutional disincentives to prevent them from doing so. First, the benefits of serving in the governing party are high. Because the legislative committee system is weak, opposition legislators possess little influence over policy or distributive benefits (Strøm 1990b). Second, governments typically have the authority to call for new elections, forcing rebellious legislators to risk their own seats at an early election (Huber 1996). Third, party leaders control a variety of electoral and party resources, allowing them to punish legislators who fail to support the government's agenda. Because of these costs, governments rarely have to face challenges from within their own party, regardless of the opposition's position. Consequently, government ministers had little incentive to support an independent central bank.

The 1946 Bank of England Bill

The postwar institutions of the Bank of England were largely determined in 1946. During the immediate postwar period, the Labour government, under Clement Attlee, sought to reshape the relationship between market and state. With planning and government management of the economy, the Labour Party hoped to achieve full employment and greater social equality. Their program involved more active use of macroeconomic policy; expansion of social services, including establishment of the National Health Service and the Family Allowance; and nationalization of vital economic institutions, including the coal, electric, gas, rail, and steel industries. Of these nationalization proposals, only the steel sector proved controversial.

As part of this program, the new Labour government proposed nationalizing the Bank of England in 1945. Since its founding in 1694, the bank's stock had been held privately. Its governor and the Court of Directors had been selected from within the bank or especially recruited by the bank. Although there had been policy cooperation between the Bank of England and the Treasury in the twentieth century, these relations were informal and uncodified. In particular, the bank's performance relied heavily on the governor's executive ability. During the interwar years, the arrangement worked well under the forceful leadership of Montagu Norman. Under Norman, the bank accepted the Treasury's control over policy. Norman once declared, "I am an instrument of the Treasury" (Fforde 1992, 15). In the management of its affairs, however, the bank considered itself "operationally and institutionally distinct from the Government" (Fforde 1992, 15).

The Labour Party had already espoused nationalizing the Bank of England during the 1930s. Many Labourites blamed Norman for failing to cooperate with MacDonald's Labour government and contributing to Labour's defeat in the 1931 elections. The 1937 manifesto *Labour's Immediate Programme* argued that the bank must be nationalized in order to integrate monetary policy with plans for a national investment policy. Labour also discussed proposals to nationalize joint stock banks to help rationalize investment. The 1945 manifesto simply stated that "The Bank of England with its financial powers must be brought under public ownership, and the operations of other banks harmonised with industrial needs."

The actual Bank of England Bill was limited and technical in nature, reflecting extensive consultation between the new Labour government and the bank during its preparation. The bill established a new Court of Directors, appointed by the chancellor, to direct monetary policy. This Court of Directors consisted of 16 individuals, including the governor and deputy governor. The court would serve five-year terms, although bank officials had requested seven-year terms (Fforde 1992). Clause 4(1) of the bill authorized the government to give directives to the bank, as "they think necessary in the public interest." Further, Clause 4(3) stated that the bank had the power to direct commercial banks, if it considered it "necessary in the public interest" and the action was "authorised by the Treasury." Finally, the bill discussed plans to compensate owners of the private stock. It made no attempt to nationalize the joint stock banks.

Discussion of the bill centered largely on two issues: Clause 4(3) and the terms of compensation for shareholders. Clause 4(3) proved most contentious. Critics charged that it was vague and gave too much authority to the Bank of England over commercial banks. They contended that the wording of the clause might allow the government to compel banks to reveal information about the private business of their clients. The government countered with amendments designed to clarify the purpose of the amendment and protect the rights of bank customers (Fforde 1992).

The terms of compensation for private shareholders also generated some challenges. Although none of the stockholders petitioned against the terms of compensation, a Commons Select Committee held hearings on their fairness. Appearing before the Select Committee on the Bank of England Bill, Treasury counsel Cyril Radcliffe went to great lengths to defend the compensation scheme (Commons 1945). This task was made more difficult because neither the chancellor nor the bank governor wanted to disclose the exact value of the bank's assets. Some members of the Labour Party complained that shareholders were overcompensated, but a party conference motion critical of the compensation terms was defeated (Craig 1982).

Overall, the plans for nationalization were relatively uncontroversial and moved through Parliament quickly (see, for example, Fforde 1992; Morgan 1984;

Thompson 1996).[2] Most saw the proposed bill as formalizing an already close working relationship between the Treasury and the Bank of England, a working relationship that had become even closer during the war effort. Hugh Dalton, Labour's Chancellor of the Exchequer, quipped that "the Old Man of the Treasury and the Old Lady of Threadneedle Street [the Bank of England], who had for some time been living in sin, were now to be married" (Pearce 1994).

Interestingly, the appointments procedure for the bank aroused little discussion. Radcliffe argued that although arrangement between the bank and the Treasury had worked well, "this is the time when what commonsense would require as the satisfactory structure as between the Bank and the Government should be put into legal form, and not left to working out by what I will call 'satisfactory chance.' . . . The time has come when the Government should avow its right to appoint the Governor, the Deputy-Governor, and the Court of Directors of this institution" (Commons 1945). During debate in the House of Lords, Lord Pethick-Lawrence pointed out that under the bill, policy decisions would be subject to parliamentary questioning, whereas in the current system, Parliament's authority over the bank was unclear.

The bill received only token opposition from the Conservatives. Winston Churchill, leader of the opposition, declared that he would not in principle oppose the bill. Most Conservative critics maintained that the present system had worked well in the past and that there was little reason to change it. These arguments did little to challenge Labour's bill. Indeed, Robert Boothby, a Conservative who had regularly criticized Norman, actually voted with the Labour government in support of the measure (Morgan 1984).

The ease with which the bill passed reflected the similarity of policy incentives faced by party politicians in Britain and the ideological coherence of the Labour Party at that time. Party legislators could trust their ministers to pursue monetary policy that benefited the party as a whole. Consequently, they had little incentive to limit the government's authority over the bank.

The Cross-National Variation of Central Bank Independence, 1970–90

Because the relationship between backbench legislators, coalition partners, and government ministers strongly influences the choice of central bank institutions, variations in that relationship across systems can explain cross-national differences in central bank independence. This section statistically tests the relationship between incentive divergence, the threat of punishment, and central bank independence.

Measurement of the Variables

Incentive Divergence

The degree of incentive divergence between legislators, parties, and ministers reflects both the distribution of constituent preferences and the configuration of electoral institutions.

Constituent Preferences. To measure the heterogeneity of constituent preferences over monetary policy, I employ the Alford index (Alford 1963). The Alford index subtracts the percentage of voters from non–working classes voting for the Left party(ies) from the percentage of blue-collar workers voting for the Left party(ies). High values reflect a high incidence of class voting. Low values indicate that class is a less-salient predictor of vote. Because low values imply that party politicians are likely to face constituents with a variety of preferences over monetary policy, the Alford index should have a negative relationship with central bank independence.[3]

Electoral Institutions. Politicians from the governing party(ies) are likely to compete in differently sized districts or at different times in systems with "strong" bicameral legislatures. Lijphart (1984) defines strong bicameralism as a situation in which both houses have roughly equal legislative powers and are selected according to different electoral rules. I use a dummy variable for countries with strong bicameralism: Australia, Germany, Switzerland, and the United States. Systems with strong bicameral legislatures should have more independent central banks.

The Threat of Punishment

The credibility of the threat of backbench legislators and coalition partners to punish the government reflects the polarization of the political system, legislative institutions, and the existence of coalition and minority governments.

Polarization. Following Powell (1982), I measure polarization as the average percentage of electoral support for extremist parties for the years 1960 to 1990. Because high levels of polarization imply that party legislators and coalition partners will be less willing to punish the government, polarization should be negatively related to central bank independence.[4]

Legislative Institutions. To capture the influence of legislative institutions, I use a dummy variable for systems with "strong and inclusive" committee systems (Powell and Whitten 1993; Strom 1990a). Because party legislators and coalition partners are more likely to withdraw their support from the government in systems with strong and inclusive legislative committees, the committee variable should have a positive relationship with central bank independence.[5]

Coalition and Minority Government. I calculated the proportion of time a country was governed by a coalition or minority government from 1960 to 1990. In systems with a high proportion of time under a coalition or minority government, the central bank will be more independent.[6]

Table 2 summarizes the independent variables and their sources. I expect independent central banks in systems with moderate Left parties (low Alford index), strong bicameralism, low polarization, strong committees, and regular coalition or minority governments.

Sample, Dependent Variable, and Methodology

The sample includes the 18 countries listed in table 1. Data availability and reliability limited the sample.

For the dependent variable, central bank independence, I used all four indices of central bank independence listed in table 1.[7] I report the results from only the average measure. Unless noted, results for all indices were similar. I used ordinary least squares (OLS) regression. I performed all calculations using Stata 5.0.

Results

The results of model I, reported in table 3, are partially consistent with the incentive divergence and potential punishment hypotheses. The Alford index has a negative, significant effect on central bank independence. Systems in which the Left parties have heterogeneous class support possess more independent central banks.[8] Systems with strong bicameral legislatures also possess more independent central banks. None of the indicators associated with potential punishment, however, is significant, although each coefficient is in the predicted direction.[9] Polarization, committee strength, and coalition/minority government are highly correlated. Although each is not individually significant, a Wald test indicates that the three variables are jointly significant at the 0.01 level of significance ($F(3, 12) = 5.17$). Model I also passes all diagnostic tests, indicating that the residuals are not serially correlated[10] (Durbin-Watson), are normally distributed (skewness and kurtosis), and are homoscedastic (Cook and Weisberg 1983). Additionally, there is no evidence of omitted variable bias (RESET).[11]

Given the joint significance of the polarization, committee strength, and coalition/minority government variables, I created a composite indicator for the threat of punishment by adding (1−polarization), committee strength, and coalition/minority government. I expect this indicator to have a positive relationship with central bank independence. The results from this equation,

TABLE 2. Independent Variables

Country	Alford Index	Strong Bicameralism	Polarization 1960–1990	Committee Strength	Coalition/ Minority Government	Punishment Index[a]
Australia	0.25	1	0.00	0	0.00	1.00
Austria	0.14	0	0.01	1	0.55	2.54
Belgium	0.20	0	0.17	1	1.00	2.83
Britain	0.33	0	0.02	0	0.02	1.00
Canada	0.01	0	0.00	0	0.32	1.32
Denmark	0.34	0	0.19	1	1.00	2.81
France	0.16	0	0.23	0	0.93	1.70
Germany	0.17	1	0.02	1	1.00	2.98
Ireland	0.13	0	0.02	0	0.61	1.59
Italy	0.15	0	0.36	0	1.00	1.64
Japan	0.15	0	0.15	0	0.20	1.06
Netherlands	0.15	0	0.06	1	1.00	2.94
New Zealand	0.32	0	0.01	0	0.00	0.99
Norway	0.28	0	0.09	1	1.00	2.91
Spain	0.20	0	0.08	0	0.00	0.92
Sweden	0.33	0	0.05	1	1.00	2.88
Switzerland	0.19	1	0.07	1	1.00	2.93
United States	0.13	1	0.00	0	0.60	1.60

[a]Computed as: (1 – polarization) + committee strength + proportion of coalition/minority government. The calculation of Austria's punishment index, for example, is: (1 – 0.01) + 1 + 0.55 = 2.54.

model II, support the hypothesis. The punishment index is significant and in the predicted direction. The Alford index and strong bicameralism variables remain significant and in the predicted direction. Model II explains 74 percent of the variance in the dependent variable for this sample. The model also passes all diagnostic tests.

Alternative Hypotheses

Given the importance of central banks for economic performance, political economists have offered several other explanations of the variation of central bank independence.

Tying the Hands

McCubbins, Noll, and Weingast (1989) argue that politicians structure bureaucracies to guarantee that their policy goals will not be overturned in the future. Similarly, Goodman (1991) claims that governments that prefer low inflation

TABLE 3. OLS Estimation of Central Bank Independence (Dependent Variable: Mean Central Bank Independence)

	I	II	III	IV	V	VI
Constant	0.52*** (0.07)	0.40*** (0.07)	0.42*** (0.08)	0.38*** (0.08)	0.39*** (0.07)	0.33*** (0.05)
Alford index	–0.73* (0.27)	–0.74** (0.25)	–0.77** (0.25)	–0.83** (0.29)	–0.78** (0.25)	
Strong bicameralism	0.22** (0.06)	0.25*** (0.05)	0.23*** (0.06)	0.26*** (0.05)	0.25*** (0.05)	
Polarization	–0.50 (0.33)					
Coalition/ minority government	0.12 (0.11)					
Committee strength	0.08 (0.08)					
Punishment index		0.09** (0.03)	0.11** (0.04)	0.10** (0.03)	0.09** (0.03)	
Trade/GDP			–0.06 (0.11)			
Capital account openness				0.02 (0.26)		
Partisanship					0.10 (0.09)	
Financial sector strength						0.15*** (0.03)
R^2	0.82	0.78	0.79	0.79	0.80	0.56
Adjusted R^2	0.74	0.74	0.73	0.73	0.74	0.54
F-Value	F(5, 12) =10.8	F(3, 14) =17.0	F(4, 13) =12.2	F(4, 13) =12.3	F(4, 13) =13.0	F(1, 16) =20.6
SEE	0.0885	0.0893	0.0915	0.0912	0.0892	0.1191
Cook-Weisberg $\chi^2(1)$	2.61	2.07	2.94	1.67	2.42	1.09
Normality	1.56	0.33	0.87	0.20	0.70	1.15
Durbin-Watson	1.76	2.10	2.07	2.02	2.09	1.70
RESET	F(3, 9) =0.73	F(3, 11) =0.76	F(3, 10) =0.86	F(3, 10) =0.84	F(3, 10) =1.02	F(3, 13) =0.97
N	18	18	18	18	18	18

$^*p < 0.05$, $^{**}p < 0.01$, $^{***}p < 0.001$, two-tailed test. Standard errors in parentheses.

and that expect a short tenure in office will adopt an independent central bank to limit the ability of future governments to manipulate economic policy. The "tying-the-hands" argument suggests that highly polarized systems or systems with highly antagonistic parties should have independent central banks. Systems with moderate centrist parties should have dependent banks because politicians can trust the opposition to pursue similar policies. The results from models I and II shown in table 3 contradict this hypothesis. Broad-based moderate Left parties (low Alford index) and low levels of polarization are associated with high levels of central bank independence.

Economic Openness

A second group argues that economic openness influences the level of central bank independence (Maxfield 1997). An open economy, dependent on international trade and foreign capital, requires an independent central bank. An independent central bank can help prevent inflation from eroding the competitive position of the economy, especially in countries that do not have floating exchange rates. An independent central bank also helps attract foreign capital and investment by demonstrating the host government's commitment to price stability (Maxfield 1997).

I tested the effect of economic openness in two ways. First, I included trade as proportion of GDP for the years 1970 to 1989. Model III in table 3 indicates that trade has no statistically significant effect on central bank independence.[12] Second, I included a measure of capital account openness based on Quinn (1997), computed by averaging his measure for the period 1973 to 1988. This measure has no statistically significant effect on central bank independence (model IV).

Partisanship

Political economists have also argued for a link between government partisanship and central bank structure. Right parties are traditionally more concerned with controlling inflation, whereas Left parties place more emphasis on employment and wealth redistribution (Alesina 1989; Alesina and Sachs 1988; Havrilesky 1987; Hibbs 1987). Consequently, Right parties will institute an independent central bank to counter inflationary pressures in the economy. Left parties will prefer a dependent bank, which allows them to manipulate monetary policy to enhance growth and employment.[13] This argument, however, suggests that new governments would reform the bank to suit their economic policy goals, implying more cross-temporal variation in central bank independence than is empirically observed.

To test the hypothesis, I created a measure of Left government strength based on Cameron (1984). The measure multiplies the percentage of cabinet seats held by Left parties by the percentage of a legislative majority held by Left parties in the legislature for each year and then averages those measures across the time period. Model V in table 3 reports the results of including the partisanship measure for the years 1970 to 1989. No statistically significant relationship between partisanship and central bank independence exists.[14]

Interest Groups

A fourth set of explanations centers on interest-group pressure as a determinant of bureaucratic structure (Moe 1989, 1990). Both Posen (1993, 1995) and Maxfield (1994) argue that the organization and political influence of a nation's financial sector strongly determine the central bank's institutional structure. Posen argues that systems in which the financial sector can organize an effective opposition to inflationary policies will have independent central banks.

To test this hypothesis, I used Posen's measure of financial sector strength, which is based on the presence of universal banking, the central bank's role in the regulation of the financial sector, federalism, and party fractionalization at the national level (model VI in table 3).[15] This measure of financial sector strength does have a positive, significant relationship with central bank independence. This model also passes all diagnostic tests. When financial sector strength was included with the variables from model II, however, the punishment index and financial sector index failed to attain significance because those two variables are correlated ($r = 0.67$; results not reported). However, the residual variance (SEE) is smaller in model II than in model VI (0.0893 versus 0.1191), suggesting that model II provides a more efficient prediction of central bank independence.

I also compared models II and VI with a parameter encompassing test (Granato, Inglehart, and Leblang 1996; Granato and Suzuki 1996). The parameter encompassing test indicates whether the substitution of one model's parameters for another's is statistically distinguishable. I used a joint F-test to test whether model II encompasses model VI (symbolically, model II ξ model VI). An insignificant statistic indicates that zero restrictions on model VI has no statistical effect on a joint model, composed of indicators from both models (i.e., model II ξ model VI). In contrast, a significant statistic signals that model II does not encompass model VI, meaning that model VI contains information that model II fails to capture. I also examined whether model VI encompasses model II. The results of the F-tests indicate that model II encompasses model

VI and that model VI does not encompass model II (see table 4). Consequently, it is possible to conclude that the variables in model II possess more predictive power than does the strength of the financial sector.

Sensitivity Analysis

Small N studies may suffer from a variety of statistical problems, including the possibility that parameter estimates are strongly affected by an individual case (Granato, Inglehart, and Leblang 1996; Jackman 1987). An observation's influence reflects both its discrepancy and leverage. Discrepancy occurs when an observation is associated with a large residual. Standardized and studentized residuals indicate which observations possess unusually large residuals. In an examination of the residuals of model II, the United Kingdom appears to be an outlier because it has a standardized residual of 2.22, outside the usual cutoff of plus or minus 2.0 (see table 5). The standardized residuals also suggest that Belgium (−1.64) and Denmark (1.65) may be outliers, although neither exceeds the cutoff point.[16]

Leverage refers to the potential for the model as a whole to be influenced by a few cases. Two statistics, Cook's Distance (D_i) and DFFITS, measure leverage (Belsley, Kuh, and Welsch 1980). A Cook's Distance (D_i) greater than $4/n$ indicates an influential observation. According to this criterion, Britain (0.49), Australia (0.30), and Denmark (0.23) are influential. A related diagnostic, DFFITS, also points to the influence of Britain and Denmark. Both Britain (1.69) and Denmark (1.02) had DFFITS values greater than the $2^*(k/n)^{1/2}$ cutoff recommended by Bollen and Jackman (1990).

Another diagnostic, $DFBETA_i$, measures the effect of deleting one observation on each parameter estimate. An absolute value of $DFBETA_i$ greater than one indicates that the observation shifts the coefficient at least one standard error (Bollen and Jackman 1990).[17] According to this criterion, Britain exerts undue influence on the parameter estimate for the Alford index (Alford $DFBETA_{U.K.} = 1.19$). None of the DFBETAs for the other independent variables exceeds the cutoff, although the punishment index DFBETA for Britain is extremely close (punishment $DFBETA_{U.K.} = -0.99$). The direction of these DFBETAs, however, indicates that Britain actually dampens the size of the coefficient for both the Alford index and the punishment index (i.e., pulls them both toward zero). That both these variables are significant even when Britain is in the sample lends credence to the results.

Overall, the diagnostics suggest that Britain and possibly Denmark are problematic cases. Does the existence of these outliers invalidate the parameter

TABLE 4. Encompassing Test

Model VI ξ Model II	Form	Test	Form	Model II ξ Model VI
5.31*	F(3, 13)	Joint model	F(1, 13)	1.24

*$p < 0.05$.

estimates of model II? Following Granato, Inglehart, and Leblang (1996), I handled these cases in a variety of ways. Table 6 compares the OLS results from model II in table 3 with a variety of estimation strategies. First, I have included a dummy variable for the influential cases (Britain and Denmark) in model 6a.[18] Second, I deleted Britain and Denmark from the sample (model 6b). In both models, the independent variables continue to be significant and in the predicted direction. As expected, the parameter estimate of the Alford index becomes even more negative, while the coefficient of the punishment index increases slightly.

I also re-estimated model II using three nonparametric techniques. The first technique employs a variant of robust regression. Robust regression produces parameter estimates that perform well even if the data slightly violate basic OLS assumptions concerning normality (Western 1995). The method I employ begins by dropping any observation that has a Cook's Distance $D_i > 1$ (no observations in my sample meet this criterion). The remaining observations are weighted according to their residuals, using Huber weights and subsequently, biweights. Weighted least squares is then used to generate new estimates. The process is iterated until the maximum change in weights drops below 0.01. Interestingly, the robust regression places zero weight on Britain and a very small weight on the Danish case (table 5). Consequently, the estimate in model 6c is similar to model 6b.

As with OLS, however, robust regression is also susceptible to highly influential observations (Western 1995). To constrain the influence of such cases, I used a simple one-bounded influence estimator suggested by Welsch (1980) and employed by Granato, Inglehart, and Leblang (1996), which uses the DFITTS values from the original OLS regression to down-weight observations.[19] The estimates, shown in model 6d, are similar to the estimates in the original OLS regressions.

Finally, I used a bootstrap technique to determine confidence intervals around the parameter estimates for each of the independent variables. Bootstrap resampling estimates the sampling distribution of a statistic, treating the sample as a population (Mooney 1996; Mooney and Duval 1993). I resampled

TABLE 5. Diagnostics and Case Weights

Country	Standardized Residual[a]	Studentized Residual[b]	Cook's Distance[c]	DFFITS[d]	DFBETA Alford Index[e]	DFBETA Strong Bicameralism[e]
Australia	–1.35	–1.39	0.30	–1.14	–0.39	–0.89
Austria	0.73	0.71	0.02	0.29	–0.16	–0.12
Belgium	–1.64	–1.75	0.10	–0.70	0.08	0.29
Britain	2.22	2.66	0.49	0.16	1.19	–0.17
Canada	1.21	1.23	0.21	0.93	–0.79	–0.25
Denmark	1.65	1.77	0.23	1.02	0.69	–0.22
France	–0.38	–0.37	0.00	–0.11	0.04	0.05
Germany	0.48	0.47	0.02	0.32	–0.03	0.23
Ireland	0.44	0.43	0.00	0.15	–0.08	–0.06
Italy	–1.31	–1.35	0.04	–0.44	0.19	0.18
Japan	0.00	0.00	0.00	0.00	–0.00	–0.00
Netherlands	–0.02	–0.02	0.00	–0.01	0.00	0.00
New Zealand	–0.86	–0.85	0.06	–0.50	–0.33	0.05
Norway	–0.86	–0.85	0.04	–0.39	–0.15	0.12
Spain	–0.41	–0.40	0.00	–0.17	–0.01	0.04
Sweden	–0.34	–0.32	0.00	–0.18	–0.11	0.04
Switzerland	0.47	0.46	0.02	0.30	–0.01	0.23
United States	0.28	0.28	0.00	0.17	–0.42	0.14

[a]Cutoff for influential observation: |Standardized Residual| > 2.0 (Bollen and Jackman 1990).

[b]Cutoff for influential observation: |Studentized Residual| > 2.0 (Bollen and Jackman 1990).

[c]Cutoff for influential observation: $D_i > 4/n$. When $N = 18$, $D_i > 0.22$ (Granato, Inglehart, and Leblang 1996).

[d]Cutoff for influential observation: $DFFITS_i > 2^*(k/n)^1/_2$. When $N = 18$, $DFFITS_i > 0.94$ (Bollen and Jackman 1990).

[e]Cutoff for influential observation: $DFBETA_i > 1.0$ (Bollen and Jackson 1990).

[f]Robust regression weights (Western 1995).

[g]Bounded-influence weights (Welsch 1980).

TABLE 6. Diagnostics on Model II Dependent Variable: Central Bank Independence (Average)

	Model 6a: Dummy Variable[a]	Model 6b: Cases Deleted[b]	Model 6c: Robust Regression[c]	Model 6d: Bounded Influence[d]	Model 6e: Bootstrapped (1000 Reps)[e]
Constant	0.45*** (0.04)	0.45*** (0.05)	0.45*** (0.05)	0.41*** (0.05)	0.40*** (0.07)
Alford index	−1.23*** (0.18)	−1.24*** (0.18)	−1.24*** (0.17)	−0.93*** (0.22)	−0.74** (0.20)
Strong bicameralism	0.27*** (0.03)	0.27*** (0.03)	0.26*** (0.03)	0.27*** (0.04)	0.25*** (0.05)
Punishment index	0.10*** (0.02)	0.11*** (0.02)	0.11*** (0.02)	0.10*** (0.02)	0.09*** (0.02)
Britain/Denmark dummy	0.25*** (0.04)				

*$p < 0.05$, **$p < 0.01$, ***$p < 0.001$, two-tailed test. Standard errors in parentheses. $N = 18$, except for model 5b ($N = 16$).

[a]Estimated with a dummy variable for the Britain and Denmark.

[b]Estimated without Britain or Denmark.

[c]Estimated using robust regression (Western 1995).

[d]Estimated using Welsch's one-step bounded influence estimator (Welsch 1980).

[e]Estimated using bootstrap resampling of the residuals with 1,000 replications.

with replacement the residuals of model II one thousand times. Model 6e presents the bootstrapped standard errors. Using the bootstrapped standard errors, I calculated the confidence intervals using the normal approximation method. For each independent variable, the 95 percent confidence interval does not span zero. The bootstrap confidence intervals therefore support the conclusions of the original OLS estimates in model II.

Each of these techniques demonstrates that the parameter estimates obtained in model II are robust. The Alford index, strong bicameralism, and the punishment index retain their significance and remain in the predicted direction.

Conclusion

Political parties provide a mechanism to account for the correlation between federalism and central bank independence. In large federal systems, party politicians face a variety of incentives over monetary policy, increasing the potential for intraparty conflicts over economic and monetary policy. The policy demands of party constituents will likely reflect regional differences in the economy, creating differences in the policy preferences of party politicians. Additionally, federal institutions force party politicians to satisfy different sets of constituents or compete for office at different times. The existence of federal veto points in the policy process—such as an upper chamber to represent the interests of regional units or powerful regional offices—means that parties must enjoy electoral success across the country, even in regions with very different economic activity, in order to control the policy process.

The information asymmetries of the monetary-policy process, however, create potential conflicts between backbench legislators, coalition partners, and cabinet ministers. The severity of these conflicts conditions politicians' incentives over the choice of central bank institutions. In systems in which politicians face different incentives over monetary policy—as in federal systems—and in which backbench legislators and coalition partners can credibly threaten to withdraw their support from the government, these potential conflicts can hurt the government's ability to remain in office. Consequently, parties in federal systems must create institutions that will help them balance the different interests and policy demands of party politicians and their constituents—institutions that can help them stay in office longer as well as build and maintain a viable electoral coalition. An independent central bank can help prevent these potential conflicts by acting as a check on the cabinet's discretion. As a result, party politicians have an incentive to choose an independent central bank.

Systems in which legislators, coalition partners, and government ministers share similar incentives over policy or in which the government's position in office is secure have a low potential for intraparty conflict over monetary policy. Party politicians have less incentive to limit the cabinet's policy discretion with an independent central bank.

The case accounts of central bank choice in Germany and Britain illustrate how these potential intraparty conflicts conditioned the choice of central bank institutions. In Germany, where federal institutions provided politicians with a variety of incentives over monetary policy, the Bundesrat vetoed plans to decrease the Bundesbank's independence in the 1950s and the 1990s. In Britain, on the other hand, where party politicians shared similar policy incentives, the political control of the Bank of England was not an issue in the 1940s. The statistical results also demonstrate that differences in political systems can account for cross-national variations in central bank independence.

The potential for intraparty conflict over monetary policy can therefore explain the cross-national variation of central bank independence in the 1970s and 1980s. While the potential for intraparty conflict reflects the configuration of political institutions (including federalism), it also is a product of the distribution of constituent preferences over economic and monetary policy. These preferences may change over time, altering the monetary-policy incentives faced by party politicians and in turn increasing the potential for intraparty conflict over monetary policy. As the potential for conflict increases, the political benefits of an independent central bank increase and pressure for central bank reform will grow. The next two chapters examine this process of central bank reform in the 1990s.

Chapter 6

Economic Internationalization, Intraparty Conflict, and Central Bank Reform

Throughout much of the postwar period, the level of central bank independence in most industrial democracies remained relatively stable. In the late 1980s and early 1990s, however, politicians in many industrial democracies reformed their central bank institutions, granting their central banks increased independence from direct political control.

I argue that this wave of central bank reform reflects long-term developments in the party systems of the industrial democracies. Changes in the policy preferences of constituents of the main governing parties and decreases in the ability of cabinet ministers to deliver promised economic outcomes increased the potential for intraparty conflicts over economic and monetary policy and in turn hurt the ability of the main governing parties to attain and retain office. Therefore, many political parties had to alter their electoral strategies and policy priorities in order to balance conflicting interests, rebuild social coalitions, and maintain electoral viability (Boix 1998; Garrett 1998a; Kitschelt 1994). Part of this strategic repositioning includes institutional reforms—reforms that are designed to reconcile diversified constituent demands while preserving the electoral success of the party. Central bank independence, I contend, represents one of those reforms.

In this chapter, I elaborate on this argument. The first section examines changes to the party systems of the industrial democracies since the 1970s, illustrating the increased potential for intraparty conflict over economic and monetary policy. This heightened potential for intraparty conflict, I argue, magnified the political benefits of adopting an independent central bank. The second section provides empirical support for this argument by examining the effect of economic internationalization and central bank independence on cabinet durability in 16 parliamentary systems between 1970 and 1992. The results show that an independent central bank protects cabinet durability, particularly under conditions of economic openness—precisely where one would expect more conflicts over monetary policy. In contrast, dependent central banks contribute to higher cabinet durability in relatively closed economies—where the potential for conflict between backbench legislators, coalition partners, and cabinet ministers is lower.

I contend that the political consequences of an independent central bank—fewer conflicts over monetary policy—can help explain variations in the timing and nature of central bank reform across the industrial democracies. Politicians in systems where economic internationalization has shortened cabinet durability have incentives to adopt an independent central bank as a way to prolong their tenure in office. Politicians in systems where cabinet durability is relatively unaffected by changes in economic openness have fewer incentives to adopt an independent central bank. Linking economic internationalization, cabinet durability, and central bank independence therefore can help explain variations in the timing and nature of central bank reform. In the third section, I evaluate these predictions.

Party System Change and Central Bank Reform

The increased potential for intraparty conflict over economic and monetary policy in the 1990s is a product of developments in the party systems of the industrial democracies. Through the 1950s and 1960s, these party systems enjoyed tremendous stability (Lipset and Rokkan 1967). Individual voters, ensconced within distinct subcultures, tended to identify closely with a particular party, helping to ensure that the main parties had stable and consistent levels of electoral support. Additionally, party systems often mirrored traditional class cleavages; that is, parties appealed either to the working class or to the bourgeoisie (with some exceptions such as Christian Democratic parties). Each party had different economic priorities, but within each party, constituents possessed relatively similar preferences over economic and monetary policy.

Since the early 1970s, however, these party systems have been in flux. Voters identify less and less with their former party affiliations. These dealigned voters cast ballots on the basis of instrumental calculations and policy programs rather than cultural attachments (Barnes 1997; Dalton, Flanagan, and Beck 1984; Lewis-Beck 1988; Lewis-Beck, Norpoth, and Lafay 1991). Consequently, vote levels for many of the traditional governing parties became less predictable from election to election (Maguire 1983; Pedersen 1983). In some systems, new parties appeared to challenge the main governing parties on both the Left (Kitschelt 1989; Richardson and Rootes 1995; Shull 1999) and the Right (Betz 1994; Kitschelt 1997). As a result, the main governing parties have pursued new electoral strategies to cope with the changing electoral environment (Kitschelt 1994; Muller and Strom 1999; Przeworski and Sprague 1986). Some parties moderated their policy positions; others became more extreme. These strategic decisions, however, often entailed internal party debate and controversy, as parties fought about how best to reshape their electoral coalitions in this new political environment.

This party-system instability reflects two developments, both related to longer-term transformations in the economies of the industrial democracies: (1) changing constituent demands over economic and monetary policy and (2) the decreasing ability of governments to deliver promised policy outcomes. Both developments increased the potential for intraparty conflict over economic policy within the main governing parties and made it more difficult for them to attain and retain office.

Changing Constituent Demands

Changes in constituent demands for economic and monetary policy are in part a consequence of three economic developments: greater economic wealth, increased economic openness, and the rise of the service sector. Each of these processes diversifies the policy incentives of politicians within the traditional governing parties.

First, the postwar period brought the industrial democracies unprecedented levels of economic development and stability. Citizens are wealthier, more educated, and have greater access to information. In many countries, a strong middle class has emerged—a middle class that does not always respond to traditional class-based political strategies (see, for example, Przeworski and Sprague 1986; Ramseyer and Rosenbluth 1993; Tarrow 1990). Economic prosperity has also allowed new issues to become prominent, including the "postmaterialist" agenda, which focuses on the environment, women's rights, and community participation (Esping-Andersen 1999; Inglehart 1997; Inglehart and Abramson 1994).

Second, increased economic openness changes constituent interests over economic and monetary policy (Alt and Gilligan 1994; Frieden 1991; Frieden and Rogowski 1996; Keohane and Milner 1996; Rogowski 1989). Economic internationalization alters the basis of economic interests from factors—primarily the worker–owner-class cleavage—to sectors, groups defined by asset-specific investments in a similar area of output. Actors within a sector have common interests that often cut across classes. For instance, both workers and owners involved in the export market may have similar policy preferences. In turn, their policy demands will differ from those of sectors that are insulated from international competition. These conflicts may center on the nature of wage bargaining (Franzese 2000; Golden, Lange, and Wallerstein 1999; Iversen 1996) or newly salient policy issues, such as exchange-rate policy (Frieden 1991).

Economic internationalization also affects the relative influence of economic sectors over economic and monetary policy (Frieden 1991). Owners of internationally mobile assets—in particular, capital—can threaten to withdraw those assets if they are dissatisfied with the government's policies. By deciding whether to invest their assets domestically or move them abroad, owners of mobile assets influence the success of macroeconomic policy and in turn, politicians' electoral fortunes. Therefore, politicians must respond to their demands if they wish to attract and retain these economic assets for their country, even if these sectors do not form part of the government's electoral coalition (Frieden 1991; Keohane and Milner 1996; Maxfield 1997). This "exit" threat increases their policy influence relative to owners of immobile factors—often labor. Consequently, the increased political power of owners of mobile assets expands the number of constituent pressures placed on politicians within the governing parties. It contributes to the possibility of conflict between legislators who appeal to asset-specific interests (e.g., workers in the home district) and cabinet ministers who have to consider the overall performance of the economy.

Third, the provision of services, rather than manufacturing, accounts for an increasingly large portion of economic production (Iversen and Cusak 2000; Krugman 1994). This trend is a result of the global overcapacity in the production of manufactured goods and in some countries, government policy. Governments in some countries have compensated for the loss of job demand in other economic sectors by expanding the service-oriented public sector (Franzese 2000; Iversen 1999; Iversen and Wren 1998). The changing sectoral composition of the economy creates a number of potential conflicts for political parties. Politicians must face difficult decisions about how to manage decline in key manufacturing sectors. Further, the wage and policy demands of the service sector, which is largely insulated from international competition, may reduce the competitiveness of exposed manufacturing interests.

These economic developments have altered the socioeconomic coalitions underlying political parties in the industrial democracies over the past 20 years (see, for example, Pempel 1998). The economic policy demands made by voters have diversified. New issues have become salient. New cleavages have emerged, reflecting divisions between exposed and sheltered sectors, manufacturing and service sectors, rising and declining industries, the private and the public sector, and between owners of mobile and specific assets. Because a party's policy reputation and voters' partisan identification evolve relatively slowly, these altered economic interests do not always line up with existing political parties. Consequently, the diversification of constituent preferences has increased the potential for intraparty conflict over economic policy. Parties must determine which constituents to satisfy and which to ignore. They must decide how to balance the policy demands of traditional constituents with appeals to new interests. These decisions entail distributional conflicts, shaping both the fortunes of affected constituents and the careers of party politicians.

Decreased Policy Effectiveness

Since the 1970s, the ability of governments to deliver promised economic outcomes has also decreased substantially. As government budget deficits ballooned in the industrial democracies, fiscal policy became less useful as a policy instrument. At the same time, the link between monetary policy and economic outcomes became less predictable. Increased economic openness during this period intensified the problems of economic management. Consequently, cabinet ministers had less ability to satisfy party legislators and their constituents, increasing the probability that backbench legislators and coalition partners would withdraw their support from the cabinet.

The emergence of high public debt in many industrial democracies limited the flexibility of fiscal policy. During the 1970s and early 1980s, many governments ran high budget deficits, increasing their public debt burden substantially (de Haan and Sturm 1994, 1997; Franzese 2000; Hallerberg and von Hagen 1999; Roubini and Sachs 1989a, 1989b; von Hagen 1992). In Italy, Ireland, and Belgium, the ratio of public debt to GDP actually exceeded 100 percent. Consequently, many governments had to devote an increasing portion of their budgets to service interest payments, limiting the possibility of expanding successful programs or launching new spending initiatives. Higher interest rates during the 1980s exacerbated this problem. Political parties were therefore severely limited in their ability to use fiscal policy to manage and expand their social coalitions. Furthermore, governments could not easily use fiscal policy to smooth short-term fluctuations in macroeconomic performance. As a result, government ministers faced a temptation to rely on monetary policy to manage the economy.

At the same time, however, established monetary-policy choices no longer produced predictable outcomes. Prior to the 1970s, monetary policy reflected the idea of the Phillips Curve, which predicted a relatively stable trade-off between inflation and unemployment. Policymakers could simply expand the economy to a point at which the cost of higher inflation balanced the benefit of lower unemployment. In the 1970s, however, both theoretical critiques and empirical evidence undermined confidence in the Phillips Curve. As a consequence, it became less clear how monetary policy affected overall economic performance—and what policies policymakers should pursue (Clarida, Gali, and Gertler 1999; Sargent 1999).

From a theoretical perspective, Friedman (1968) noted that the existence of a long-run Phillips Curve requires that economic agents not anticipate the level of inflation when negotiating their wage contracts, an unrealistic assumption about individual behavior. If economic agents build inflation expectations into their wage demands, then a long-run trade-off between inflation and unemployment does not exist. The best outcome a policymaker could achieve would be to keep employment near the level it would be if firms and workers had expectations of nonaccelerating inflation.

In the short run, on the other hand, a trade-off between unemployment and inflation is possible. Monetary expansions can affect real economic variables—growth, employment—if economic agents are surprised by policy changes (Lucas 1972). The economic boom, however, will last only until economic agents have adjusted their inflation expectations. It is a point of debate in the literature how long this adjustment takes—and as a result, how much the economy benefits (Granato 2000; Hall and Franzese 1998; Iversen 1998; Krugman 1994).

Even as economists attacked the Phillips Curve theoretically, events were undermining it. During the 1970s, the industrial economies suffered from stagflation—a combination of high inflation and high unemployment—an outcome unexplained by the Phillips Curve. Ironically, therefore, as growing public debt forced policymakers to rely on monetary policy for macroeconomic management, the consequences of monetary policy became less predictable—and the policy guidelines for policymakers more opaque.

During this period, the industrial economies also became more exposed to the international economy. International trade continued to grow (Milner and Keohane 1996). Financial-market deregulation sharply increased capital mobility as well (Goodman and Pauly 1993; Kapstein 1994; Quinn and Inclan 1997; Simmons 1999). These increased levels of economic openness exacerbated the problems of policy management. Openness exaggerates the economic and social consequences of policy actions (Franzese 2000; Frieden 1991). Advances in technology shorten the time lag between policy choices and policy outcomes. Policymakers must therefore respond more quickly and more accurately to exogenous shocks in order to meet the demands of their constituents.

Additionally, the volume and pace of international markets can overwhelm many national policy tools (Andrews 1994). By the early 1990s, for example, transactions in international currency markets totaled well over $1 trillion each day, dwarfing the reserves of any individual country and limiting the ability of countries to affect the exchange rate through market intervention. As a result, national macroeconomic policies are often less effective in delivering policy outcomes (Goodman 1992; Goodman and Pauly 1993).

Fewer barriers to international economic activity also reduce national policy autonomy, making it more difficult for political leaders to manage the macroeconomy. Both monetary and fiscal policy can be affected by increased openness (Clark 1999; Clark and Hallerberg 2000; Oatley 1999; Simmons 1994). According to the Mundell-Fleming conditions, maintaining a fixed exchange rate in a world of capital mobility will limit the ability to use monetary policy for domestic-policy objectives. With floating exchange rates and capital mobility, however, fiscal policy may become less effective (Frieden 1991; Milner and Keohane 1996).

Decreased policy effectiveness hurt the ability of cabinet ministers to achieve promised economic outcomes—with predictable political consequences. Poor economic performance led to sharp electoral losses for incumbents. Parties that were in office during the stagflation of the 1970s were exceptionally hard hit, losing their reputation for capable economic management.

Socioeconomic Change, Intraparty Conflict, and Institutional Reform

The combination of diversified constituent demands and decreased policy effectiveness increased the possibility of intraparty conflict over economic and monetary policy during the 1980s and 1990s—conflicts that threatened the ability of the main governing parties to win and retain office. Indeed, intraparty conflicts occurred throughout the industrial democracies and across the ideological spectrum.

In Left parties, traditional working-class constituents battled not only export interests but also middle-class postmaterialists and public-sector workers for control of party programs (Kitschelt 1994, 1999). In Germany, the Social Democratic–led government of the 1970s and early 1980s was divided between moderates and trade unionists, contributing to the collapse of the government in the early 1980s. In Britain, the Labour Party splintered as it adjusted its policies in the wake of Thatcher's victory in 1979. The Labour Party originally pulled leftward, prompting some moderates to leave the party in 1981 to found the more centrist Social Democratic Party. After another electoral defeat in 1983, Labour Party leaders struggled to pull the party back toward the center—a long and tumultuous process that culminated with the election of Tony Blair in 1997. In France during the early 1980s, François Mitterrand's decision to maintain the commitment to the EMS involved sweeping changes to the Socialists' constituent base. By pursuing economic *rigueur,* Mitterrand rejected a focus on blue-collar constituents and reached out to middle-class professionals in the nontradables sector, creating conflict and dissension within the party (Frieden 1994; Loriaux 1991). In the United States, Democratic Party centrists and trade unionists battled over trade and environmental issues (Shoch 2000).

Right parties faced similar conflicts. The Italian Christian Democrats suffered internal battles over the best response to union militancy and the economic shocks of the 1970s, pursuing stop-go policies that alternately sought to appease the unions and then tighten macroeconomic policy. In Britain, policy conflicts between Tory Wets and radical free-market Thatcherites divided the Conservative Party during the 1980s and 1990s (Hall 1986). The Republican Party in the United States exhibited similar divisions.

Although these conflicts often centered on economic and monetary-policy issues, they represented more fundamental concerns about the long-term trajectory and viability of these parties. Changes in both the policy preferences of constituents and the government's policy efficacy meant that parties were operating in a new political environment—an environment that not only challenged parties to maintain their traditional constituents but also provided them with opportunities to expand their electoral coalitions.

One strategy to enhance the party's fortunes in this changed political environment involved the support of institutional reform. Institutional reform can provide outlets for the representation of new interests, demonstrate policy commitment to affected constituents, or enhance policy effectiveness. Institutional reforms can therefore potentially help parties balance the interests of party politicians with divergent policy incentives and reestablish an electoral coalition. Where the increased potential for intraparty conflict threatened the ability of parties to win and maintain office, party politicians had incentives to pursue institutional reform.

I argue that central bank reform reflects such calculations. A more independent central bank can help parties overcome internal party divisions over policy. First, it acts as a check on the cabinet's policy discretion. The policy information furnished by a more independent central bank provides credible assurances about the cabinet's policy behavior to backbench legislators, coalition partners, and constituents. A more independent central bank also enhances monetary-policy effectiveness. It signals to economic agents that monetary policy will be insulated from excessive partisan and electoral manipulation (Cukierman 1992; Hall and Franzese 1998; Maxfield 1997). Consequently, economic agents will adjust their behavior more quickly, improving policy efficacy. Making the central bank more independent does, of course, entail some political costs: the cabinet loses the ability to manipulate policy for short-term electoral or partisan gain. But where intraparty conflicts threaten the party's ability to win and stay in office, the political benefits of an independent central bank outweigh these costs.

In particular, I argue that economic internationalization has increased the political value of an independent central bank. Internationalization diversifies constituent demands and decreases policy effectiveness, increasing the possibility of intraparty conflict. In systems where these conflicts threaten the parties' ability to attain and retain office, politicians have more incentive to adopt an independent central bank. In contrast, where the configuration of domestic institutions prevented intraparty conflict from hurting the parties' ability to remain in office, politicians had fewer incentives to adopt an independent central bank. In these systems, central bank reform will be delayed or put off entirely.

Economic Internationalization, Domestic Institutions, and Cabinet Durability

In this section, I examine cabinet durability in parliamentary systems to show that the political value of an independent central bank is higher under conditions of increased economic openness.[1] Economic internationalization—increased capital mobility and exposure to international trade—has increased the possibility of policy conflict between backbench legislators, coalition partners, and cabinet ministers, making cabinets less durable. An independent central bank, however, can prevent some of these potential conflicts and as a consequence help politicians prolong their position in office. If independent central banks do prevent conflict over monetary policy, I expect cabinets in parliamentary systems with independent central banks to survive longer than cabinets in similar systems with dependent central banks.

Cabinet Durability

The political-science literature argues that cabinet duration is a function of the cabinet's attributes, such as majority status and number of parties in the coalition, and the bargaining environment, such as the fragmentation of the party system and party-system polarization (Alt and King 1994; King, Alt, Burns, and Laver 1990; Laver and Schofield 1990; Warwick 1994). Two other factors are also likely to influence expected cabinet duration: the diversity of policy incentives faced by politicians in the governing party(ies) and the ability of the government to determine policy outcomes. The divergence of policy incentives promotes conflict between and within the governing parties. If politicians within each party face different incentives over economic policy, it is more difficult not only to form a government but also to keep it together. Legislators will be more likely to withdraw their support from the cabinet if their policy demands are not met. Consequently, the more diverse the interests in the governing party(ies), the less stable the government.

The government's ability to influence economic performance also influences cabinet duration. Government ministers need to deliver policy outcomes in order to maintain the support of backbench legislators and coalition partners. If government ministers do not have the capability to produce promised outcomes—if, for instance, the link between policy and outcomes is unclear or vulnerable to external shocks—dissatisfied backbenchers and coalitions partners may bring down the government. Therefore, the more the government can shape economic outcomes, the longer the expected cabinet duration.

I argue that the divergence of policy incentives within the governing party(ies) and the government's policy effectiveness is a function of economic internationalization and the configuration of domestic political institutions.

Economic Internationalization

As previously discussed, economic internationalization diversifies constituent demands over economic and monetary policy and reduces the ability of cabinet ministers to deliver promised economic outcomes. Both of these developments increase the likelihood that backbench legislators and coalition partners may withdraw their support from the government, leading to shorter cabinet duration. Therefore, systems with higher levels of exposure to the international economy will have shorter cabinet duration.

I measure economic internationalization along two dimensions (Milner and Keohane 1996). The first dimension reflects barriers to the movement of economic assets across borders. Increased economic internationalization implies fewer restrictions on the movement of capital and traded goods across borders, including no capital controls, full convertability of currencies, no restrictions on the current account, and no tariff or nontariff barriers to trade. As a proxy for this variable, I use a measure of *capital account openness* compiled by Quinn (1997). This variable ranges from 1.5 (high restrictions) to 4 (no restrictions).[2]

The second dimension reflects the degree of exposure to the international economy. I measure this by the sum of imports and exports as a proportion of gross domestic product. This *trade openness* variable ranges from 18 percent to 148 percent of GDP. I expect both capital account openness and trade openness to have a negative effect on cabinet durability.

Domestic Institutions

Domestic institutions mediate the effects of economic internationalization on cabinet durability (Garrett and Lange 1996). Three sets of institutions influence this relationship: coalition and party-system attributes, the level of unionization, and the institutional status of the central bank.

Coalition and Party-System Attributes

According to the political-science literature, cabinet durability is a function of coalition attributes and party-system attributes (Alt and King 1994; King, Alt, Burns, and Laver 1990; Laver and Schofield 1990; Warwick 1994). Coalition attributes reflect the majority status of the government and the number of parties in the government. According to the literature, single-party majority governments tend to be most durable, minimum-winning coalitions slightly less durable, and oversize and minority governments least durable.

I include dummy variables for *government type* in the analysis: single-party majority, minimum-winning coalition, oversize coalition, single-party minority, and coalition minority.

Party-system attributes include fragmentation of the political system and political polarization. Political scientists argue that the more fragmented and polarized the political system, the shorter the expected cabinet duration. I include a variable for party-system *fractionalization,* which measures the number of effective political parties in the system (Rae 1971). This variable should have a negative effect on cabinet durability. *Polarization* is measured by the electoral support for extremist parties. More support for extremist parties also implies shortened duration.

Unionization

The level of unionization influences the relationship between economic internationalization and cabinet durability. At both high and low levels of unionization, cabinet durability will be high. Moderate levels of unionization, however, may hurt cabinet durability.

First, consider the effect of unionization on the diversity of policy incentives within the governing coalition. At one end, strong centralized unions decrease the diversity of policy demands faced by politicians in the governing parties. Large encompassing unions can coordinate the particularistic demands of workers or firm-level unions, even in situations where workers have different market interests (Garrett 1998a; Lange and Garrett 1985; Olson 1982). As a result, governing politicians will face more coherent policy demands in systems with strong unions. The coherence of these policy demands will reduce the potential for policy conflict within the governing party(ies) and therefore contribute to higher cabinet durability.

At the other end of the spectrum, where unions are weak, politicians face working-class constituents with a wider variety of policy interests, but these workers lack the organizational power to press their claims. Politicians in the governing parties will not face strong pressure to respond to union demands. Union weakness will therefore reduce the potential for policy conflict and help increase cabinet durability.

In systems where unionization is moderate, however, workers will likely have both a greater variety of policy interests and significant organizational power. The diversity of these demands—and the ability of the unions to press their claims—provides politicians within the governing parties with conflicting incentives over economic policy, which in turn shortens cabinet durability.

The level of unionization will also have a curvilinear effect on the government's policy effectiveness. High levels of unionization with centralized wage bargaining may enhance the government's policy effectiveness. Strong unions can better coordinate a response to changes in government macroeconomic policy (Franzese 2000; Garrett 1998a; Hall and Franzese 1998; Iversen 1998, 1999; Lange and Garrett 1985; Scharpf 1987). This coordination deters militant wage behavior, which in turn can improve real economic performance. Very low levels of unionization, on the other hand, may also improve the government's policy effectiveness by facilitating market adjustments to government policy. Weak unions do not have the organizational strength to prevent wages from adjusting quickly to market-clearing levels.

At moderate levels of unionization, however, unions cannot coordinate wage demands or facilitate wage adjustments to policy changes. As a result, the government may have to pursue overly tight monetary policy to signal its commitment to low inflation and induce wage moderation among workers (Cukierman 1992). This will hurt the government's policy effectiveness—and its ability to hold a governing coalition together.

I include a variable measuring the level of *unionization* in the economy as the proportion of unionized workers in the work force.[3] I also include the squared value of unionization.

The effect of unionization on cabinet durability will also depend on the level of trade openness. Unions in open economies may be less able to coordinate the policy demands and policy response of their members (Iversen 1996). Consequently, I include interaction terms between trade openness and the unionization variables.

Central Bank Independence

Independent central banks will help increase cabinet durability in the face of economic internationalization. First, an independent central bank helps alleviate potential conflicts over monetary policy between politicians by helping to check the cabinet's discretion over monetary policy. Second, an independent central bank also strengthens the government's policy effectiveness by providing credibility to the government's policy choices (Cukierman 1992). An independent central bank therefore should increase cabinet durability.

I include a measure of *central bank independence*. Because systems with independent central banks should have longer cabinet duration than systems with dependent central banks, the coefficient should be positive.

The effect of central bank independence on cabinet durability will also vary according to the openness of the economy and the organization of economic interests. First, in systems with full capital mobility, an independent central bank will provide credibility with international markets. I include an interaction term by multiplying capital account openness by central bank independence. At higher levels of capital openness, I expect central bank independence to have a stronger positive effect on cabinet durability.

Second, independent central banks will also affect cabinet durability based on the organization of interests within the economy. In particular, independent central banks can better deter militant wage behavior where unions are organized (Franzese 2000; Hall and Franzese 1998; Iversen 1998). To capture this effect, I multiplied central bank independence with the unionization*trade openness interaction variables.

Partisanship

The partisanship of the government may affect the relationship between economic internationalization and cabinet durability. However, the literature does not offer a clear prediction. Recent work suggests that economic internationalization will likely shorten the expected duration of Left governments more than Right governments. The socioeconomic consequences of economic internationalization will more likely cause conflict within the Left's traditional constituent base (Garrett 1995; Golden, Langer, and Wallerstein 1999; Milner and Keohane 1996). Economic internationalization creates divisions between workers in sectors exposed to international competition and those insulated from the international economy (Iversen 1996). Additionally, internationalization enhances the policy influence of financial interests, a constituent not in the traditional Left social coalition. These developments will likely create tension and policy conflict in Left parties and lead to less-stable governments.

On the other hand, Left governments have enjoyed long tenures in the many small, open economies of western Europe (Katzenstein 1985). These parties have used corporatist bargaining and extensive welfare states to insulate their constituents from international economic volatility and create stable political systems (Cameron 1978; Lange and Garrett 1985).

I include a measure of Left government strength based on Cameron (1984). I do not expect that partisanship will influence cabinet durability by itself. However, I do expect the consequences of economic internationalization to be more apparent in Left governments. Consequently, I multiplied this variable with three other variables: capital restrictions, trade openness, and central bank independence.

Table 7 contains the summary statistics for all the variables employed in the empirical analysis.

Sample, Dependent Variable, and Methodology

Sample

The sample includes 182 cabinets from 16 countries: Australia, Austria, Belgium, Britain, Canada, Denmark, Finland, France, Germany, Ireland, Italy, Japan, the Netherlands, New Zealand, Norway, and Sweden.[4] The sample extends from approximately 1970 to 1992. For each country, the sample begins

TABLE 7. Descriptive Statistics

Variable	Mean	Standard Deviation	Minimum	Maximum
Cabinet durability	0.55	0.32	0.041	1
Time to election	39.46	13.70	3	59
Single-party majority	0.23	0.42	0	1
Single-party minority	0.21	0.41	0	1
Oversize coalition	0.21	0.43	0	1
Minimum-winning coalition	0.21	0.41	0	1
Fractionalization	0.69	0.10	0.41	0.87
Polarization	0.13	0.12	0	0.42
Trade openness	63.64	29.41	18.01	148.68
Capital account openness	2.84	0.64	1.5	4
Central bank independence	0.33	0.14	0.17	0.69
Unionization	0.48	0.17	0.10	0.84
Partisanship (Left)	0.34	0.42	0	1.31
Inflation	8.09	4.79	0.47	23.58
Unemployment	5.51	3.28	0.17	16.7

N = 182

with the first cabinet installed after 1970 and ends with the last cabinet that dissolved in the early 1990s. The sample includes no censored data.

The number of cabinets varies substantially across the countries in the sample. Canada and Germany had the fewest governments (7 each), whereas Italy and Belgium had the most governments (20 and 18, respectively).

Dependent Variable

For the dependent variable, I could simply use the number of months that a cabinet is in office. Constructing the dependent variable in this manner, however, leads to complications that could bias the results. First, countries have different constitutionally mandated electoral terms—36, 48, or 60 months—that define the maximum number of months a government can hold office. If the dependent variable is simply the number of months in office, I would not be able to discern whether a cabinet that lasted 36 months completed its maximum term or if the cabinet ended prematurely. Second, measuring the dependent variable as the number of months in office obscures the durability of cabinets that do not form at the beginning of the electoral term. Consider two hypothetical cabinets in a system with a 48-month electoral term. The first cabinet forms immediately after an election and serves two years before collapsing. The second cabinet forms with only two years left before a mandated election and then serves out its maximum term.

If the dependent variable were measured as months in office, both would be counted as 24 months, even though the latter served its maximum term.

To overcome these issues, I constructed a dependent variable that measures cabinet duration as the proportion of the maximum term available when the cabinet takes office. For example, a cabinet that lasts 36 months out of a possible 48 would score a 0.75. A cabinet that formed only 12 months before constitutionally mandated elections and survived for those 12 months is coded 1.

I include a control variable, *time to election,* measuring the maximum number of months that a government could potentially be in office.[5] For example, in a country with a 60-month electoral clock, a government that formed immediately after an election would score a 60 because it could potentially be in office for 60 months. A government that formed with only one year left before constitutionally mandated elections would receive a 12 because it could be in office for only 12 months. The longer the potential time a government can be in office increases the possibility that a government will collapse during its term. Consequently, I expect this variable to have a negative coefficient.

Methodology

I employ simple OLS regression. But cross-country differences in cabinet durability, potential problems with serial correlation and high-influence observations, and a skewed dependent variable suggest that simple OLS will produce inefficient parameter estimates. Consequently, I also use three alternative estimators.

The first challenge to OLS is that instances of cabinet durability within a certain country may not be independent of one another. The literature on cabinet formation, as well as clear cross-national differences in cabinet duration, suggests that country-specific factors, such as similar political institutions or practices, will affect all cabinets in that country. As a consequence, there may be unequal variation in cabinet durability across countries. For example, cabinet duration in Italy may differ a great deal, whereas the length of cabinets in Germany is relatively similar. To address this issue, I also run the model using OLS regression with robust (Huber-White) standard errors. This method assumes that observations are independent across countries but not necessarily independent within countries.

A second concern arises from the possibility of serial correlation in the residuals; that is, the errors may be related to one another, either across countries or over time. For example, the duration of a cabinet in Italy at time t is likely to be related to the duration of prior cabinets in Italy because those observations share a similar political environment. To correct for this, I use OLS regression with panel-corrected standard errors and panel specific AR(1) as suggested by Beck and Katz (1995, 1996).

Third, OLS regression is vulnerable to outlying or influential observations. These observations can cause marked changes in parameter estimates. Both the skewed distribution of the dependent variable and distinct patterns of cabinet durability across countries suggest that outliers may be a problem. Consequently, I estimate the model using a variant of robust regression.[6] Robust regression provides unbiased and efficient parameter estimates even when there are significant departures from normality.

I report the results from all four estimation strategies. Although OLS is the most conservative estimation technique and should have the largest standard errors, comparison of the standard errors across the four models provides an important robustness check.

Results

Table 8 contains the statistical results. Column entries are parameter estimates, and standard errors are in parentheses. Models I, II, and III are estimated using OLS. Models IV, V, and VI are estimated using OLS with robust standard errors, OLS regression with panel-corrected standard errors and panel specific AR(1), and robust regression, respectively.

Model I provides a baseline model of cabinet duration, based solely on attributes of the governing coalition and the party system. The model as a whole is statistically different from zero. Time to election, fractionalization, and polarization are statistically significant and, as predicted, negative. The negative coefficient on the time-to-election variable indicates that the longer potential term in office, the less likely the cabinet is to last the entire period. Consistent with the literature, the estimates for the fractionalization and polarization variables indicate that more heterogeneous party systems produce cabinets that survive for shorter times. Surprisingly, none of the government types is statistically different from zero.

Model II includes the central bank independence variable. The parameter estimates for the attributes of the governing coalition and the party system remain similar. The central bank variable is, as predicted, positive and significant. According to the results, systems with independent central banks have higher levels of cabinet durability. For a hypothetical government beginning a potential four-year term in office, increasing the level of central bank independence from 0.2 (about one-standard deviation below the mean) to 0.5 (about one standard deviation above the mean) increases expected durability by about four months.

Models III–VI add variables capturing economic internationalization, domestic institutions, and the interactive terms. Interestingly, inclusion of these

TABLE 8. Models of Cabinet Durability

Variable	I	II	III	IV	V	VI
Constant	1.36*	1.18*	2.14*	2.14*	2.14*	2.19*
	(0.25)	(0.27)	(0.76)	(0.63)	(0.78)	(0.77)
Time to election	–0.006*	–0.006*	–0.004*	–0.004*	–0.004*	–0.004*
	(0.002)	(0.002)	(0.002)	(0.002)	(0.001)	(0.002)
Single-party majority	0.10	0.16	0.30*	0.30*	0.30*	0.31*
	(0.10)	(0.10)	(0.11)	(0.08)	(0.08)	(0.11)
Single-party minority	0.05	0.08	0.07	0.07	0.065	0.098
	(0.08)	(0.08)	(0.09)	(0.06)	(0.07)	(0.09)
Oversize coalition	0.04	0.08	0.13	0.13*	0.13	0.15
	(0.08)	(0.08)	(0.09)	(0.06)	(0.08)	(0.09)
Minimum-winning coalition	0.14	0.16**	0.23*	0.23*	0.23*	0.25*
	(0.08)	(0.08)	(0.09)	(0.09)	(0.09)	(0.09)
Fractionalization	–0.83*	–0.73*	–1.26*	–1.26*	–1.26*	–1.36*
	(0.31)	(0.31)	(0.43)	(0.35).	(0.34)	(0.43)
Polarization	–0.64*	–0.56*	–0.055	–0.055	–0.055	–0.14
	(0.22)	(0.22)	(0.36)	(0.40)	(0.25)	(0.37)
Central bank independence		0.30**	–1.12	–1.12	–1.12	–2.31
		(0.16)	(1.42)	(1.17)	(1.23)	(1.43)
Unionization			–4.99	–4.99	–4.99	–3.43
			(3.29)	(3.41)	(3.37)	(3.32)
Unionization squared			7.75	7.75	7.75*	6.05
			(4.08)	(4.22)	(3.82)	(4.10)
Partisanship (Left)			0.62*	0.62*	0.62*	0.62*
			(0.31)	(0.22)	(0.27)	(0.31)
Trade openness			–0.006	–0.007	–0.006	–0.002
			(0.01)	(0.01)	(0.01)	(0.01)
Capital account openness			–0.07	–0.07	–0.068	–0.11
			(0.11)	(0.06)	(0.10)	(0.11)
Trade × Left			0.01*	0.01*	0.01*	0.01*
			(0.003)	(0.003)	(0.003)	(0.003)
CBI × Left			–0.09	–0.09	–0.09	–0.07
			(0.47)	(0.40)	(0.40)	(0.48)
CBI × Capital account openness			0.43	0.43	0.43	0.68*
			(0.32)	(0.25)	(0.29)	(0.32)

(continued)

terms makes the government-type variables statistically significant. (The omitted category is coalition-minority governments). Additionally, the magnitudes of the government-type parameter estimates are consistent with the literature. Single-party majority governments and minimum-winning coalitions are the most durable. Both single-party minority and coalition minority governments are least durable. Party-system fractionalization remains significant and in the predicted direction, but polarization becomes statistically insignificant.

TABLE 8.—*Continued*

Variable	I	II	III	IV	V	VI
Capital account openness × Left			0.02	0.02	0.02	–0.005
			(0.09)	(0.07)	(0.06)	(0.09)
Unionization × trade openness			0.06	0.06	0.06	0.02
			(0.06)	(0.06)	(0.06)	(0.06)
$Unionization^2$ × trade openness			–0.095	–0.095	–0.095	–0.042
			(0.07)	(0.07)	(0.07)	(0.07)
CBI × unionization × trade openness			–0.004	–0.004	–0.004	0.043
			(0.04)	(0.02)	(0.03)	(0.04)
CBI × $unionization^2$ × trade openness			–0.002	–0.002	–0.002	–0.068
			(0.054)	(0.038)	(0.047)	(0.054)
Tests of joint significance						
Model	9.86*	9.16*	5.62*	67.93*	515.25*	7.81*
Openness			2.36*	7.43*	35.94*	3.90*
Trade openness			2.92*	8.39*	27.82*	4.39*
Capital account openness			1.35	1.60	8.88*	2.57*
CBI			0.63	2.71**	5.25	1.87**
Left			3.10*	3.70*	15.35*	4.24*
Unionization			3.71*	11.13*	47.35*	5.32*

Note: Tests of joint significance are for combinations of the following variables:
Model: for the model as a whole.
Openness: all capital account and trade variables.
Trade openness: trade openness, trade openness × unionization, trade openness × $unionization^2$, CBI × trade openness × unionization, CBI × trade openness × $unionization^2$, trade openness × Left.
Capital account openness: capital account openness, CBI × capital account openness, capital account openness × Left.
CBI: CBI, CBI × Left, CBI × capital account openness, CBI × trade openness × unionization, CBI × trade openness × $unionization^2$.
Left: Left, trade openness × Left, CBI × Left, capital account openness × Left.
Union: unionization, $unionization^2$, trade openness × unionization, trade openness × $unionization^2$, CBI × trade × unionization, CBI × trade openness × $unionization^2$.
For Models I–IV and VI, tests of joint significance are *F*-tests. For Model V, test of joint significance is Chi(2) test.
[a]Models I–III: OLS regression
[b]Model IV: OLS regression with robust standard errors
[c]Model V: OLS regression with panel-corrected standard errors and panel specific AR(1)
[d]Model VI: robust regression
*$p < 0.05$, **$p < 0.10$
$N = 182$ for all models.

The standard errors across models III–VI are fairly consistent. As expected, the OLS standard errors (model III) tend to be slightly larger. With a few exceptions, none of the interaction terms is individually significant. T-statistics test whether a parameter estimate is statistically different from zero holding all other variables constant. With interactive terms, however, this is not

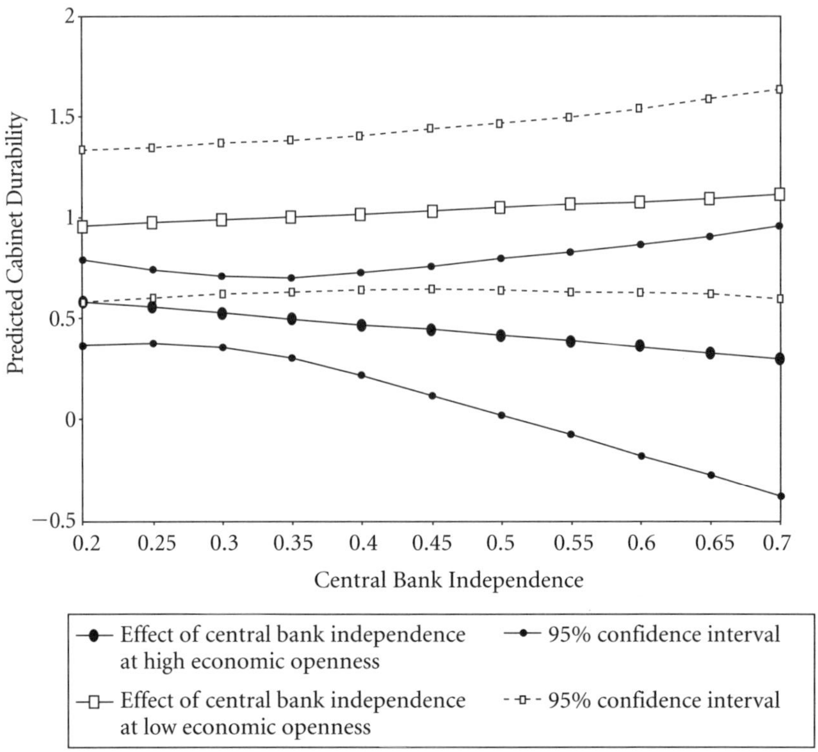

Fig. 3. Effect of central bank independence on cabinet durability

really possible. Instead, I test for the joint significance of different sets of variables. These tests, included in table 8, indicate that most sets of variables are jointly significant. But again, the OLS estimates appear to be the least efficient of the four models.

The interactive terms, however, make interpretation of individual variables difficult. Consequently, I present the results graphically. Figure 3 shows the effects of central bank independence on cabinet durability. Holding all other variables constant, I generated predicted values of cabinet durability using the sample range of central bank independence (King, Tomz, and Wittenberg 2000). The x-axis represents the range of variation for the central bank independence variable. The y-axis represents the predicted values of cabinet duration.

I have argued that central bank independence is likely to improve cabinet durability where conflicts over monetary policy are likely—that is, in an open economy. In other words, there is an interactive effect between central bank independence and the level of economic openness. Thus, holding other variables at their means, I varied the level of economic openness. To calculate predicted cabinet durability in a closed economy, I restricted capital account openness to be at its lowest level in the sample (1.5) and trade openness to be one standard deviation below its mean (30 percent of GDP).

The line in figure 3 marked "Effect of CBI at low economic openness" illustrates how central bank independence (CBI) affects cabinet durability in a closed economy. The slope of this line is negative. In a closed economy, central bank independence shortens cabinet durability; that is, higher levels of central bank independence lead to shorter cabinet durability.

The line marked "Effect of CBI at high economic openness" indicates how central bank independence affects cabinet durability in an open economy. Here, I restricted capital account openness to be at its highest level in the sample (4) and trade openness to be one standard deviation above its mean (100 percent of GDP). The slope of this line is positive, indicating that central bank independence actually increases cabinet durability in an open economy; that is, an independent central bank helps prolong cabinet durability in situations where conflicts over economic policy are very likely.[7] In other words, higher levels of economic openness increase the political value of an independent central bank.

Discussion: Explaining Patterns of Central Bank Reform

Politicians will want to reform their central bank when it is in their interest to do so. Because they are interested in attaining and retaining office, if institutional reform can help the government survive longer, politicians are likely to pursue those reforms. Where central bank reform is unlikely to increase cabinet durability, politicians will have less incentive to reform the central bank. The results indicate the conditions under which an independent central bank provides higher levels of cabinet durability. Consequently, they can provide predictions concerning the conditions under which politicians are likely to pursue reform.

The implications for central bank reform shown in figure 3 are straightforward: increased economic openness provides an incentive for politicians to adopt an independent central bank. Under conditions of low trade and capital account openness, politicians will prefer a dependent central bank because that institutional arrangement provides them with the highest levels of expected cabinet duration. At higher levels of economic openness, however, politicians

TABLE 9. Economic Openness and Central Bank Reform

Country[a]	Reform Date	Trade Openness[b]	Capital Account Openness[c]	Union Density[c]	Government Partisanship[e]
Italy	1981; 1992	0.38	3.42	0.33	Center-Right
New Zealand	1990	0.54	3.50	0.42	Left
Belgium	1993	1.43	3.16	0.55	Center-Left
France	1993	0.45	3.08	0.10	Right
Spain	1994	0.35	3.00	0.21	Left
Britain	1997	0.51	4.00	0.38	Left
Sweden	1998	0.59	3.16	0.83	Left
Ireland	1998	1.12	2.83	0.35	Center-Right
Japan	1998	0.20	2.50	0.25	Right
Australia		0.34	3.00	0.59	
Norway		0.75	2.92	0.54	

[a]Countries that ranked with less than 0.50 on the average scale of independence are included.
[b]Exports plus imports as a proportion of GDP in 1990.
[c]Average measure of capital account openness, 1985–1990. 1 = closed; 4 = open (Quinn 1997).
[d]Proportion of unionized workers in the workforce in 1990 (Golden, Lange, and Wallerstein 1998).
[e]Government partisanship is for date of reform.

can increase their expected cabinet durability by adopting an independent central bank. Table 9 reports the level of economic openness in 1990 for a subsample of systems with relatively dependent central banks—that is, systems in which central bank reform was likely. A comparison of the level of trade openness and capital account openness for reforming and nonreforming countries indicates that countries that reformed early in the 1990s tended to have higher levels of openness than late reformers or nonreformers.

The choice of central bank institutions, however, depends not only on the openness of the economy but also on the level of unionization. Figure 4 illustrates the interactive effect of unionization and central bank independence on cabinet durability under different conditions of economic openness. The x-axis is the level of unionization and the y-axis is predicted cabinet durability.[8] The four lines represent different levels of central bank independence (independent, dependent) and economic openness (open, closed).[9]

Consider first the two lines marked "closed economy." As expected, unionization has a U-shape effect on cabinet durability; that is, low and high levels of unionization contribute to higher cabinet durability than moderate rates of unionization. But in a closed economy, a dependent central bank produces higher expected cabinet durability at all levels of unionization. This difference

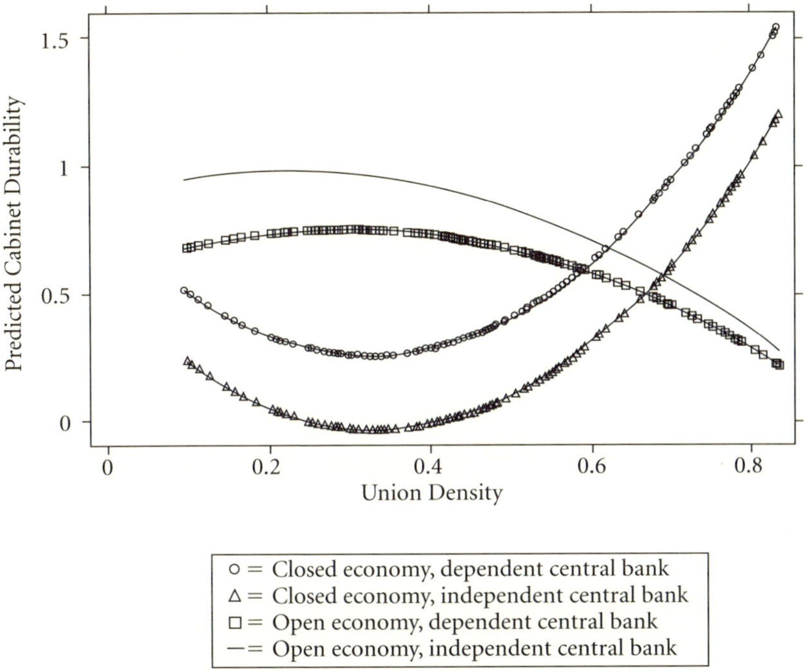

Fig. 4. Effect of unionization on predicted cabinet durability

is statistically significant; for closed economies, central bank independence hurts cabinet durability regardless of unionization.

At high levels of economic openness, however, the situation is reversed. Moderate levels of unionization provide the highest predicted cabinet durability, and high union density hurts cabinet durability. Further, in an open economy, an independent central bank produces higher predicted cabinet durability, although this effect diminishes at higher levels of unionization. At high levels of unionization in an open economy, the institutional status of the central bank appears to have no effect on expected cabinet durability.[10] Highly organized union organization may already coordinate policy demands and enhance policy effectiveness, making an independent central bank unnecessary. Therefore, in open economies with high levels of unionization, politicians have less incentive to support an independent central bank than in systems with lower levels of unionization.

These results suggest that systems with high levels of unionization and economic openness will be slower to adopt an independent central bank. In fact, the

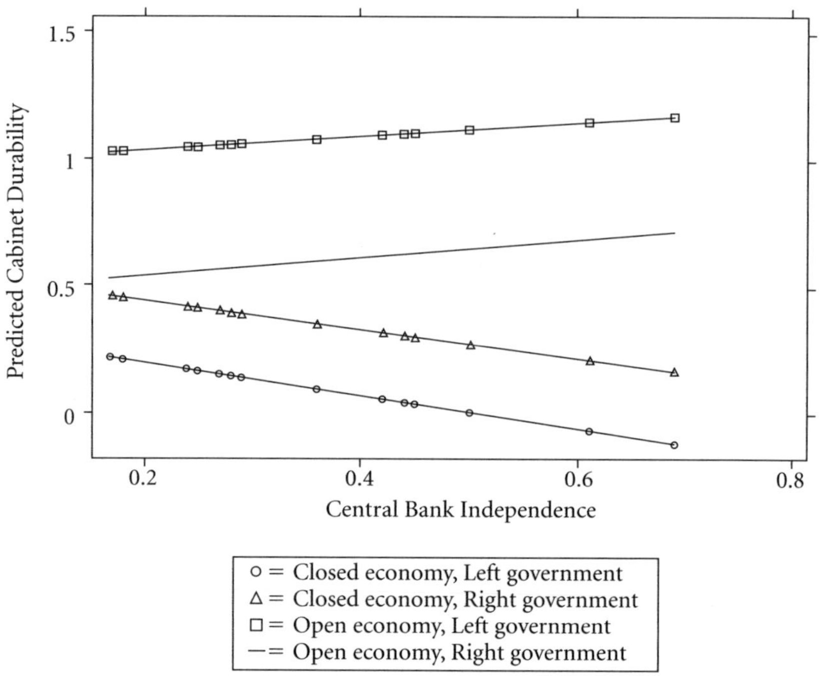

Fig. 5. Effect of central bank independence on predicted cabinet durability for different levels of partisanship and economic openness

countries that reformed their central banks in the early 1990s—France, Italy, New Zealand, and Spain—tend to have relatively low levels of unionization (see table 9). Countries with higher levels of unionization, such as Norway and Sweden, did not reform their central banks during this time period.

Figure 5 shows the effect of central bank independence on expected cabinet durability for different levels of economic openness and partisanship.[11] According to the results, economic openness actually helps the cabinet tenure of Left governments.[12] This may reflect the success of Left parties in small open democracies (Katzenstein 1985; Lange and Garrett 1985). The results also indicate that central bank independence affects expected cabinet durability for both Left and Right governments in the same manner. In a closed economy, central bank independence has a negative relationship on expected cabinet durability for both Left and Right governments. For an open economy, central bank independence has a slightly positive affect on cabinet durability regardless of partisanship.

The results imply that government partisanship does not affect the probability of central bank reform. Under conditions of economic openness, both Left and Right governments benefit from an independent central bank. Indeed, central bank reform has occurred under both Left and Right governments (see table 9). In New Zealand, Spain, Britain and Sweden, Left governments instituted independent central banks. In Italy, a Center-Right government initiated central bank reform. In France, a Right government carried out the central bank reform, although the Socialists had also endorsed central bank reform in the 1993 election campaign.

Conclusion

In one sense, the findings in this chapter are not particularly controversial. As with much of the recent literature in international political economy, I make a connection between increased economic internationalization and central bank reform. What is different is the mechanism that links internationalization and central bank reform. Much of the literature contends that economic openness—particularly international capital mobility—presents an external constraint on policymakers, forcing them to choose certain types of policies and institutions, including an independent central bank.

Instead, I provide an explicitly political mechanism—cabinet durability—to link internationalization and reform. Increased economic openness alters the policy preferences of constituents in the electoral coalitions of the traditional governing parties, creating the potential for policy conflict among constituents and among party politicians. Economic internationalization also decreases the ability of the government to deliver macroeconomic outcomes. Both of these developments are likely to shorten cabinet durability and hurt the ability of the traditional parties to maintain their position in office.

Party leaders therefore have to consider policy innovations and institutional reforms to ensure that party legislators with different interests will still cooperate with one another to keep the party in office. Because an independent central bank can help prevent conflicts between party politicians with different incentives over monetary policy, central bank reform is one way for party politicians to overcome the potential conflicts created by economic internationalization and protect the party's viability. Central bank reform represents a response by party politicians to the electoral dealignment brought about by increases in economic openness.

Linking economic internationalization, central bank independence, and cabinet durability helps account for the timing of central bank reform in the late 1980s and early 1990s. Despite international economic shocks—the end of the Bretton Woods monetary system and the oil shocks—and high levels of domestic inflation in the 1970s and early 1980s, politicians in most countries did not attempt to reform their central bank institutions. The stability of central bank institutions reflects the continuity of political incentives within the major parties. Although the economic shocks of the 1970s began to change constituent interests, electoral dealignment did not occur immediately. Voters continued to support the political party with which they identified. Party politicians continued to court traditional social coalitions for electoral support. Consequently, political leaders had little incentive to adopt an independent central bank.

By the mid-1980s, however, the political consequences of economic internationalization were apparent—the interests of the electoral coalitions underlying the traditional governing parties had changed enough to create sustained conflicts over economic and monetary policy. Where this electoral dealignment threatened the ability of the governing party(ies) to remain in office, party leaders moved to grant the central bank more independence. Where the social and economic consequences of internationalization did not threaten the ability of the governing party(ies) to hold office, politicians had less incentive to choose an independent central bank. The next chapter details the cases of Italy, where politicians moved early to grant the Bank of Italy more independence, and Britain, where central bank reform was delayed until the late 1990s, to illustrate the argument.

Chapter 7

Party System Change and Central Bank Reform in Italy and Britain

Throughout the industrial democracies, economic internationalization has created potential conflicts over economic and monetary policy within the leading governing parties. Increased levels of economic openness have altered the policy preferences of key constituent groups, diversifying the demands made on these parties. At the same time, the ability of parties in office to deliver promised outcomes has also declined. These developments threaten the traditional parties' ability to attain and retain office. Consequently, many parties have modified their electoral and policy strategies in order to reshape their electoral coalitions and maintain electoral viability. Central bank reform is one component of this change in party strategy. A more independent central bank can help prevent intraparty conflicts over monetary policy and enhance the government's policy effectiveness, helping parties meet the political challenges of economic internationalization.

In this chapter, I illustrate this argument by discussing central bank reform in Italy and Britain. In both countries, the economic and political developments of the 1970s and 1980s created the potential for conflict within the governing parties. In Italy, divisions over economic policy within the ruling coalition and changes in the political strategy of the Communists endangered the dominant position of the Christian Democratic Party in the late 1970s. In Britain, both the Labour and Conservative parties suffered from intraparty conflicts brought about by economic change in the 1970s and 1980s.

As these internal divisions threatened the viability of the major parties, pressure to grant the central bank more independence increased in both countries. In Italy, the Christian Democrats initiated the "divorce" of the Bank of Italy in 1981, freeing it from some of its obligations to finance the government's budget deficit. Italy's politicians continued to grant the bank increased authority for monetary policy through the 1980s and 1990s, even as the Italian party system crumbled. In Britain, central bank reform was delayed. An independent central bank would have seemed to complement the Thatcher government's monetarist policies in the early 1980s. Yet the Conservative government resisted demands for an independent Bank of England because, in part, Britain's majoritarian institutions protected the cabinet's position in office. Not until the election of a Labour government in 1997 was the central bank granted control over policy instruments.

In both countries, central bank independence was part of a larger process of policy and institutional reform—reforms designed to maintain and extend the social coalitions underpinning the main parties and protect their security in office. Around the time of the divorce, the Christian Democrats proposed reforms in a number of other issue areas, including regional, fiscal, and industrial policy. In Britain, the Labour government held referenda on the establishment of regional parliaments and studied electoral reform. The coincidence of monetary reform and other political reform supports the argument that changes to the party system conditioned the choice of central bank institutions in the 1990s.

This chapter examines the Italian and British cases in more detail. The first section discusses political and economic developments in Italy leading up to the divorce. The second section focuses on Britain and debates over central bank reform in the 1990s.

Central Bank Reform in Italy

Since World War II, the Christian Democratic Party played a predominant role in the Italian party system. But the economic shocks of the 1970s exposed deep divisions within the party and the ruling coalition, leaving the Christian Democrats politically vulnerable. The Christian Democrats responded with a series of reforms, including the divorce of the Bank of Italy, designed to revitalize the party's fortunes. The reforms, however, were not enough to rescue the party.

This section first discusses the position of the Christian Democratic Party in the Italian political system. It then examines the political response to the economic shocks of the 1970s, which left the Christian Democrats in a precarious position. Finally, it investigates the divorce of the Bank of Italy and its consequences.

The Dominant Christian Democrats

In the postwar period, the Christian Democratic Party dominated Italian politics. Although the party never commanded a legislative majority, it consistently won the highest number of votes and seats in the system. And although cabinets changed with almost alarming frequency, Christian Democrats always held the most important ministries. As the major party in government, the Christian Democrats benefited from Italy's strong export-led growth during the 1950s and 1960s, obtaining a reputation for competence and skill in economic-policy management.

Despite their reputation in economic matters, Christian Democratic politicians did not share similar economic-policy incentives. The Christian Democrats' appeals of religion, anticommunism, and patronage attracted constituents with a wide range of interests over monetary policy, including Catholics, farmers, trade unionists, shopkeepers, artisans, small business, and big business (Sani 1987; Tarrow 1990; Wertmann 1987). During the 1960s and 1970s, the growing divide between the modern industrial north and the agrarian south also strained the Christian Democrats. As a result of these divisions, the Christian Democratic Party was notoriously factionalized (Spotts and Weiser 1986; Wertmann 1981).

The frequency of coalition governments created another potential source of conflict over economic policy. The Christian Democrats had to rely on smaller parties to form a government, including the Socialists, Liberals, Republicans, and Social Democrats. The Socialists possessed a policy program sympathetic to union demands. The other parties had economic-policy platforms generally closer to those of the Christian Democrats.

Bargaining between the Christian Democratic factions and the small parties, rather than expertise or merit, determined the distribution of cabinet portfolios. Because the prime minister could not choose or dismiss cabinet ministers, each minister possessed a high degree of autonomy (Laver and Hunt 1992; Tarrow 1990). As a result, factions and parties that were dissatisfied with policy were forced to withdraw their support from the entire government, contributing to the frequency of government turnover throughout the period. This high turnover also hurt government ministers' policy credibility because few ministers served in office long enough to gain the expertise necessary to forecast policy outcomes.

As a consequence of the potential for policy conflict within the ruling coalition, most small parties and even some Christian Democratic Party members supported a central bank that was more independent of government control. For example, in 1975, the resignation of Bank of Italy governor Guido Carli sparked heated debate about an appropriate successor not only between parties but also within the Christian Democratic Party. The Christian Democratic candidate, Ferdinando Ventriglia, was opposed by the Communists, Socialists, Republicans, and some Christian Democrats (including Neno Andreatta, who, as Treasury minister, later initiated the divorce of the Bank of Italy). Eventually, the Christian Democrats decided to support the bank's internal candidate, Paolo Baffi (Goodman 1992). Again in 1979, following Baffi's resignation, the Christian Democratic–led government settled on the bank's internal candidate, Carlo Ciampi, rejecting outside candidates because of their political affiliations.

Despite the diverse policy incentives faced by the Christian Democratic–led coalition, the Christian Democrats' position as the dominant governing party was almost unassailable. Backbenchers and coalition partners could (and often did) withdraw their support from the cabinet, but the configuration of the Italian party system prevented an alternative coalition from forming without the Christian Democrats. Any alternative would have had to include the Communist Party, the Christian Democrats' main rival. But the Communists' radical economic program prevented the smaller parties and dissatisfied voters from leaving the Christian Democratic camp. Because the Christian Democrats' position in office was secure, party leaders had little incentive to open the policy process to scrutiny. Although the party faced constituents with a variety of interests over monetary policy, these constituents and their backbench representatives could not credibly threaten to punish the party by defecting—the Communists were simply too extreme. Party leaders therefore had no need to increase the transparency of their monetary-policy decisions with an independent central bank. As long as the Christian Democratic leadership was confident of the party's predominant position, the bank would be dependent.

Developments in the late 1960s and 1970s, however, jeopardized the party's dominance. First, Italy's unions became radicalized in the late 1960s, particularly in the northern industrialized regions. The strong economic growth in those regions had lowered unemployment, creating a tight labor market. Workers began to organize unions and increase strike activity. This militancy exploded in the "Hot Autumn" of 1969, a series of strikes and demonstrations that paralyzed the Italian economy. As a consequence, labor not only attained higher real wages, but it also pressured the government for expanded public spending on social services and increased regulation of the labor market (Lange and Vannicelli 1982; Reyneri 1989).[1]

Second, the Communist Party, Italy's second-largest party, moderated its economic position in an effort to get into office. In 1973, the Communists announced the "Historical Compromise," changing the party's goal from replacing the Christian Democrats to cooperating with them (D'Alimonte 1999; Lange 1980). The Communists hoped to emulate the German Social Democrats, who gained legitimacy by first serving in a grand coalition before leading their own coalition. The Communists thought the move would appeal to the growing number of centrist voters and demonstrate their coalition potential to other parties. As part of their strategy, the Communists espoused macroeconomic discipline, supporting austerity plans and negotiating with the unions to keep wages down. At the same time, they began to emphasize postmaterialist and left-libertarian issues (LaPalombara 1981).

These developments exacerbated tensions both within the Christian Democratic Party and between the Christian Democrats and their coalition partners, particularly the Socialists. Within the party, labor militancy increased the influence of the prolabor wing of the party as some party leaders feared that denying union demands would increase the power of the Communists. Within the governing coalition, the Socialist Party became more outspoken in defense of union interests. These policy divisions in the ruling coalition prevented a consistent and coherent government response to the economic shocks of the 1970s. Instead, the government's stop-go policy choices plunged Italy into a prolonged economic crisis that tarnished the Christian Democratic Party's reputation and set the political context for central bank reform.

Economic Performance and Political Conflict in the 1970s

In the early 1970s, Italy's economy was not well positioned to weather the coming economic shocks. The combination of higher wages and government spending brought about by union militancy increased domestic demand, just as the Bretton Woods system collapsed. While the rest of Europe prepared to enter the European Exchange Arrangement (Snake), the lira was left alone to float and quickly depreciated. The Christian Democratic–led government, however, continued accommodative economic policies to appease the trade unions and the Socialists, creating an inflationary surge. In addition, the first oil shock in the fall of 1973 quadrupled oil prices, causing further deterioration of the current account.

Acting on the advice of the central bank, Ugo La Malfa, the Republican Treasury minister, requested a standby loan from the International Monetary Fund (IMF). The terms of the IMF program, although less restrictive than usual, provoked a government crisis. The Socialists complained that the terms were too harsh. The Christian Democrats, however, decided to accept the conditions after foreign banks announced that they would refuse loans to Italy unless the government adopted the package. The Socialists reluctantly went along because they did not want to jeopardize an upcoming referendum on marital divorce.

Under the IMF package, Italy received access to a credit line of over 1 billion dollars. In return, the Italian government agreed to restrict the growth of domestic credit and reduce its nonoil current account deficit. Additionally, loans from other sources, including the European Community and Germany, soon materialized, motivated in part by a desire to prevent the Communists from coming to power. The policies worked better than expected. Economic activity declined sharply in the last half of 1974, and the slowdown continued through 1975. The nonoil current account deficit was eliminated by the third quarter of 1974, well ahead of schedule.

Nevertheless, the government did not sustain economic and monetary discipline. Beginning with the May 1974 Divorce Referendum, the Christian Democrats suffered a string of defeats in local and regional elections. These electoral swings encouraged the Socialists, who called for expansionary economic policies and, anathema to the Christian Democrats, Communist participation in government. The fragile center-left coalition quickly disintegrated, and the Christian Democrats barely managed to find support for a minority government.

Consequently, the Christian Democrats decided to loosen economic and monetary policy in late 1974. Despite warnings from the Bank of Italy, the Christian Democrats lowered the discount rate, abolished limitations on imports, and created new facilities to finance exports.[2] The government also negotiated an agreement with the Bank of Italy, giving the bank the right to tender Treasury bills at auction as long as the bank purchased all unsold bills. This agreement helped establish a private market in government securities, an institution that would facilitate control of the money supply (Goodman 1992; Padoa-Schioppa 1987). But the bank's obligation to purchase all unsold bills left monetary policy vulnerable to the government's fiscal profligacy. Additionally, the Treasury determined the floor price for each auction, implicitly setting a ceiling on interest rates.

As a consequence of this rapid monetary expansion, inflation took off and the lira depreciated. Two events turned these deteriorating economic conditions into a crisis. First, the U.S. government ruled that U.S. banks had to treat all loans to Italian state-owned companies as loans to the Italian government. Because U.S. banks were restricted in the amount of lending they could extend to a single customer, this decision blocked Italy's access to new loans (Goodman 1992). Second, the Socialists withdrew their support from the Christian Democratic minority government in January 1976. The possibility of government instability raised serious questions about economic policy, both domestically and abroad. Pressure on the lira intensified. Because the Bank of Italy's reserves were already low, the lira was allowed to float freely. In response, the caretaker government and the bank moved to tighten monetary policy. The government also began negotiations with the IMF for a second standby loan.

The crisis formed the backdrop for the 1976 elections. The Christian Democrats maintained their position as the top party in Italy, winning almost 39 percent of the vote, similar to their proportion in 1972. The Communists' vote share, however, jumped seven percentage points, to over 34 percent of the vote. After the election, the Christian Democrats attempted to form a new government, based on the traditional center-left alliance with the Socialists. The Socialists, however, were not eager to serve in government. The Communists, on the other hand, called for a government of national emergency. Complicating the situation, the United States and Germany threatened to cut off financial assistance if the Communists participated in government.

After much negotiation, Christian Democrat Giulio Andreotti formed a minority government based on the cooperation of all the major parties, including the Communists. In return for consultation on policy decisions, the Republicans, Liberals, Social Democrats, Socialists, and Communists agreed to abstain from votes of no confidence. For both the Christian Democrats and the Communists, the strategy represented a gamble. In return for short-term cooperation, the Christian Democrats risked giving the Communists a new legitimacy with potential coalition partners and the public. For the Communists, implicit cooperation with the Christian Democratic government provided them with an opportunity to broaden their appeal by demonstrating a commitment to responsible economic policies, but the strategy risked alienating traditional constituents (Tarrow 1981).

The lira came under renewed attack in September 1976, forcing the government to turn again to the IMF. This time, however, the IMF placed strict requirements on any promise of assistance, demanding tight restriction of the money supply and limitations on domestic credit, including the level of the government deficit, in order to bring inflation and the current account deficit under control. Further, the IMF sought limits on increases in labor costs. Here, the Communists' close relations with the trade unions helped the government negotiate these restrictions (see, for example, Goodman 1992, LaPalombara 1981). Although a second letter of intent was signed in April 1977, Italian authorities did not draw on the standby credit. Instead, an unexpected downturn erased the current account deficit. Further, inflation dropped to 12 percent in 1978. Consequently, the government never had to achieve the targets for domestic credit and the budget deficit that it had negotiated with the IMF.

The Communists' support for the government, however, began to alienate their core supporters, especially workers and younger voters. Faced with declining membership and losses in regional elections in 1978, the Communists forced a showdown with the Christian Democrats by demanding formal participation in the government. Predictably, the Christian Democrats refused the request, ending the government of national unity and precipitating new elections in 1979 (Penniman 1981).

During the campaign, the Christian Democrats took a hard line against the Communists, reflecting the reassertion of the party's right wing (Lange 1980; Tarrow 1981). In the elections, the Christian Democratic vote share remained steady, but the Communists' vote share dropped to about 30 percent. The Christian Democrats were able to form a center-left coalition with the Socialists, leaving the Communists out of government.

Although the Christian Democratic Party had survived the 1970s, its position as Italy's dominant party was not as secure. The economic shocks had revealed conflicts among the Christian Democrats' main constituents over policy. Union supporters clashed with those who wanted a more disciplined policy. Firms and unions exposed to the international economy called for different policies than those insulated from international competition. The diversity of these constituent demands contributed to intraparty conflicts over the direction of economic policy.

The Christian Democrats' reputation for competence also suffered. Voters became increasingly dissatisfied with the government's management of economic policy and disillusioned with the political infighting, pervasive corruption, and incompetence of Italy's traditional parties (Barnes 1984; Lange and Tarrow 1980; Sani 1981; Tarrow 1989). Moreover, much of the Christian Democrats' continued electoral success depended on patronage, an appeal that did not help them attract support from young educated professionals or immigrants from rural and southern areas, two groups that grew rapidly during the 1960s and 1970s (Tarrow 1990).

Combined with the moderation of the Communist Party, these developments increased the possibility that the Christian Democrats would lose office, due either to a coalition defection or to an electoral defeat. Confronted with that possibility, the Christian Democrats embarked on a new strategy in the late 1970s and early 1980s that entailed significant reforms in a variety of issue areas, including fiscal policy (Della Salla 1988), regional policy (Putnam 1993), and industrial policy (Ferrera 1989; Locke 1995). The Christian Democrats also pursued monetary reform by joining the EMS in 1979 and by making the Bank of Italy more independent in 1981.

Monetary-Policy Reform: The EMS and the Divorce

Both monetary reforms were designed to help revitalize the Christian Democrats and maintain their dominance of the Italian party system. Reformers hoped that these commitments would enforce discipline on the party and provide a consistency to economic policy that would improve the macroeconomic environment. Moreover, these new institutions could verify that the Christian Democrats were pursuing coherent, responsible economic policies. Maintaining the value of the lira within the EMS would signal the government's commitment to tighter monetary policy (Bernhard 1998). A more independent Bank of Italy would help the fiscal crisis and allow central bankers an increased freedom to provide information about consequences of the government's policy decisions—a credible source of information that if handled properly, would benefit the Christian Democrats politically. Together, these reforms could help restore the Christian Democrats' reputation among voters tired of the trade unions and the party's vacillating response to the economic shocks of the 1970s.

Italy's decision to join the EMS reflected both European and domestic concerns. At the European level, many Italian politicians recognized that nonparticipation would risk Italy's position within the European Community. Domestically, the costs and benefits of participation were less clear. Whereas some Christian Democrats saw membership in the EMS as a way to enforce discipline on monetary policy, other Christian Democrats and the Communists opposed participation, arguing that the adjustment costs would be too high and that Italy would be unable to pursue its own economic policies (Ludlow 1982). Interestingly, the Bank of Italy echoed similar reservations about Italy's participation in the EMS, fearing that influential trade unions and persistent budget deficits would make domestic adjustment difficult and that the weakness of the Italian economy would make the lira a target for speculation (Goodman 1992).

The Christian Democratic government's commitment to the EMS was soon tested. In 1979, the economy faced two new shocks: a second oil crisis and a sudden restriction in U.S. monetary policy. The tightening of U.S. policy placed downward pressure on all European currencies, including the lira. Unlike past responses to exchange crises, however, the Christian Democratic–led government decided to tighten monetary policy to maintain the value of the currency.

The new monetary discipline, however, did not dampen inflation, which remained at about 20 percent in early 1980. The combination of high inflation and a fixed exchange rate hurt the competitiveness of Italian exports. Despite pressure from Italian firms, including Fiat, and from unions affected by restructuring, the government and the central bank refused to devalue the lira. The public, too, seemed exasperated by the trade unions. In response to union strikes at Fiat in September 1980, Fiat workers organized a massive counterdemonstration demanding their right to work. The so-called March of 40,000 marked a turning point in union influence over economic policy (Padoa-Schioppa 1987). Although the government eventually asked their EMS partners to devalue the lira in February 1981, they accompanied the devaluation with an increase in interest rates and limitations on imports, again reflecting the Christian Democrats' support of tighter monetary policies. The Italian government devalued the lira several more times during the 1980s, but participation in the EMS provided a clear measure of the government's commitment to macroeconomic discipline for markets, politicians, and the public. That policy transparency helped discipline monetary policy and bring inflation levels down.

The second reform, the divorce of the Bank of Italy, was precipitated by yet another change in government. In early 1981, a scandal led to the collapse of the Christian Democratic–led government, forcing the resignation of a number of prominent Christian Democratic ministers. Unlike other government collapses, however, the scandal emboldened the smaller parties to press for greater responsibility in the government. Bettino Craxi, leader of the Socialists, sought the prime minister's position. Many Christian Democrats, however, found his candidacy unacceptable. Eventually, the ruling coalition settled on Giovanni Spadolini, leader of the tiny Republican Party, as a compromise; Spadolini and the Republicans had a reputation as the "conscience" of Italian politics. Spadolini became the first non–Christian Democratic prime minister in the postwar period. Nino Andreatta, a reform-minded Christian Democrat, became the Treasury minister.

With Spadolini's approval, Andreatta issued an administrative decree freeing the bank from its obligation to purchase unsold government debt. Because Andreatta anticipated opposition from the Socialists, he used this method to avoid a parliamentary debate. Interestingly, the Communists supported the divorce, continuing their strategy of courting centrist voters and potential coalition partners. The trade unions and export manufacturers were largely silent on the measure (Goodman 1992). Only the Socialists opposed the divorce, arguing against the inevitability of higher interest rates. They were isolated, however, and did not press the issue. Nevertheless, bank officials discouraged the government from introducing a bill in parliament to guarantee central bank independence, not wanting to risk their status in an open debate (Goodman 1992). The divorce sparked other changes to the bank and monetary policy. In

1983–84, Italian monetary authorities decided to phase out the use of credit ceilings, enhancing the importance of the bank's monetary targets as a guide to overall monetary policy. The Treasury also allowed the bank to have the primary responsibility for the determination of the monetary targets (Goodman 1992; Padoa-Schioppa 1987).

Despite the divorce, the government retained ways to finance deficit spending. It could still borrow up to 14 percent of total expenditures from the Bank of Italy. Beyond that limit, the government could ask parliament to authorize an "extraordinary advance" from the bank. It soon became apparent that monetary financing was to be a source of friction between the bank and the government, especially because the Treasury fixed the price of bonds on the primary market. In the fall of 1981, the Treasury lowered interest rates on short-term securities to ease the debt burden. The bank, however, feared inflation and raised interest rates for short-term securities on the secondary markets. With a higher interest rate on the secondary market, investors refused to purchase Treasury bills on the primary market, and the Treasury soon ran out of funds. To prevent a total collapse of the bond market, the bank agreed to purchase all the Treasury bills at auction (Goodman 1992). A few months later, a political dispute over how best to pay off Italy's huge debt precipitated a cabinet dissolution, causing the demand for Treasury bills to fall dramatically. Again, the bank acted as a residual purchaser of the government's securities to prevent a crisis.

The bank's actions in the bond markets, however, fueled inflation. Additionally, the government's borrowing had exceeded its statutory limit. Exasperated, the bank ceased all purchases of government securities in December 1982, forcing the government to appeal to the parliament for an extraordinary advance. The parliament easily and quickly passed the government's request. The bank's refusal to purchase more government securities therefore did not prevent the government from financing the deficit. But it did compel the government to acknowledge responsibility for its fiscal policy. Through an explicit vote, Italy's politicians had to declare that their actions were contributing to the national debt.

The divorce did not solve Italy's fiscal crisis. Indeed, government deficits increased throughout the 1980s. Italy's public debt-to-GDP ratio exceeded 100 percent by the late 1980s. The percentage of the deficits financed by monetary creation, however, decreased (Goodman 1992). Without monetization of the deficit, Italy's politicians were required to accept responsibility for the protracted fiscal crisis. Their inability to deal with this problem throughout the 1980s fueled voter discontent with the traditional ruling parties.

Evaluating Central Bank Reform

Changes to the Bank of Italy's institutional status therefore mirrored long-term developments in Italy's political system. The economic shocks of the 1970s, especially increased labor militancy, exacerbated tensions within the governing parties, creating potential conflicts between factions in the Christian Democratic Party and its coalition partners. At the same time, the Christian Democrats' dominant position in the political system began to erode. The increasing vulnerability of the Christian Democrats led them to support a series of institutional reforms, including the divorce, as a way to reinvigorate their political fortunes. Reformers hoped that closer scrutiny of economic policy-making would help enforce discipline on the party and limit the policy conflicts that had dogged the party during the 1970s.

The reforms did help improve Italy's inflation performance: inflation rates dropped from over 18 percent in 1981 to less than 5 percent in 1986. But instead of restoring the Christian Democrats' reputation for effective economic management, the reforms called attention to the Christian Democrats' inability to solve Italy's tough economic questions, particularly the national debt problem. Reformers had figured that the divorce would compel the party to deal with the fiscal crisis. By the late 1970s, however, the Christian Democrats had come to depend on patronage to hold together their core constituencies—an appeal that directly contradicted the need for fiscal discipline. Many party politicians were reluctant to risk their seats and the party's fortunes by abandoning a source of certain votes to achieve deficit reduction, an objective with a nebulous political payoff. Instead of demonstrating the Christian Democrat's commitment to macroeconomic responsibility, therefore, the divorce actually exposed the party's futile response to the fiscal crisis.

The continued failure of the Christian Democrats to address Italy's fundamental economic problems contributed to voters' dissatisfaction and disillusionment with Italy's traditional parties. Throughout the 1980s, the vote share of the Christian Democrats declined (Barnes 1984; Leonardi 1987). New single-issue and regional political parties emerged, giving voters other outlets for their frustration. Under the weight of corruption scandals, increasing regional disparities, and voter dissatisfaction, the political system disintegrated in the late 1980s and early 1990s. In a series of referenda in the early 1990s, voters approved a new mixed proportional representation–majoritarian electoral system. Designers of the system hoped to promote the establishment of two broad-based party blocs, preventing the type of one-party dominance that had marked Italian politics since the end of World War II.

The popular demand for reform demonstrated that Italy's party system had not adjusted to the new political and economic environment. The old parties, particularly the Christian Democrats, simply could not accommodate the diversity of interests created by economic modernization and internationalization. Instead of modifying their appeals to attract new constituents, the Christian Democrats relied on their traditional patronage appeal and pursued an inconsistent policy program. Increased levels of economic openness during this period simply magnified the consequences of the government's weak and vacillating policies. As result, the Christian Democrats and Italy's postwar party system simply dissolved in the face of popular discontent.

The Bank of Italy's reputation, however, made it a symbol of national unity during the political crises of the 1990s. The bank remained one of the few institutions in Italy untouched by scandal. Indeed, its governor, Carlo Ciampi, was called upon to form a government in May 1993 in the midst of the political upheaval. Ciampi's government implemented electoral reform and attempted to bring the public deficit under control. After the collapse of the Berlusconi government in December 1994, another former central bank official, Lamberto Dini, formed an emergency government of nonelected technocrats. (Dini had also served as Treasury minister in the Berlusconi government.) Although many did not expect the Dini government to last, Dini successfully shepherded a new budget, pension reform, and modification of regional electoral laws through parliament (*The Economist*, 12 August 1995).

The Bank of England Reform

In Britain, as in Italy, the economic shocks of the 1970s and 1980s created sharp divisions within the Labour and Conservative parties over economic policy. Britain's majoritarian institutions, however, ensured that these conflicts did not threaten the cabinet's position in office, making reform less urgent than in Italy. Indeed, the Conservative government blocked a bill to increase the independence of the Bank of England in 1993–94. Nevertheless, growing tensions within the Conservative Party and the fiasco of being forced from the EMS in 1992 created pressure for a more transparent monetary policy. After winning election in 1997, the incoming Labour government moved quickly to grant the central bank authority over interest rates. The reform was designed to solidify Labour's diverse social coalition and enhance its reputation as a responsible moderate party.

This section first explains the divisions within both the Labour and Conservative parties. It then discusses the conflict over British participation in the

EMS and the consequent bill to increase the Bank of England's independence. Finally, it examines the response to the Labour government's proposal of a more independent central bank.

The Labour Party and the Economic Shocks of the 1970s

Throughout the 1950s and 1960s, British economic policy reflected cross-party support of Keynesian demand management (Alt 1979; Britton 1991; Hall 1986; Kavanaugh 1987; Scharpf 1987). In return for wage restraint, the government would strive to lower unemployment, increase social spending, and strengthen the unions' bargaining position with employers. At the same time, however, sterling's position as a reserve currency made the balance of payments vulnerable to international speculation. The government would pursue expansionary policies to increase employment levels but then quickly slam on the brakes due to balance of payments pressures. This stop-go pattern to macroeconomic policy deterred investment and confidence, hurting long-term economic growth. Indeed, since World War II, Britain's economic competitors have outperformed it in almost every category.

The economic shocks of the 1970s shattered this cross-party consensus and exposed deep divisions within each party over economic policy. For the Labour Party, these divisions centered on the relationship between the party and the trade unions. In 1975, following the first oil crisis, the Trade Unions Congress (TUC) voluntarily restrained wage increases to help the Labour government (Scharpf 1987). In return, the Labour government initiated pro-labor legislation, repealing the Conservatives' Industrial Relations Act, expanding safety, health, and pension benefits, and freezing rents in council housing. The balance-of-payments situation, however, continued to deteriorate as British inflation remained high. To counter the growing crisis, the government demanded more wage restraint in 1976. Although unemployment had increased, the TUC again agreed to moderate its wage demands.

In early 1976, however, the pound came under heavy attack in international financial markets. The Bank of England quickly used up all its reserves and exhausted its access to international credit in defending the pound. Import prices increased dramatically, contributing to an inflationary surge. As in Italy, the government turned to the IMF for access to a special longer-term loan. The IMF agreed to the loan on the condition that the government tighten its fiscal and monetary policies.

Following the 1976 pound crisis, James Callaghan, the new leader of the Labour government, was determined to bring inflation under control.[3] The government tightened fiscal policy and requested that the TUC limit wage increases again in 1977. The TUC, however, argued that the working class had already borne enough costs. Unemployment was still increasing. And although inflation had begun to fall in 1977–78, the government had rescinded some regulations designed to insulate the working class from inflation, including food subsidies and price controls. Consequently, the TUC leadership did not push the guideline on the rank and file.

The following year, the Callaghan government demanded that unions limit their demands to a 5-percent wage increase. By this time, however, union membership had become dissatisfied with the government and with wage restraint. Skilled workers in particular felt that they had accepted a disproportionate share of the adjustment burden. The government's request also divided the party, the increasingly radical left wing arguing against the government's orthodox economic policies. The TUC decisively rejected the government's plan and opted for free collective bargaining. Private-sector unions concluded agreements for large wage increases, making up for the years of restraint. The government, however, held firm against the public-sector unions. This conflict exploded in 1978–79's "Winter of Discontent" as the unions staged a series of strikes that crippled public services throughout Britain.

The widespread dissatisfaction with the Labour government's macroeconomic performance and its conflicts with the unions swept the Conservatives into office in May 1979. Labour responded to its defeat by moving leftward, calling for more radical Socialist programs, including nationalization of key industries and disarmament (Kavanaugh 1987; Kitschelt 1994). As a result, centrists exited the party to form the Social Democratic Party in 1981, a party that eventually merged with the Liberals. Interestingly, Labour's middle-class constituents supported the Socialist agenda more than did the working class; an exodus of working-class voters contributed to Labour's crushing defeat in 1983 (Crewe 1985).

Thatcher and the Tory Wets

The Thatcher government entered office in 1979 intent on not just controlling inflation but also reshaping the entire relationship between state and economy. The government's program consisted of three interrelated initiatives: monetarist management of macroeconomic policy, labor-market deregulation, and privatization. First, in macroeconomic policy, the government rejected the Keynesian consensus in favor of a monetarist approach, tightening fiscal policy and raising interest rates. In the 1980 budget, the government announced the Medium Term Financial Strategy (MTFS), a plan to target monetary aggregates over a four-year period. Interestingly, the Bank of England provided only reluctant support for the government's macroeconomic policies, fearing the real economic consequences of dogmatic overreliance on a single indicator (Britton 1991; Hall 1986). Additionally, the Bank of England had to dissuade the government from pursuing wholesale reform of the banking system, arguing that reform would make the relationship between monetary policy and the money supply impossible to predict (Britton 1991).

Second, the Thatcher government sought to break the power of the trade unions. The government favored free collective bargaining, whereby firms and unions could coordinate their expectations around the monetary target. Wage agreements out of line with economic conditions would simply result in unemployment. Not content with eroding the unions' market power, the government also passed legislation weakening unions' bargaining position with employers and increasing members' influence over their leadership. It also challenged public-sector unions, successfully closing a number of labor disputes, including a violent conflict with the mine workers in 1984–85. Both economic and political reasons motivated the government's anti-union strategy; the strategy not only opened up the labor market, but it also injured the Labour Party's main constituency.

Third, the Thatcher government rolled back the state's role in the economy, privatizing nationalized industries and reducing government regulation. The government also made nationalized firms more efficient, laying off thousands of workers and closing plants. Again, the government's motivation reflected both economic and political concerns. Selling council flats to their occupants attracted working-class constituents to the Conservative Party (Garrett 1992). Additionally, the government's method of privatization encouraged small new investors to purchase shares on the theory that shareholders were more likely to vote Conservative. Finally, the windfalls from privatization and North Sea oil raised substantial revenues, limiting the tax burden.

The immediate consequence of the Thatcher program was a deep recession. Between 1979 and 1981, unemployment doubled, quickly climbing above 9 percent. In 1980, the GDP declined by more than 2 percent. Inflation began to fall, but not nearly as quickly as the Thatcherites had hoped. Despite the fact that the British inflation rate was well above the OECD average, the pound appreciated on international currency markets, reflecting high interest rates, North Sea oil revenues, and investor confidence in the government's monetarist resolve. The high exchange rate, however, had devastating consequences for British manufacturers, who were priced out of international markets. Manufacturing output fell by over 15 percent (Britton 1991).

The deep recession exposed divisions within the Conservative Party between the radical free-market Thatcherites and Tory "wets." Whereas the Thatcherites preferred the efficiency of the market to state intervention, the "wets" supported the traditional Keynesian consensus surrounding economic policy and the welfare state and felt an obligation to provide a social safety net to all classes of British society. Indeed, the government's MTFS received harsh criticism from the Treasury and Civil Service Committee in Parliament, despite its Conservative majority. Their report argued that the MTFS "was not soundly based," and it proposed a less dogmatic approach to economic and monetary policy (Britton 1991). Within the cabinet, some ministers disputed the government's tight fiscal policies, pressing for more expansionary policies. In spring 1981, however, Thatcher asserted her dominance of the party organization. After she failed to secure her preferred spending cuts in the budget, Thatcher responded by dismissing her moderate or "wet" ministers, replacing them with more loyal monetarists (Hall 1986).

By mid-1981, the economic recovery had begun, helping Thatcher solidify her position. Increases in domestic demand provided a spark for the economy, benefiting the construction and service sectors. In contrast, manufacturing and export sectors remained mired in a slump due to the weakness of the world economy. Unemployment also remained stubbornly high because productivity growth led the recovery. Nevertheless, the Conservative government capitalized on the economy, the Falklands victory, and the disarray of the Labour Party to win the 1983 elections decisively.

During the next few years, the economy continued to grow while inflation fell. With inflation seemingly under control, the government loosened both fiscal and monetary policy. From 1986 to 1988, Chancellor Nigel Lawson produced a series of expansionary budgets. In monetary policy, Lawson ceased to rely on monetary targets and instead shadowed the D-mark. To maintain the parity, the government actually had to lower interest rates. These policies helped ensure another Conservative victory at the 1987 elections.

The government's confidence in its ability to manage the economy, however, dulled them to the possibility of renewed inflation. The combination of increased consumer spending, expansionary budgets, and lower interest rates increased inflationary pressures in the economy. Between 1987 and 1990, the inflation rate more than doubled, increasing from 3.7 percent to 9.3 percent. The subsequent debate about how best to regain control over inflation further divided the Conservative Party and led to Thatcher's downfall.

The Conflict over EMS Entry

During the 1980s, the foreign-policy cleavage surrounding Britain's relationship with Europe reemerged, creating tensions within the major parties, especially the

Conservatives. With the disinflationary success of EMS member states and Britain's poor inflation performance in the late 1980s, discussions soon centered on the question of British participation in the EMS. Advocates of participation, including Lawson and most other party leaders, argued that joining the exchange-rate mechanism (ERM) would provide the macroeconomic discipline necessary to regain control over inflation and enhance the government's anti-inflation credibility with markets and the public. Additionally, participation would allow Britain to influence any negotiations over economic and monetary union. Thatcher and her allies, however, remained opposed, arguing that participation in the ERM would sacrifice policy-making autonomy to Germany. Thatcher turned increasingly to her personal economic advisor, Sir Alan Walters, for advice, ignoring Lawson's policy judgments and party sentiment.

The conflict between the prime minister and the chancellor climaxed in October 1989 with Lawson's resignation. His resignation speech to the House of Commons noted his disagreements with Thatcher and advocated entry into the EMS. Surprisingly, Lawson also stated that he had proposed a "fully worked-out" plan for an independent Bank of England to Thatcher in 1988, when inflation had begun to rise (*Financial Times*, 2 November 1989; *The Economist*, 4 November 1989; Elgie and Thompson 1998; Lawson 1992).[4] Thatcher had rejected the proposal, arguing that it would appear to indicate "failure" in the battle against inflation (Thatcher 1993, 706).

Under increasing pressure from her party, Thatcher finally agreed to join the ERM in October 1990. Thatcher's belated acceptance of EMS entry, however, was not enough to maintain the party's support. The inflationary surge of the late 1980s, her imperious nature, and a number of other missteps, including the poll tax, made Conservative MPs wary of fighting the next election under her leadership. In November 1990, party MPs did not give her their full support during a leadership challenge, and she resigned. The party settled on John Major as their next leader.

British entry into the EMS, however, had come at an inopportune time. In an effort to enhance the anti-inflation credibility of its exchange-rate commitment, the government entered the system at a parity higher than what many economists argued was justified by economic fundamentals. Moreover, with the tightening of German monetary policy after unification, the government had to maintain high interest rates to sustain the pound's value in the system, prolonging the economic slowdown long after inflation had been controlled. Both Major and his chancellor, Norman Lamont, pressed the Germans to cut rates, but their demands were ignored. Despite the economy, however, the Conservatives won a surprising electoral victory in April 1992, giving Major a small working majority in Parliament.

The Conservatives' good fortune did not last long. Amid concerns about the disparity of economic fundamentals across Europe and ratification of the Maastricht Treaty, currency traders attacked the EMS in September 1992. Both the British pound and the Italian lira were forced to leave the ERM (Bernhard 1998; Cameron 1993; Cobham 1994; Gros and Thygesen 1998). The Major government, which had issued public assurances about the pound's value prior to the crisis, had to backtrack on its statements, losing credibility not only with markets but also with the public and its own backbenchers.

In the wake of the crisis, Lamont sought to reestablish the cabinet's trustworthiness. In October 1992, he announced that the government would establish a public medium-term inflation target. If the government missed the target, it would have "to explain how this had arisen, how quickly it intended to get back within the range, and the means by which it could achieve this" (*Financial Times*, 9 October 1992). Further, he proposed a new role for the Bank of England: monitoring the government's pursuit of the inflation target. The bank would publish an Inflation Report, a critique of and prescription for monetary policy. Although the Treasury would see the report prior to publication, the Treasury would not be able to modify it. By making monetary policy more transparent, Lamont "could hope to convince the electorate and the markets that decisions, even if ultimately wrong, were being made for good, rather than bad, reasons" (Elgie and Thompson 1998, 78).

Lamont and Major, however, disagreed about how to handle monetary policy in the short term. Lamont favored maintaining interest rates in order to meet the new inflationary target. Major, on the other hand, saw interest-rate reductions as a way to shore up his dwindling support within the electorate and within his own party. Against the chancellor's wishes, Major ordered a series of interest-rate cuts in late 1992 and early 1993. Over the spring, it became evident that the two men had very different ideas about monetary policy, and in May 1993, Major fired Lamont and replaced him with Kenneth Clarke. In his resignation speech to the House of Commons, Lamont, echoing Lawson, voiced his support for a more independent central bank.

Central Bank Independence Blocked

The resignations of Lawson and Lamont placed the Bank of England's institutional status on the public agenda. As a result, the Commons Select Committee on the Treasury began hearings on the institutional status of the Bank of England (*Guardian*, 5 May 1993). The select committee, including MPs from all three major parties, sought information not only on the bank's independence but also on its supervisory role in the Bank of Commerce and Credit International (BCCI) scandal and the bank's actions during Britain's exit from the EMS in September 1992.

During the hearings, the committee heard testimony from Lawson (pro-independence) and Lord Healey, the ex-Chancellor of the Labour government in the late 1970s (anti-independence) (*Financial Times*, 8 July 1993). A number of prominent economists also issued a report, sponsored by the Centre for Economic Policy Research, calling for independence (*Guardian*, 18 November 1993). The new governor of the Bank of England, Eddie George, argued for increased autonomy.

The committee's final report, published in December 1993, argued for an independent Bank of England, proposing institutions similar to the newly reformed Reserve Bank of New Zealand (*Guardian*, 17 December 1993). Under the proposal, the government would determine inflation targets, and the bank would be obliged to set interest rates to meet those targets. Bank policy would be determined by a Monetary Policy Committee, whose members could not hold positions outside the bank. The proposal also included institutional safeguards designed to enhance the bank's accountability to Parliament. First, the bank's governor would have to appear regularly before the select committee to answer questions about the conduct of monetary policy. Additionally, the government would have the authority to override the bank's price-stability objective "temporarily and in exceptional circumstances." Finally, unlike in New Zealand, the House of Commons would have to approve the government's inflation target.

The proposal met with opposition from both the Conservative and Labour frontbenches and from the extremes of both parties.[5] Prime Minister Major made it clear that the report was a "dead" issue. Opponents argued that monetary policy entailed distributive questions best determined by the voters through their representatives. Consequently, elected politicians, not central bankers, should control interest rates. Opponents also doubted the effectiveness of the institutions designed to hold the Bank of England accountable for its actions. They did not trust the bank to be truthful during its testimony nor did they believe that the Commons was capable of effective oversight. Finally, critics of the proposal noted that, "of the 30 memorandums submitted to the [Treasury] committee, 21 were from central banks—so it was hardly likely they would contest the idea that price stability does not conflict with employment and growth, or that independent central banks are the best means to achieve that end" (*Guardian*, 17 December 1993).

Nevertheless, Conservative MP Nicholas Blugden, a member of the Select Committee, attempted to place the committee's report on the legislative agenda, proposing "The Bank of England (Amendment) Bill." His arguments in favor of the bill emphasized the informational role of an independent central bank: "The whole object of these proposals is to achieve openness and to ensure that when a Government says it is doing one thing, it cannot give directives to the Bank which may do something quite different. My proposal does not prevent the Government giving instructions to the Bank to let inflation rip, but merely means that, if they do that, it has to be done openly and everybody has to understand the consequences. . . . We want a bit of openness between the House and the Government" (*Guardian*, 29 January 1994).

Both Conservative and Labour leaders opposed the proposal and prevented it from further consideration. Only the Liberal Democrats formally supported the reform. Opposition to the bill, I contend, reflected the government's incentives over the central bank. Although the Conservative Party possessed constituents with a growing variety of preferences over monetary policy and increasing conflict within the party, Britain's majoritarian political institutions still encouraged MPs to toe the party line and support their frontbench leaders. In other words, the institutions of the Westminster system insulated the governing party's tenure from the political consequences of economic internationalization.[6] Because the governing party had little reason to fear that its supporters would withdraw their support, they had no reason to support a more independent bank.

The Ken and Eddie Show

The growing pressure for an independent bank, however, contributed to changes in the relationship between the government and the Bank of England. Already, people had noticed that the bank's governor had become more outspoken in his criticism of government (*Guardian*, 20 May 1991, 1 November 1991, 17 December 1993). With the increasing divergence of policy views within the governing parties, the governor could be sure to find a supportive audience. The appointment of Eddie George as governor in January 1993, one of the bank's inflation hawks, helped ensure that the bank would continue to espouse restrictive policies.

In fall 1993, Chancellor Kenneth Clarke proposed several more institutional changes to increase the transparency of policy while keeping the ultimate authority for interest-rate decisions with the chancellor. First, the bank would cease to submit its Inflation Report to the Treasury prior to publication. Consequently, differences between the bank's policy analysis and the government's own evaluations would become more public. Second, Clarke allowed the bank to determine the exact timing of interest-rate changes he requested. Finally, in spring 1994, after negotiations with the bank, Clarke decided to publish the minutes of the monthly meetings between the Treasury and the bank after a six-week delay. In these meetings, the bank advised the chancellor about monetary policy before the chancellor took any action on interest rates. The publication of the minutes would help provide transparency to monetary policy and hold the bank accountable for its policy information (*Guardian*, 11 April 1997).

Coming out of the recession of the early 1990s, both the Bank of England and the government advocated relatively accommodative policies. In September 1994, however, the bank issued warnings about the inflationary pressures of an overheating economy and called for an interest-rate hike. Clarke reluctantly acquiesced and supported interest-rate increases in December 1994 and February 1995 as well. But as the Conservative Party's approval ratings continued to decline, Clarke felt that he could not afford to continue to raise interest rates, touching off a series of public disagreements between the Treasury and the bank—a melodrama dubbed the "The Ken and Eddie Show" by the popular press. Beginning in May 1995 and continuing through the summer, Clarke ignored the bank's warnings of higher inflation and refused to raise interest rates (*Business Week*, 5 June 1995, 7 August 1995). Most Conservative MPs agreed with the chancellor's actions, fearing the political fallout of dampening the economic upturn. Currency markets did not punish the chancellor either. Although the pound depreciated soon after Clarke began to chart his own course, it soon restabilized due to changes in the position of the U.S. dollar.

In December 1995 and January 1996, Clarke cut interest rates further, hoping to maintain a robust economy in the run-up to the next election. In spring 1996, however, the bank forecast an inflationary surge on the horizon. But the chancellor continued to cut interest rates. Finally, by October, it was apparent that inflation was accelerating. Clarke and George agreed to raise interest rates by 0.25 percent. At the same time, however, the pound began to appreciate on international currency markets. Arguing that the appreciation would dampen any potential inflation, Clarke resisted the bank's advice to raise rates from December 1996 through March 1997, the six months preceding the next general election, helping to preserve the economic recovery.

Despite the bank's warnings of impending inflation, Clarke's position enjoyed solid support within the Conservative party. This support reflected the similarity of policy incentives for party politicians created by the institutions of the Westminster system. In Britain's centralized unicameral system, party politicians run for office all at once. Consequently, only the economic conditions at the general election matter for the party's success. Any medium-term negative consequences of the chancellor's strategy—for example, higher inflation or tighter monetary policy after the election—would not hurt the party because party candidates would not stand until the next general election, and by that time the government would have had an opportunity to reinvigorate the economy. Because Conservative Party members had similar electoral incentives, they supported Clarke rather than the bank's policy position.

New Labour, New Bank of England

The economy's performance, nonetheless, was not enough to save the Major government at the May 1997 election. Tired and divided over the question of Europe, the Conservatives lost badly to the Labour Party. But it was a new Labour Party that took office under Tony Blair—one that had responded to the changes in the electorate by becoming more centrist, inclusive, and moderate while still attempting to retain its working-class constituents.

The political and economic environment had changed considerably since Labour had last held office. The size of the manufacturing sector, shrinking through the 1970s, decreased drastically during the 1979–81 recession. Instead, the service sector replaced heavy industry as the dynamic engine of economic growth, creating regional disparities between the declining industrial north and the booming service-oriented south. Consequently, new sectoral conflicts replaced the union-management division, pitting service against manufacturing, profitable sectors against declining industry, and sectors exposed to international competition against sectors producing for the domestic market.

These developments challenged the long-term viability of the Labour Party's traditional emphasis on unions and the working class. After sharply moving to the left in the early 1980s and losing badly to the Conservatives, Labour Party leaders began to pull the party toward the center—a slow and difficult process. Centrist leaders and entrenched party interests clashed repeatedly over policy changes and reforms to internal party organization that limited trade-union influence. These divisions between radicals and moderates prolonged Labour's reputation as a party of special interests and contributed to electoral losses in 1987 and surprisingly, in 1992. Finally, with the ascent of Tony Blair as party leader, the moderates were solidly in command. Nevertheless, the leaders of "New Labour" faced a difficult balancing act. With the socioeconomic developments of the 1970s and 1980s, the Labour Party had to build and maintain a very different social coalition than its predecessors—a coalition that included not only the remainder of the traditional working-class base but also the middle class, new sectoral interests, business, and centrist voters.

New Labour's party program was clearly designed to appeal to that coalition. The policy agenda emphasized middle-class concerns such as education and improvements to the National Health Service. The Labour government also advocated substantial institutional reforms. It supported referenda in Scotland and Wales on whether to establish regional parliaments. Devolution would not only enhance Labour's support in those regions, but it would also allow the national party to pass responsibility for potentially divisive policy issues to regional governments. Additionally, the Labour government formed a commission to explore electoral reform. The commission proposed an alternative vote system combined with additional member constituencies, a compromise between the traditional first-past-the-post system and proportional representation (*The Economist,* 31 October 1998). The government promised action on the proposal after the next election. These policies and reforms were designed to help the Labour Party build a viable electoral coalition among constituents with heterogeneous economic policy preferences.

I argue that Labour's reform of the central bank fits with this strategy of party building. The Labour Party manifesto promised monetary reform, although it fell short of calling for complete independence: "We will reform the Bank of England to ensure that decision-making on monetary policy is more effective, open, accountable and free from short-term political manipulation." In particular, party leaders proposed the establishment of a monetary-policy committee to advise the governor, who, in turn would advise the chancellor. This committee, they contended, would help make monetary policy more representative of Britain's economy.

But in a surprise move just after the election, new Chancellor Gordon Brown announced that he was giving "operational responsibility" for setting interest rates to the Bank of England. While the government would determine the inflation target, the central bank would control day-to-day management of interest rates to achieve that target.[7] Further, decisions about interest-rate changes would be taken by a new nine-member monetary-policy committee, consisting of the governor, two deputy governors, and six other members. Four of the six nonexecutive members were to be appointed by the chancellor for three-year terms. A reformed Court of the Bank of England, composed of individuals from industry, commerce, and finance, would supervise the committee to determine whether it "was collecting proper regional and sectoral information for the purposes of monetary policy formation." The bank would also give reports to the House of Commons through the Treasury select committee (*Financial Times,*

7 May 1997; *Guardian,* 7 May 1997; *Parl. Deb.*, Commons, 5s, 295:508). Later in May, Brown stripped the bank of its responsibility to supervise the banking sector, transferring those duties to the Securities and Investments Board (*Financial Times,* 21 May 1997; *Guardian,* 21 May 1997).

The reform reflected the Labour Party's desire to solidify its potentially fragile social coalition. In announcing the reform, Brown explained, "We must remove the suspicion that short-term party political considerations are influencing the setting of interest rates" (*Financial Times,* 7 May 1997). In parliamentary debates, he emphasized that the reforms would make monetary policy more representative of Britain's diverse economy: "The [Monetary Policy] Committee will be responsible for taking full account of regional and sectoral information in its monetary policy decisions. . . . The Court [of the Bank] will be substantially reformed, so that it is able to take account of the full range of industrial and business views in this country, and for the first time it will be fully representative of the whole of the United Kingdom" (*Parl. Deb.,* Commons, 5s, 294:508). These institutional changes were clearly designed to enhance the bank's credibility not only with markets, but also with the public. By moving to grant the Bank of England more independence, the Labour Party's leadership sought to prevent potential conflicts over monetary policy from dividing the party and also to reassure constituents about its commitment to moderate economic policies.

Labour's announcement enjoyed a largely positive reception from a variety of actors. Predictably, the major financial press, *The Financial Times* and *The Economist,* praised the decision, as did *The Guardian.* Financial markets, which might have been expected to be hostile to a Labour government (Herron 2000), also reacted favorably. In the wake of the chancellor's decision, the pound appreciated and the stock market rose. Most dramatically, British government bond prices made their biggest one-day gains in more than five years, indicating that market actors expected a reduction in long-term inflationary pressures (*Financial Times,* 7 May 1997). Consequently, the Labour government would enjoy lower long-term interest rates, freeing up some public money for new spending projects.

Business, another group not traditionally associated with the Labour Party, also welcomed the announcement. The Confederation of British Industry (CBI) and the Institute of Directors issued statements applauding the reform. Adair Turner, director general of the CBI, stated, "We very much welcome this move. We would like to see macro-economic policy become independent of politics and we see this as a step in the right direction" (*Financial Times,* 7 May 1997). During parliamentary debates, several Labour MPs reported that businesses in their constituencies approved as well. MP Lawrence Cunliffe (Leigh) stated, "In my part of the world, the largest industrial region in the north-west, the bosses are backing Labour: in the latest poll of industrialists, 88 per cent. responded in support of the Chancellor. . . . That is an independent response to an independent bank system" (*Parl. Deb.*, Commons, 295:1059). Similarly, first-time Labour MP Ivor Caplin (Hove) said, "I know from my postbag that many businesses in my constituency are solidly behind his [the Chancellor's] decision" to make the Bank more independent (*Parl. Deb.*, Commons, 5s, 295:1067).

Financial and business interests were not the only ones to endorse the reform. Many citizens also approved the decision. Helen Liddell, economic secretary to the Treasury, stated, "it was not just universal acclaim from the City and the financial institutions, but universal acclaim from the people. As recently as Saturday, at Shotts highland games—hardly the usual scenario for talking about monetary policy—I was assailed by people wanting to congratulate the Government on their decision on the Bank of England" (*Parl. Deb.*, Commons, 5s, 295:1076).

But not everyone was pleased with the chancellor's decision, particularly the traditional elements of the Labour Party (*Financial Times*, 7 May 1997). These left-of-center MPs complained that they had been surprised and betrayed by the announcement. Diane Abbott (Hackney, North and Stoke Newington), who emerged as one of the most reasoned opponents of independence, quipped, "Why do not we simply sub-contract the entire economy to Goldman Sachs?" (*Parl. Deb.*, Commons, 5s, 295:1059).[8] Dennis Skinner (Bolsover) complained, "I cannot understand, however, in a world economy that offers very few financial levers to any incoming Government, why . . . the first thing a Labour Government do—without a manifesto commitment in precise terms—is hand over one of the most important financial levers to the enemy" (*Parl. Deb.*, Commons, 5s, 294:518).

These complaints, however, represented "old" Labour and did not fit with the party's new emphasis on moderation and inclusion. Indeed, supporters of central bank independence attacked the complaints of Labour extremists as antithetical to the party's interests. Stephen Timms (East Ham) argued:

> An article . . . written by one of my hon. Friends describes the decision as "delivering policy to the enemy" and "a gesture which . . . conciliates only our enemies." The decision also conciliates many people who are not our enemies; many who wanted a new Labour government who would be radical and trustworthy, and who feel that this is what they have got. The new Government will not play fast and loose with people's money, and it would

> be a fatal error to believe that only our enemies would be anxious if it were otherwise. To be successful, do not the new Government have to consign to the dustbin the idea that large parts of the economy constitute our enemy? Such an idea can only be recipe for the disastrous and debilitating strife that has so damaged Labour Governments in the past. We would fail if we went down that road again. We are on a different road now, and we shall succeed. We want partnership, not warfare. (*Parl. Deb.,* Commons, 5s, 295:1064)

Clearly, reformers hoped that making the central bank more independent would cement Labour's electoral coalition and prevent monetary policy from dividing the party.

Debating the Bill

Parliamentary debates about the Bank of England Bill centered on three issues: the Bank of England's accountability, the policy consequences of such a move, and Britain's participation in the single currency. Unlike debates over nationalizing the bank in 1946, a considerable portion of the debate in 1997 focused on the bank's governance structure. Even MPs who supported making the bank more independent questioned whether the government's proposal gave the chancellor too much influence over the bank—an unsurprising concern in a party with diverse constituents and backbenchers who did not necessarily share the chancellor's policy preferences. MPs pressed the government to allow the Treasury Select Committee to hold confirmatory hearings for appointments to the monetary-policy committee. Labour MP Giles Radice (North Durham), a supporter of the bill, asserted that the select committee would hold such hearings: "The fact we can and shall do it [hold hearings]—even without formal powers being written into the Bill—could influence the Chancellor were he thinking of putting his granny or whoever on to the Monetary Policy Committee" (*Parl. Deb.,* Commons, 5s, 300:747). MPs further complained that the three-year term for committee members was too short, giving the "perception that they could be put under pressure" by the Chancellor (Malcolm Bruce, Gordon, Liberal Democrat [*Parl. Deb.,* Commons, 5s, 300:752]). Finally, MPs did not believe that the Treasury Select Committee had enough resources to hold the bank responsible. Diane Abbott, speaking against the bill, stated, "We cannot seriously believe that the Treasury Committee, with two and a half special advisers, can hold to account the Monetary Policy Committee and the battalions of economists behind Eddie George" (*Parl. Deb.,* Commons, 5s, 300:765)—a view that was echoed by many of the bill's supporters. The government, however, contended that the bill already contained enough measures to ensure the accountability of both the bank and the chancellor, including reporting requirements and increased transparency.

The second issue centered on the policy consequences of the bank's independence. Critics on both sides of the aisle expressed concern that the bank would impose a deflationary bias on the economy, hurting growth and employment unnecessarily. Former Chancellor Kenneth Clarke argued, "In recent years, the Bank of England has not been very good at forecasting inflation. The Bank has always overestimated the likely upside inflation risk. . . . The Bank always fears the worst and reacts accordingly, which is what will cause damage" to the real economy (*Parl. Deb.*, Commons, 5s, 300:738). The bill's supporters repeatedly countered that lower and more stable levels of inflation would foster investment and growth, helping to restore Britain's competitiveness.

The third topic of debate focused on Britain's participation in the single currency. Euro-skeptics in both the Conservative and Labour parties complained that making the central bank more independent was a covert step toward entry into the single currency. Conservative MP Sir Peter Tapsell (Louth and Horncastle) stated, "The Bill is intended as a halfway house towards our economy being managed by a European central bank. . . . It is a further constitutional retreat along the road to a single European currency and the sacrifice of British parliamentary self-government to the bureaucracies of a federal Europe" (*Parl. Deb.*, Commons, 5s, 300:758). The Chancellor, however, emphasized that the reform was not a stepping stone to the single currency: "The Government's decision to give the Bank operational responsibility for setting interest rates is a British solution, designed to meet British domestic needs for stability. Decisions on EMU will be taken if and when required, and will have to be agreed by Cabinet, Parliament, and the people" (*Parl. Deb.*, Commons, 5s, 295:87). He added that his reforms did not entirely meet the requirements for central bank independence in the Maastricht Treaty.

The bill passed, but it generated internal dissension for both the Labour and Conservative parties. In the Labour Party, many old-guard MPs were clearly hostile to the bill, although they were not numerous enough to block it. On the other side, the Conservatives officially opposed the bill, although some privately approved of the measure. (Former chancellor Norman Lamont openly endorsed the proposal.) Only the Liberal Democrats supported making the bank more independent with little intraparty conflict.

In the first year of the Labour government, therefore, party leaders successfully launched a series of institutional reforms, including a more independent central bank and regional devolution. These reforms helped the party balance new interests with their traditional core constituencies and establish a reputation for good governance, a reputation that was reflected in the high approval ratings given to the Blair government during the early part of its term.

Central Bank Independence and Political Reform

The economic shocks of the 1970s and 1980s changed constituent preferences over economic and monetary policies, contributing to electoral dealignment in many industrial countries. The erosion of the traditional social coalitions underpinning the governing party(ies) diversified the policy demands placed on politicians, creating distrust among party politicians. At the same time, governments became less able to deliver promised economic outcomes. Faced with changing constituent bases, less-committed electoral support, and new political challengers, the major parties had to adjust their strategies to maintain their viability. They needed to build new social coalitions that embraced the diversity of economic interests yet continued to appeal to their core constituents.

Central bank reform represents a response to such political pressures. A more independent central bank can help prevent intraparty conflicts over monetary policy from threatening the party's ability to win and retain office. It also demonstrates a commitment to a variety of constituents, helping the party hold together a diverse social coalition. In both Italy and Britain, political parties made the central banks more independent as part of a strategic calculation to help them compete in a changed economic and political environment. Further, in both cases, central bank independence was adopted amid other major reforms—devolution, legislative reform, and even electoral reform.[9] With these institutional changes, party leaders were seeking ways to ensure the party's political survival.[10]

The combination of central bank independence and political reform in Italy and Britain is not a mere coincidence.[11] The same factors underlying central bank reform—changes in constituent demands and increases in intraparty conflict—also increase the possibility of political reform. In fact, monetary reform and political reform are linked in other countries as well. In New Zealand, the adoption of an independent central bank in 1989–90 nearly coincided with the popular rejection of the majoritarian electoral system in 1992–93. Prior to the 1990s, New Zealand had possessed a typical "Westminster" system, with two-party competition between the Labour Party and the National Party. When the National Party won the 1990 election,[12] it honored a pledge it had made in opposition to hold a referendum on the electoral system (*The Economist*, 26 September 1992). In 1992, voters rejected the first-past-the-post electoral system, supporting mixed majoritarian–proportional-representation system.[13]

The coincidence of central bank reform and electoral reform suggests a similar underlying cause: politicians are seeking to insulate themselves from the political consequences of economic internationalization. Established political parties are using these institutional reforms to balance conflicting interests, rebuild social coalitions, and maintain electoral viability. Central bank independence, therefore, is more than just a "technical" solution to an economic problem. Rather, the institutional status of the central bank reflects how political parties choose to aggregate citizen demands and in turn, how those demands shape public-policy choices—fundamental questions about the nature of democracy in a capitalist society.

Chapter 8

Europe's Commitment to the Single Currency

After more than a decade of stagnation, the European Community enjoyed a revitalization in the 1980s. The 1986 Single European Act made concrete plans for the completion of the internal market, a goal established in the 1950s, by the end of 1992. Unlike any European initiative before it, the "1992 program" captured the public's imagination and generated widespread excitement.

Buoyed by this enthusiasm, Europe's leaders looked to take another big step toward full political integration. So in December 1991, in the Dutch town of Maastricht, they signed the Treaty on European Union, committing themselves to the creation of an Economic and Monetary Union with a single currency for all participating countries. The treaty laid out an explicit timetable for the transition to the single currency—by January 1999 at the latest. It required member states to meet specific economic performance indicators, the "convergence criteria," by that time in order to qualify for participation. These criteria set limits for inflation rates, interest rates, budget deficits, the level of government debt, and exchange-rate stability and were designed to ensure that participating countries would have sufficiently similar economies to guarantee a successful transition. The treaty also included an "opt-out" clause, which allowed member states not to join the single currency if they did not desire to do so. Finally, the treaty called for a single European central bank, independent of direct political control, to manage monetary policy.

Yet instead of solidifying public acceptance of European integration, the treaty met with widespread skepticism. Difficulties with ratification and a currency crisis within the EMS quickly eroded confidence in the plan. Moreover, the convergence criteria prolonged a Europe-wide recession throughout the entire 1990s. Despite sluggish economic growth and rising unemployment, member-state governments were forced to pursue fiscal restraint to meet the targets for budget deficits (no more than 3 percent of GDP) and debt levels (no more than 60 percent of GDP). In turn, the popularity of member-state governments suffered.

As a result, the single currency remained in doubt throughout the 1990s: Would member states follow through on the plan? Which member states would qualify under the convergence criteria? What countries would choose not to participate? As late as 1997, one observer wrote, "The Treaty of Maastricht sets a clear timetable: a single currency will come into being no later than 1999. It may seem that all that remains is to watch the countdown before lift-off. Nothing is further from the truth. Power in the boosters is not assured; last minute checks reveal a number of blinking red lights; and politico-economic pressures are building up to dangerous levels. Public support for the euro is lukewarm at best" (Wyplosz 1997, 16).

Nevertheless, politicians in Europe remained committed to the Maastricht plan. And in January 1999, the single currency, the euro, came into existence. Eleven of the 15 member states participated (Britain, Denmark, and Sweden opted out; Greece was judged not ready to join). In light of the uncertain consequences of the single currency, the short-term political costs of complying with the convergence criteria, and the economic slump, this commitment is remarkable. Why did politicians adhere to the single currency?

I argue that this commitment reflects in part the incentives and constraints faced by political parties in western Europe. With the diversification of constituent policy demands and decreased policy discretion under the EMS, the political value of controlling national monetary policy had declined in the 1980s. Instead, politicians perceived that delegating monetary policy to the European level could help manage intraparty conflicts over economic policy and allow them to rebuild social coalitions. The promise of these domestic political benefits helps explain the commitment to the single currency.

This chapter first reviews traditional explanations of the origins of the Maastricht Treaty, which focus on international and state-level interests. The second section explores the debates and uncertainties surrounding the Maastricht Treaty during the 1990s. The third section discusses how the single currency can help political parties win and retain office. The fourth section explores the implications of the single currency for the future of the EU.

Origins of the Single Currency

Political economists studying the EU have used the traditional frameworks of neofunctionalism, intergovernmentalism, and international state competition to explain the move to a single currency.[1]

Neofunctionalism

Neofunctionalist arguments emphasize the leadership of European institutions and the role of "spill-over" in the process of integration: successful supranational management of a policy area requires integration in complementary policy areas. As the supranational institution acquires responsibility for an increasing range of issue areas, public loyalty gradually transfers from national governments to the supranational institution.

According to this perspective, the single currency was the result of pressures for further integration brought about by the single-market program. The European Commission's report, *One Market, One Money* (Emerson et al. 1991), argued that a single currency was necessary to achieve the full benefits of the single market. Without a single currency, member states could still resort to competitive devaluations to make their goods more attractive within the internal market. Other member states might respond by reerecting trade barriers. Only a single currency could secure the internal market against such exchange-rate manipulation.

Indeed, after Britain and Italy exited the EMS in September 1992, their currencies plummeted against the remaining EMS states. Consequently, British and Italian products flooded into France. In response, the French government requested special restrictions on the British and Italian imports in contradiction of the internal market (Eichengreen 1993a).

Intergovernmentalism

Intergovernmentalist arguments view the EU as an agreement between member states. In particular, bargaining between the large states—Germany, France, and Britain—shapes the EU's development (Moravscik 1991, 1998). These arguments point to three factors to explain the Maastricht agreement: the perception of German economic hegemony in the EMS, the pan-European policy consensus on the need for price stability (McNamara 1998), and interstate bargaining surrounding German unification (Sandholtz 1993).

As the EMS hardened in the 1980s, member states had to mimic German monetary policies in order to maintain the value of their currencies. These asymmetries created political tension within the EU. French and Italian policymakers complained about their lack of policy discretion. Recognizing the opportunity to reshape European monetary cooperation, German foreign minister Hans-Dietrich Genscher in early 1988 proposed a single currency with an independent central bank, similar to the Bundesbank. His proposals led to the formation of the Delors Committee to study the issues surrounding the transition to and management of a single currency.

The Maastricht Treaty offered a way for France and Italy to reduce German dominance of monetary policy, and at the same time, it provided assurances to inflation-phobic German leaders that the single currency would not produce higher inflation rates.

International State Competition

A third set of arguments contends that international competition, particularly from the United States and Japan, is the driving force behind European integration (Sandholtz and Zysman 1989). In particular, the history of monetary cooperation in Europe represents an attempt to insulate European economies from the fluctuations of the U.S. dollar (Henning 1998).

In the postwar period, the Bretton Woods system of fixed exchange rates helped to restore trade and economic growth within Europe. As strains appeared in the system in the 1960s, the European Community began to explore alternative arrangements for ensuring exchange-rate stability within Europe (Eichengreen 1993a; Maes 1992). The collapse of Bretton Woods in the early 1970s ushered in a de facto international system of floating exchange rates. Europeans responded first by establishing the Snake, a loose agreement to limit exchange-rate fluctuations within Europe, and later by forging the EMS (Goodman 1992; Ludlow 1982; Oatley 1997). Extreme gyrations in the value of the U.S. dollar during the 1980s provided renewed impetus for European monetary cooperation (Henning 1998). The single currency would not only protect the internal market from U.S.-generated exchange-rate instability but also create a rival international currency that could enhance Europe's international political standing (Bergsten 1999).

Although each of these perspectives emphasizes a different aspect of the origins of the single currency, they share an international relations approach to European integration, focusing on issues of national sovereignty, supranational institutions, and transnational cooperation. Without a more complete understanding of domestic politics and the incentives faced by political parties in Europe, however, they cannot explain why politicians remain committed to the Maastricht Treaty in face of severe short-term political costs.

The Uncertainty around EMU in the 1990s

Instead of extending the popular enthusiasm for the EU generated by the 1992 program, the Maastricht Treaty ushered in a decade of doubt and uncertainty about European integration. Commentators immediately questioned the economic desirability and political feasibility of a single currency. Currency market volatility and sluggish economic growth in the early 1990s compounded reservations about the future of the single currency.

The Economic Desirability of a Single Currency

The Maastricht Treaty plans for EMU sparked fierce debates about whether the single currency would constitute an economic boon to European economies or become an economic fiasco.[2] Economists evaluated every aspect of EMU: prospects for participation, the impact on member-state economies, the future of the euro as an international currency, monetary-policy transmission mechanisms under a single currency, convergence issues in accounting and banking regulation, and the operation of the ECB. Many of the early controversies focused on two issues: whether the EU constituted an "optimal currency area" and the single currency's implications for fiscal policy.

Optimal Currency Area

The single currency implied one monetary policy for all participating countries. Each member state would forego the use of national monetary policy and exchange-rate changes to counter localized economic shocks. The real economic costs of relinquishing these instruments depended on the degree of economic similarity between participating member states and the existence of other means of adjustment, particularly cross-border factor mobility. Regions with similar economies and high levels of cross-border factor mobility are better suited for a common currency than less-integrated economies (McKinnon 1963; Mundell 1961; Tavlas 1993).

To determine whether Europe represented an optimal currency area, economists examined the similarity of member-state economies, the adjustment mechanisms available to member states, and the impact of EMU on trade.

Economic analysis of the similarities of member-state economies found that despite convergence, significant differences remained in their vulnerability to external shocks (Bayoumi and Eichengreen 1993, 1997; Eichengreen 1992; Frankel and Rose 1996). Complicating these analyses, however, was uncertainty about how the completion of EMU would affect the long-term dynamics of economic development within and across member states.

Analysis of the adjustment mechanisms in the member states was also not encouraging for the EMU project. Researchers found that labor mobility both within and between member states was low relative to the United States

(Eichengreen 1993b; Obstfeld and Peri 1998). Although the Single European Act had eliminated legal restrictions to the free movement of people within the EU, linguistic and cultural barriers to migration remained. The results implied that labor-market adjustments to local shocks would be difficult, producing sharp regional disparities in unemployment. Further, economists noted the existence of fiscal stabilizers in the United States to facilitate cross-regional adjustment. Federal tax and transfer payments automatically shifted money from prosperous regions to sluggish ones (Bayoumi and Masson 1995; Fatas 1998; Kletzer 1998; Obstfeld and Peri 1998; Sala-i-Martin and Sachs 1992). Although estimates of these effects varied substantially, economists agreed that the small EU budget would be inadequate to perform such a function under EMU, particularly if there were limits on the amount of fiscal stabilization that could take place at the member-state level.

The single currency would help reduce transaction costs between member states, potentially increasing trade, but these benefits appeared to be relatively small. Eliminating the need to convert currencies would save money, but even according to proponents, these savings would constitute only a fraction of 1 percent of Europe's overall GDP (Emerson et al. 1991). The single currency could also increase cross-border trade and investment by reducing exchange-rate uncertainty. But again, research suggested that these gains would be relatively minor because the EMS had already reduced exchange-rate volatility, and the existence of forward markets allowed traders to hedge against currency risk (Frankel and Rose 1996). Perhaps the largest impact was the psychological benefit of a single currency rather than a system of fixed exchange rates. Although a fixed exchange-rate system operated like a single currency in many ways, a chance always remained that a participating country would devalue its currency. A single currency would be the only way to preclude this possibility and guarantee the single market.

Comparing these costs and benefits, most economists concluded that Europe did not yet represent an optimal currency area. The risks of such a venture seemed to outweigh the nebulous and uncertain economic benefits.

Fiscal Implications

Many economists also recognized that the single currency would affect fiscal policy in the member states. The single currency would create a tension for fiscal-policy management (Eichengreen 1998; Wyplosz 1997). According to some economists, without the ability to alter exchange rates, member states would have to rely on a more active fiscal policy to facilitate economic adjustment. Other economists, however, maintained that fiscal policy would need to be closely coordinated under the single currency to ensure price stability. Excessive budget deficits in a single member state could force the European Central Bank to bail out that country by monetizing its debt, leading to inflation throughout the eurozone.

Reflecting German concerns, the Maastricht Treaty emphasizes fiscal discipline as a cornerstone of the EMU. The convergence criteria established an economically arbitrary standard for budget deficits and national debt (Buiter, Corsetti, and Roubini 1993). But the treaty itself was vague about how to ensure fiscal discipline after the single currency had been implemented—an issue that was not resolved until the Growth and Stability Pact in December 1996. Moreover, the economic impact of these requirements remained unclear (Hallett, Hutchison, and Jensen 1999). Eichengreen and Wyplosz (1998) estimated that the Stability Pact would not significantly hurt output in any one year, but the cumulative effect over a 20-year period could produce output losses of 5 to 9 percent of GDP. Finally, political economists recognized that fiscal-policy discretion at the member-state level also represented a critical issue for national sovereignty and democracy within the EU.

Political Feasibility

A second set of issues centered on the political feasibility of EMU. The Maastricht Treaty laid out not only a timetable for monetary union but also the economic criteria necessary to qualify for participation. Meeting the convergence criteria would require substantial policy adjustments for many states, particularly in fiscal policy. In high-debt states such as Belgium and Italy, compliance would necessitate extraordinary budgetary restraint (Garrett 1998b; Hallerberg 1999; McNamara 2000). Throughout the 1990s, academic and media speculation centered around what countries would eventually participate, how strictly the criteria would be enforced,[3] and, if some member states were excluded from the final stage, how a "two-speed" Europe would function.

Public apathy toward the single currency also called into question whether countries would make the necessary policy adjustments to comply with the treaty.[4] In northern Europe, support for the single currency was at best soft, particularly in Germany. German citizens worried about the inflationary consequences of the single currency and were loathe to give up the D-mark, a symbol of German strength and stability. In Italy and Spain, the idea of a single currency was more popular. Many Italians perceived that the single currency would help promote fiscal responsibility as well as political accountability. European business did support EMU, although few considered it as pressing an issue as the completion of the internal market. As a result, business did not make the single currency a priority in the way that they had demanded the 1992 program.

The lack of strong public support for the treaty became evident during the ratification process in Denmark and France. In accordance with Danish law, the treaty had to be approved by a popular referendum.[5] Although Denmark has traditionally been skeptical about European integration, the major parties endorsed the treaty. Extreme parties on both the Left (Socialist People's Party) and the Right (Progress Party) encouraged a no vote. In June 1992, Danish voters rejected the treaty by a slim margin (50.7 percent voted no; 49.3 percent voted yes). Although polls leading up to the referendum had indicated that the vote would be close, both Danish and EU leaders were shocked by the result.[6]

In France, President Mitterrand had scheduled a referendum on the Maastricht Treaty for September 1992. In early summer 1992, opinion polls indicated a majority in favor, but as the campaign developed, support began to slip. Again, opposition to the treaty came from the extremes of the political spectrum. Both the Communists and the National Front urged a no vote. The nationalist Rally for the Republic was divided over the issue. Although party leader Jacques Chirac declared his (grudging) support for the treaty, he also said that party members were free to vote as they pleased. The Socialists and the Union for a Democratic France solidly supported the treaty. But the economic recession and other Socialist policy blunders hurt the reception of the government's recommendation. The final vote approved the treaty, but only by a precarious margin (51 percent versus 49 percent).

German Unification and the EMS Crisis

Economic and political events in the early 1990s created even more questions about the viability of the single-currency project. In particular, the shock of German monetary unification created new tensions for European monetary relations.

German Unification

The Maatstricht Treaty negotiation debates occurred around the collapse of communism and the reunification of West and East Germany. On 1 July 1990, monetary unification took place, followed quickly by full unification on 3 October 1990. While unification sped the treaty negotiations toward their conclusion (Dinan 1999; Marsh 1992), the German government's strategy of unification shaped not only the treaty's immediate reception but also Europe's economy and monetary relations in the 1990s.

Few had anticipated the costs of integrating East Germany into the German economy. The generous terms of exchange given to East Germans, as well as extensive transfer payments and subsidies, unleashed inflationary pressures in Germany (as well as unemployment and a loss of competitiveness in the eastern regions).

In order to stave off these domestic inflationary pressures, Germany tightened its monetary policy. Higher German interest rates, however, raised the interest-rate floor for all the EMS member states. As a result, the German policy strategy exacerbated a recession throughout Europe, hurting growth and employment rates across the continent.

The European Monetary System

The institutions of the EMS provided for currency realignments to respond to divergences in economic performance across member states. In the early years of the EMS, realignments occurred relatively frequently, but as macroeconomic performance converged during the 1980s, realignments happened less often. Prior to 1991, the last realignment had occurred in 1987. Since then, a number of currencies, including the lira (Italy), the peseta (Spain), and the pound (Britain), had gradually become overvalued (Gros and Steinherr 1992; Johnson and Collignon 1994). The twin shocks of the Maastricht Treaty and German monetary unification placed further strains on the EMS. As a result, a general realignment was necessary to adjust to the new economic situation.

Despite the economic pressures for a realignment, however, member states refused to adjust the values of their currencies. I argue that the domestic political costs of devaluation contributed to the reluctance of member-state governments to pursue a general realignment. By the early 1990s, the perceived political costs of devaluation had increased in each of the major EMS member states: France, Italy, Britain, and Spain. These governments were already unpopular with the public, reflecting in part the Europe-wide economic recession. Moreover, each government had invested considerable political capital in defending its currency's parity. An about-face on the issue of devaluation would damage the government's credibility with the public in the short term and hurt the prospects for participation in the single currency in the long term.[7] Given that each of the governments was due to hold elections in the early 1990s, a currency realignment could have had devastating political consequences—costing them not only public approval but also their positions in office.

The September 1992 Crisis

The Maastricht Treaty requirements for the transition to EMU turned the weakening economic conditions into a crisis. The treaty's convergence criteria required that a member state have no devaluations for at least two years to qualify for the single currency. Currency traders knew that several currencies were overvalued and that a general realignment was imminent given the treaty's timetable. Furthermore, the problems surrounding the treaty's ratification, including the controversial public referenda in Denmark and France, created uncertainty about the future of monetary union. Consequently, in September 1992, currency traders placed extra pressure on weak currencies, making a "one-way bet" that these currencies would be devalued (Buiter, Corsetti, and Pesenti 1998; Cobham 1994; Gros and Thygesen 1998; Johnson and Collignon 1994).

Rather than devalue, governments faced two options: they could continue to push up interest rates, or they could exit the system. Higher interest rates would maintain exchange-rate stability with the D-mark, but these rates would also contribute to the deepening economic recession. Exiting the system, on the other hand, would ease the recessionary pressures. Politicians could also use the EMS as a scapegoat for the economic slump, possibly helping defray the political costs of breaking their commitment to the system. Exiting the system, however, did carry some risks, including higher inflation and increased doubt about the member state's commitment to the Maastricht timetable. Each option—devaluation, maintaining the parity, or exit—carried potential costs. The political circumstances of each government determined its response to the speculative attack.

In Britain, the high interest rates necessary to maintain the parity had hurt the Conservatives' approval ratings by exacerbating a private-debt crisis. Because home ownership is widespread in Britain and mortgages are tied to current interests rates, government popularity is highly sensitive to interest rate changes (Clarke and Stewart 1995; Garrett 1992). Although devaluation might have eased these pressures, Prime Minister John Major had assured the markets and the public that the government would not devalue, claiming it was his intention to make the pound the anchor currency of Europe. A reversal on devaluation would have shaken public confidence in his government and unleashed criticism from the anti-Europe wing of his own party. Instead, exit became the least-objectionable option, despite its potential costs. Leaving the system allowed the government to lower interest rates and spark an economic recovery. The move also appealed to Conservative euro-skeptics.

Italy suffered from a public debt crisis. Throughout the early 1990s, the Italian debt-to-GDP ratio was over 100 percent. The lira's weakness in the EMS stemmed in part from the inability of Italian politicians to address the fiscal crisis. To preserve the value of the lira in the face of market pressure, Italian policymakers needed to raise interest rates. At the same time, however, higher interest rates would worsen the debt problem—the very reason that currency traders were reluctant to hold the lira in the first place. A devaluation would have made currency traders unlikely to hold lira in the future and reinforced the popular image of government incompetence. Instead, exit became the most palatable option for the Italian government.

In contrast, the Socialist government in France remained within the system, reflecting both domestic and international political calculations. Domestically, the Socialist government could campaign for the upcoming elections, due in spring 1993, on few other economic successes besides the *franc fort.* Although a currency realignment might have eased the recession, a devaluation would have suggested that the economic hardships endured by the Socialists' constituents had been in vain. Additionally, voters might have interpreted devaluation as a cynical ploy that sacrificed long-term economic goals for short-term political gains.

International interests prevented the Socialists from exiting the system entirely. Leaving the EMS would have doomed the EMU project and ensured continued German dominance of European economic and monetary policy. French institutional reforms, particularly capital market liberalization (de Boissieu and Pisani-Ferry 1998; Loriaux 1991) and the tight monetary policies of the 1980s, reflected in part a desire to establish France as Germany's equal in European economic affairs. Exiting the system would have indicated continued French subordination to German economic leadership, making those reforms a failure.

Despite their defense of the franc, the Socialists lost the 1993 elections badly, dropping from 35 percent of the vote in 1988 to only 19 percent. Shortly after the new Conservative government took office in the summer of 1993, it sought modifications in the EMS. In August, EU finance ministers announced a widening of the exchange rate bands to plus or minus 15 percent, up from the original 2.25 percent.

The Sluggish 1990s

After the ratification problems and the EMS crisis, political leaders seemed to lose confidence in European integration. Instead, they focused more on their own domestic problems—both economic and political.

Germany's economic policy strategy continued to hamper growth throughout the EU. Unemployment remained stubbornly high in most member states. The convergence criteria, however, made it difficult for European policymakers to respond to the situation with traditional policy tools. They could not devalue their currency or lower interest rates. Nor could they pursue fiscal stimulus—indeed, the criteria required many states to reduce budget deficits. As a result, the weak economy dragged on throughout the entire decade.

Member-state governments also suffered from domestic political problems. Most dramatically, the Italian political system collapsed under public outrage at corruption scandals and the inefficacy of government policy, producing both electoral reform and a revamped party system. Political change in other member states was less spectacular but still left governments with only weak mandates. In France, Mitterrand remained president through the mid-1990s, but the Socialist Party had been decimated in the 1993 elections, leading to another government of cohabitation. Although John Major's Conservative Party surprisingly won the 1992 British elections, his government appeared devoid of new policy ideas and was severely divided over the question of Europe. In Spain, the Socialist government under Felipe Gonzalez endured a number of corruption scandals before losing office in 1996.

As a consequence of this economic and political weakness, member-state governments were less enthusiastic about the process of European integration. Instead of taking large steps toward political integration, member states seemed content to consolidate the status quo. In 1995, for instance, member states replaced outgoing European Commission president Jacques Delors, an energetic visionary, with Jacques Santer, a low-key figure unlikely to press for major innovations. And although the Maastricht Treaty called for another intergovernmental conference in the mid-1990s, the result of the conference, the Amsterdam Treaty, contained no major initiatives.

Nevertheless, preparation for the single currency proceeded apace. In December 1995, the European Council abandoned the idea of launching the single currency in 1997 but reaffirmed its commitment to the 1999 date. Further, it initiated studies concerning political and economic issues after the single currency had been adopted. This led to the Stability and Growth Pact, adopted in December 1996, a measure designed to ensure that governments would continue to pursue fiscal discipline after the initiation of the single currency. Under the agreement, governments that ran "excessive" budget deficits were subject to fines (Buti, Franco, and Ongena 1998; McNamara 2000). The following year, the council agreed to the establishment of the "Euro-X" council of finance ministers to coordinate economic policy within the eurozone.

With these actions, it became increasingly apparent that Europe's leaders were serious about their commitment to the single currency. Indeed, the May 1998 European Council decision to approve 11 member states for membership in the single currency, in doubt as late as mid-1997, had become widely anticipated in the early months of 1998. The only controversy surrounded who would be appointed as the first head of the ECB. French president Jacques Chirac objected to the favorite, Wim Duisenberg, the head of the Dutch central bank, and proposed a French candidate, Jean-Claude Trichet. After much wrangling, a compromise was reached that allowed Duisenberg to assume the post, provided he resign early to allow Trichet to succeed him. On 1 January 1999, therefore, the euro came into being.

That politicians carried out their commitment to the euro is remarkable, particularly given the circumstances: sluggish economic growth, high levels of unemployment, public apathy toward the single currency, weak popular approval ratings, unruly currency markets, and the political difficulty of complying with the convergence criteria. Each of these factors could have derailed the single currency. Indeed, throughout much of the decade, commentators and economists remained skeptical about whether the euro would happen. But Europe's politicians surprised many by pushing forward with the single currency. One commentator observed, "Member states' determination to proceed with EMU regardless was one of the most striking aspects of European integration in the 1990s" (Dinan 1999, 159). What explains politicians' commitment to the euro?

Political Parties and the Single Currency

The transition to the single currency entailed some severe short-term costs for Europe's politicians: slow economic growth and high unemployment, the need to make painful budget cuts, and a loss of popular approval (Garrett 1998b). Yet the politicians followed through on EMU. I argue that their commitment reflects in part the domestic political benefits of the single currency.

As with the incentives for adopting an independent central bank, changes in constituent preferences and monetary-policy efficacy helped make monetary union possible in the 1990s. The fragmented social coalitions of the major parties in the member states had increased the potential for intraparty conflicts over monetary policy. Additionally, participation in the EMS had limited the macroeconomic policy options available to member states. Monetary policy was constrained by the need to maintain the exchange rate. Furthermore, the structure of the EMS left member states vulnerable to speculative currency attacks, as in the 1992 crisis. These attacks had the potential not only to undermine the single market but also to hurt the government's credibility with the public. With the diversification of constituent preferences and policy restrictions imposed by the EMS, therefore, the political value of controlling national monetary policy had decreased.

Delegating monetary policy to the European level could in turn help parties rebuild their social coalitions and protect their electoral fortunes. Most obviously, the single currency would remove a potentially divisive policy issue from the agenda of domestic politics. Although monetary policy had always been a relatively blunt instrument for maintaining social coalitions and fine-tuning the national economy, changes in constituent preferences had made it even more contentious. The single currency would help parties avoid intra-party conflicts over monetary policy and allow them to emphasize other issue areas to appeal to potential voters.

Additionally, the single currency would help guarantee the single market and presumably improve economic growth. Higher rates of economic growth would increase tax revenues and create new employment opportunities—all of which would benefit the major political parties in the long run. Beyond these benefits, the single currency promised to help Europe's political parties in two less-intuitive ways.

Speculative Currency Attacks

First, the single currency would insulate national politicians from international currency and financial markets. With increased capital mobility, currency traders could exert extreme pressure on currencies in the EMS and force governments to pursue policies that hurt their popularity with constituents (Bernhard 1998; Clarke and Stewart 1995; Garrett 1992; Leblang and Bernhard 2000). Certainly, the September 1992 crisis was a clear example of how currency market unrest could hurt a government's approval ratings.

But as far back as the mid-1980s, policymakers had recognized the potential for speculative attacks within the EMS—and their deleterious consequences for domestic political support. Indeed, European leaders judged that the January 1987 realignment, the last realignment prior to the 1992 crisis, had been caused by market turmoil, rather than macroeconomic divergence among the member states (Gros and Thygesen 1998). In response, they negotiated the Basle-Nyborg agreement in September 1987 to help prevent future speculative attacks. Nevertheless, it became increasingly apparent that currency markets were simply growing too powerful to be deterred. The only way that Europe's politicians could insulate themselves from the political consequences of these shocks was to adopt a single currency.

Fiscal Policy

Second, the single currency helped politicians pursue fiscal retrenchment. During the 1980s and early 1990s, many member states suffered from exploding budget deficits and high public debt (de Haan and Sturm 1994; von Hagen 1992). Yet these states remained overcommitted to the maintenance of the welfare state (Franzese 2000; Iversen and Cusak 2000). Consequently, government taxes and spending constituted ever-larger portions of the economy. Many governments accumulated debt at an enormous pace (see fig. 6). During the early 1990s, debt-to-GDP ratios exceeded 100 percent in Italy, Belgium, and Ireland and rose substantially in Germany, France, and Spain. These countries simply could not sustain their fiscal positions. Instead, European politicians faced the unpleasant prospect of cutting budgets and reducing public services—tasks that were necessary regardless of the convergence criteria.

The Maastricht plans for a single currency, however, helped politicians tackle the fiscal situation. The single currency provided an incentive—participation in the single currency—for member states to pursue fiscal discipline (Hallerberg 1999; Hallerberg and von Hagen 1999). Failure to make headway on the budgetary question would mean exclusion from the euro—with a loss in political prestige and influence within the EU.

Furthermore, the convergence criteria helped politicians justify politically sensitive budget cuts to their publics by framing those decisions as critical to participation in the European project. Program reductions and tax increases were redefined as "actions necessary to join the single currency and remain in the forefront of European integration." Politicians could take credit for producing a budget in compliance with the 3 percent limit, rather than defend themselves for chopping public services and benefits. The clear, if economically arbitrary, criteria also provided the public with a baseline with which to measure and monitor the government's progress. Politicians, especially in southern Europe, used the convergence criteria to defend these dramatic changes in fiscal policy (de Haan, Moessen, and Volkerink 1999; Hallerberg 1999; McNamara 2000; Pitruzello 1997). By 1998, budget deficits in all member states met the 3 percent criterion of the Maastricht Treaty.

Finally, participation in the single currency promised the possibility of lower long-term interest rates for member states. As the fiscal positions of member states improved, long-term interest rates declined. Indeed, the spread between yields on long-term German bonds and bond yields for other member states fell throughout the 1990s (see fig. 7). Long-term interest rates dropped even further once the single currency came into being, and remained lower than in non-euro countries. These lower interest rates provide some medium-term relief from the burden of servicing public debt.

The fiscal imbalances of the 1980s and early 1990s limited the ability of political parties to use fiscal policy to expand their appeals or manage the economy. The convergence criteria provided a pretext to cut their spending com-

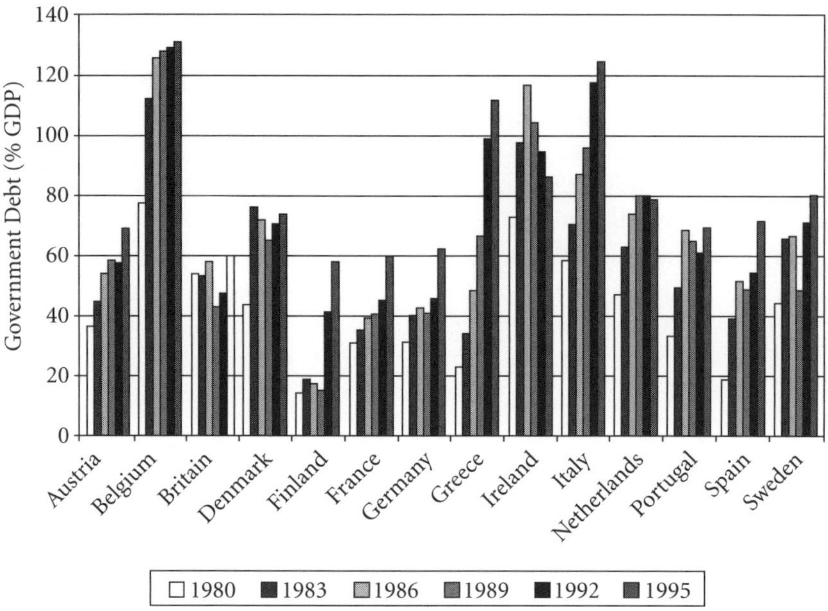

Fig. 6. Public debt in the European Union

mitments. As a result, many countries joined the single currency in an improved fiscal position. Although the size of budget deficits is restricted under the Growth and Stability Pact, fiscal policy may actually become a more flexible policy tool. Political parties would then have the ability to build their support bases by maintaining existing programs or even paying for new ones.

Losing Autonomy?

The single currency does involve a formal transfer of sovereignty to the European level. Politicians lose the ability to use monetary policy toward domestic objectives or to combat asymmetric shocks. But politicians in many member states perceived that they already had little monetary-policy autonomy under the EMS—they were limited by the need to maintain parity with the D-mark. Monetary policy throughout Europe, therefore, reflected German priorities, rather than national policy objectives.

While the single currency also implies that no member state would have monetary-policy autonomy, the structure of the European Central Bank allows national representatives (in the form of central bank governors) to participate

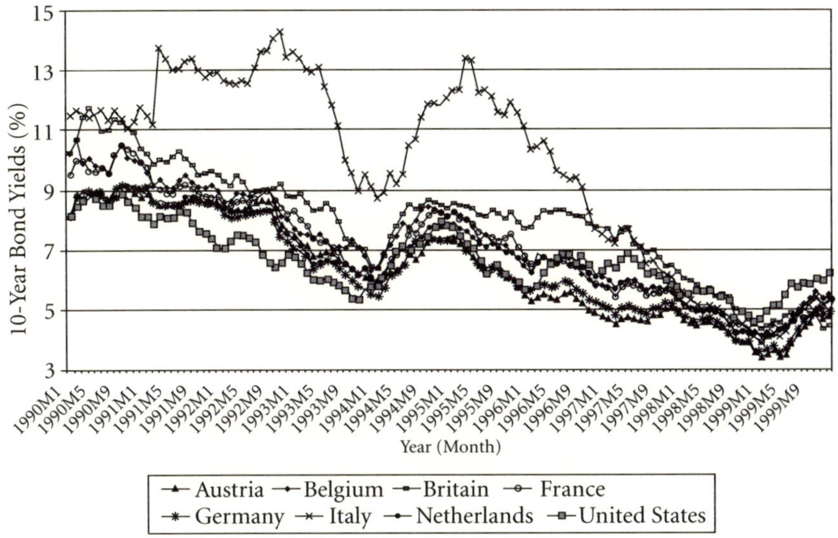

Fig. 7. Bond yields in selected EU countries

in the formulation of monetary policy. Although these governors are not supposed to take instructions from any political body, their participation in the policy process means that each member state has a voice in formulating monetary policy. Consequently, European monetary policy could reflect a balance of regional concerns and interests. Moreover, without direct political interference, this balance would be achieved without a temptation to manipulate monetary policy for short-term electoral gain.

The single currency therefore entails potential benefits for the main governing parties in the member states while the costs—in terms of lost policy autonomy—are not that large. The single currency removes a potentially divisive issue from national political debate, insulates politicians from international currency markets, and helps them tackle fiscal retrenchment. As a result, the single currency provides parties in the EU with an opportunity to rebuild and reshape their electoral coalitions. These benefits can help explain why politicians remained committed to the single currency despite the short-term political costs.

Implications for the European Union

Economic and monetary union will create new sets of interests within Europe. Given the economic diversity of Europe's member states (and even regions within the member states), a single monetary policy for all of Europe—with an emphasis on price stability—will benefit some sectors and hurt the prosperity of others. The response of both national-level politicians and European institutions to these economic and political challenges will shape the course of European integration, determining both its pace and direction.

Winners and Losers: A Dynamic Process

The euro will, of course, generate "winners" and "losers" (Frieden 1998). Tight monetary policy, for instance, would keep inflation low and the euro strong on international currency markets but adversely affect the interests of import competitors and exporters. An accommodative monetary policy would stimulate domestic growth and help European goods compete on international markets but weaken the euro's potential to become an international reserve currency.

These policy conflicts, however, are not a simple one-time dilemma for Europe's politicians. Sectoral interests and policy demands will develop over time, as economic conditions evolve and economic agents change their behavior under the new regime. The completion of the single market with a single currency will produce dramatic and perhaps unpredictable consequences for Europe's economy. Dealing with the political implications of this dynamic process will be a formidable task for Europe's politicians.

Labor-market organization, for instance, is one of the key factors shaping economic performance under the single currency. Research on national economies suggests that the real economic consequences of the euro will depend on the structure and behavior of labor unions in the wage-bargaining process (Franzese 2000; Hall and Franzese 1998; Iversen 1998; Soskice and Iversen 1998; Wallerstein 1998). Where unions are organized and wage bargaining is coordinated, unions will respond more effectively to monetary-policy signals from the European Central Bank and as a result keep unemployment low. A more decentralized bargaining process, where workers are less able to coordinate their wage demands, may lead to higher unemployment. Because union organization and wage-bargaining processes still vary tremendously across Europe (Golden, Lange, and Wallerstein 1998), the single currency may produce regional disparities in unemployment. How labor responds to these developments remains to be seen.

European capital markets have also undergone a transformation over the past decade due to technological change, the completion of the internal market, and the introduction of the euro. Traditionally, European business and industry relied on debt-based financing from large commercial or quasi-public banks

(Loriaux 1991; Zysman 1983). But in the 1990s, European stock markets became larger and more developed. Ownership of shares has become more widespread. In (western) Germany, for example, the number of households holding stock doubled between 1997 and 2000, jumping from 10 percent to 21 percent (*The Economist,* 8 July 2000). Additionally, the number and visibility of cross-border mergers and acquisitions—uncommon in the postwar period—have increased dramatically over the past 10 years and will continue to grow. These developments in European capital markets are likely to alter business practices throughout Europe—and change the policy demands faced by political parties.

These changing interests present political opportunities and challenges at both the domestic and European levels. At the domestic level, parties can build on these interests to reshape and reform their social coalitions. But given the uncertain consequences of the EMU project, the possibility exists of a political reaction against the single currency and Europe. At the domestic level, politicians will need to incorporate the "losers" of the euro into social coalitions that support European integration, perhaps compensating them with side payments or concessions in other issue areas.

The European Central Bank: A Democratic Deficit?

European institutions will also need to respond to these new and changing interests. But the experience of independent central banks at the national level suggests that current EU institutions are insufficient to meet these political challenges. At the national level, independent central banks operate in political environments. Successful monetary policy rests on the interaction of cabinets, legislators, and central bankers. The central bank's policy actions reflect the balance of interests in the cabinet and the legislature—that is, the interests of the bank's political principals—and the fact that the bank's independence can be overturned by those principals. In turn, those political leaders are ultimately accountable for the successes and failures of economic policy. Voters can signal their approval and disapproval of monetary policy through the ballot box.

Furthermore, in countries with independent central banks, strong legislatures allow bargaining and compromise among affected constituents. These inclusive and representative political institutions bring together labor, business, financial, and regional interests—the winners and losers of monetary policy—to voice their policy demands. These actors can design compensatory mechanisms for the losers to ensure their continued support for the system. These political institutions therefore help guarantee support for an independent central bank.

European political institutions, however, lack similar mechanisms of political control, accountability, and representation (Berman and McNamara 1999; Buiter 1999; Issing 1999). The identity of the ECB's political principals remains vague. Indeed, the Maastricht Treaty places so much emphasis on protecting the central bank's independence that it fails to establish which political actors are responsible for a Europe-wide monetary policy. Additionally, the configuration of European institutions does not provide voters with significant control over the policy process. Consequently, the public does not know whom to hold accountable for monetary policy. Finally, Europe's representative institutions, particularly the European Parliament, are notoriously weak. The Parliament lacks the authority to develop and implement agreements between policy winners and losers.

During the Maastricht negotiations, Germany did attempt to link EMU with further political integration. Both Kohl and the Bundesbank advocated closer political union to cope with the political consequences of EMU (Marsh 1992). Bundesbank president Schlesinger argued, "A monetary union will prove permanent only if there is a dominant political will to take social measures to deal with the serious economic effects. . . . In the last resort, this will call for political union too" (Marsh 1992, 244). An official Bundesbank statement on monetary union, authored by Hans Tietmeyer, stated, "A monetary union is an irrevocably sworn cofraternity—'all for one and one for all'—which, if it is to prove durable, requires, judging from past experience, even closer links in the form of comprehensive political union" (Marsh 1992, 242).

German proposals for further political union, however, were not adopted in the Maastricht Treaty. Indeed, some observers dismissed the linkage as an attempt to thwart the single currency by attaching conditions that the Germans knew other member states would find unacceptable. But the German position reflects an understanding of the role of an independent central bank in a democratic system, as well as an awareness that strong political institutions are a necessary component of economic and monetary success. The German proposal sought to empower European's political institutions, giving them the responsibility and authority to foster the success of the EMU project.

EMU and the Future of European Integration

The lack of political control, accountability, and effective representation at the European level raises questions about the role of an independent ECB in a Europe composed of democratic states. Yet it is not clear how those implications will play out.

On the one hand, without adequate political integration, the potential conflicts created by a single European monetary policy may threaten the sustainability of a single currency and even the viability of the EU itself. Political entrepreneurs in the member states may use the ECB as a scapegoat, blaming it for economic hardships and unemployment. These entrepreneurs might foster a popular backlash against the EU and seek to reestablish national-level strategies of economic adjustment. This type of appeal is already evident in the emergence and popularity of New Right parties throughout Europe (Kitschelt 1997; Betz 1994).

A more optimistic (and more probable) outcome, however, is that Europe's leaders will decide that the single currency requires further political integration to remain viable. This political integration will likely include a strengthened role for the European Parliament, giving it authorities and responsibilities more akin to a national legislature. Doing so would create a political environment with clearer lines of accountability between elected representatives and an independent ECB and allow the European Parliament to determine the range of acceptable policies for European monetary policy. These institutional reforms would represent a major step toward political integration.

But perhaps the most important consequence of the euro for political integration will be a change in citizen psychology and identity. Money is a powerful symbol. In a modern nation, it is one of the few things that citizens have in common, perhaps the most familiar symbol of their shared political bonds. Each time individuals make a purchase, they are reminded of that national identity and citizenship. The circulation of euro notes will affect how individuals identify themselves. The euro is a tangible sign of a common political unit, a symbol that Germans and Finns and Italians all share. Paying for a beer or a coffee with a euro will help those individuals think of themselves as Europeans. Ultimately, that change in citizen attitudes will have the greatest effect on the long-term prospects for political integration and the transfer of sovereignty from the nation-state to the European level.

Conclusion

Shortly after the 1992 crisis, I interviewed a number of European economists, central bankers, and European Commission bureaucrats about monetary relations in Europe and the future of the single currency. Many expressed confidence in the Maastricht Treaty, lauding its economic benefits and recognizing it as a large step toward political integration. But just as many voiced concerns about the single currency: the convergence criteria are too strict; the convergence criteria are not strict enough; states will not have the political will to carry out the necessary fiscal reforms; a skeptical public will not accept the new currency; the single currency will cause permanent regional disparities; the single currency will limit national sovereignty and thus stunt democratic choice and accountability.

After listening to the litany of complaints about the single currency, I asked these individuals whether, given their objections, the single currency would happen. In almost every case the answer was the same: "Yes, it will happen. . . . It will happen because the politicians want it to happen."[8] Some cited international and security issues as driving concerns, particularly the need to cement Germany's presence in the EU and preserve peace for the long term. But many argued that the politicians were more concerned about their own political fortunes than sound economic practice.

Although international concerns obviously affected the negotiation of the Maastricht Treaty, it is important not to overlook how domestic political conditions shaped politicians' interests over the single currency. The diversification of constituent preferences and decreased policy flexibility under the EMS reduced the political value of controlling national monetary policy, providing a context for the transition to a single currency. Delegation of monetary policy to the European level in turn could help political parties by removing a potentially divisive issue from intraparty politics, insulating them from the political consequences of currency speculation and providing some political breathing space on fiscal policy. As a result, Europe's politicians have an opportunity to rebuild and reshape their electoral coalitions.

This opportunity, however, also represents a challenge. The single currency will unleash new interests and new policy demands. Regions and sectors that suffer under EMU may create a backlash against the euro and further political integration. European politicians will need to meet these new demands and incorporate these new interests into both the domestic and European political systems. How well Europe's politicians meet this challenge will determine the success of the euro experiment and the future of the European Union.

Chapter 9

Conclusion

The wave of central bank reform in the late 1980s and 1990s represents a remarkable change in how countries administer monetary policy. Among the industrial democracies, an independent central bank has become the norm rather than the exception. In most countries, elected officials no longer control interest rates or the money supply but entrust the management of these policy instruments to central bank bureaucrats. Although politicians still possess the ultimate responsibility for monetary policy, their means of influencing monetary policy are now less direct. Nowhere is this more evident than in the EU, where member-state politicians have given up national control over monetary policy in favor of an independent European Central Bank.

These reforms have occurred in the context of economic internationalization. With improved communication and transportation, economies have become more closely integrated over the past 40 years. The volume and pace of cross-border transactions have increased dramatically. While unprecedented levels of wealth in the industrial democracies have accompanied the internationalization of product and capital markets, increased economic openness has also brought pressure for economic change. Global overcapacity in manufactured goods, for example, has accelerated the process of deindustrialization.

Political economists have also noted a variety of domestic-policy changes and institutional reforms concomitant with economic internationalization, including central bank reform, European integration, and fiscal retrenchment. But the mechanism connecting increased economic openness to these political developments is not clear. Some argue that the need to attract scarce international capital drives reform. Other political economists suggest that the capital mobility allows markets to punish states for certain policies, forcing them to choose "market-friendly" policies. Still others suggest that economic competition between states pushes them to pursue institutional reform.

Instead of these mechanisms, I emphasize the role of political parties to link economic internationalization with domestic reform. Political parties supply central bank institutions. They will choose institutions that will help them win and retain office.

Economic internationalization changes the incentives of political parties over central bank institutions. First, economic openness alters constituent preferences over economic and monetary policy (Frieden 1991; Frieden and Rogowski 1996; Rogowski 1989). Second, increased internationalization makes it increasingly difficult to gauge the relationship between policy choices and their consequences, hurting the government's ability to control the macroeconomy and deliver promised outcomes.

These developments have eroded the social coalitions of the major parties in the industrial democracies (see, for example, Boix 1998; Ramseyer and Rosenbluth 1994; Rosenbluth 1996). These parties could once count on stable electoral support, but voters have become more instrumental, casting ballots on the basis of policy performance rather than cultural identity. Moreover, economic interests fall increasingly along sectoral lines rather than traditional class-based cleavages, with conflicts between exposed and insulated sectors, manufacturing and service sectors, rising and declining sectors, and the public and private sectors. The diversification of constituent demands has increased the possibility of intraparty conflicts over economic and monetary policy, hurting the ability of these parties to hold office.

Although this changed political environment makes it difficult to maintain their constituent base, it also presents opportunities for parties to court new sectors and new interests. In order to maintain their political viability, therefore, parties must decide which voters to pursue and then design policies to appeal to those constituents. Parties must determine how to balance the demands of their traditional support base with the electoral opportunities created by changes in the political environment. These strategic decisions are often difficult and contentious, pitting different interests against one another.

One way for parties to overcome these potential intraparty conflicts is to support institutional reform. Reform can provide representation to new interests, reassure constituents about the party's intentions, or allow the party to shed responsibility for divisive issues. In turn, these reforms can help parties reassemble and maintain new social coalitions. Electoral reform, devolution, and delegation of policy authority to the EU represent a political response to the diversification of constituent demands and reduced policy effectiveness.

Central bank reform, I argue, is another one of these strategic reform experiments designed to help parties overcome intraparty conflicts. Because an independent central bank can challenge the cabinet's policy choices, it enhances the cabinet's accountability. Party politicians and constituents can rely on an independent central bank to monitor the cabinet's policy behavior. Further, an independent central bank can also justify the cabinet's policy choices in the face of unpopular economic outcomes, helping to prevent party politicians and constituents from withdrawing their support from the cabinet. The political credibility of an independent central bank can therefore help parties solidify their electoral base and keep the party in office, even where party legislators and constituents face different incentives over monetary policy.

That political credibility helps explain the association between central bank independence and federalism during much of the postwar period. In federal systems, parties typically need to appeal to constituents with a variety of monetary policy preferences, reflecting regional differences in economic activity. Further, the institutions of federalism tend to provide party politicians with different policy incentives. Parties in federal systems therefore relied on an independent central bank to help them manage these potential intraparty conflicts over policy.

With the diversification of constituent preferences and decline in policy effectiveness, parties in the late 1980s and 1990s sought to use the political credibility of an independent central bank to help them prevent intraparty conflicts and rebuild their constituent base. Political parties will remain committed to these independent central banks as long as the banks continue to help them appeal to constituents with diverse economic policy preferences.

Political parties will reduce the independence of a central bank if the bank loses a policy dispute with the cabinet or if the bank challenges a policy action that enjoys widespread support within the party. These scenarios are more likely where the party(ies) in government appeals to constituents with similar policy preferences or if party politicians have similar policy incentives. Central bankers, however, are strategic actors in the policy process. They are unlikely to risk their institutional status by challenging the cabinet under those circumstances. As a result, central banks are likely to retain their formal independence for quite some time—even if it means central bankers sacrifice some behavioral autonomy.

Central Bank Independence and Democratic Governance

Many discussions of monetary reform close by noting the irony of central bank independence in democratic societies (e.g., Alesina 1989; Keech 1996). Independent central banks may improve inflation performance, but they are usually criticized as secretive undemocratic institutions, unaccountable to politicians and to the public.

This book has demonstrated the opposite in several respects. First, I have argued that the economic-policy success of countries with independent central banks depends as much on the bank's political principals as it does on the bank's institutional structure. An independent central bank does not "depoliticize" monetary policy. In countries with independent central banks, monetary policy remains a source of partisan conflict and tension. Both qualitative and quantitative empirical accounts indicate that politicians play a large role in determining monetary policy in these countries. An independent central bank therefore does not prevent politicians from influencing monetary policy.

Instead, an independent central bank changes the manner in which politicians affect monetary policy. In countries with a dependent central bank, central bankers are responsible to the cabinet only, allowing the cabinet to determine the course of monetary policy. With an independent bank, the bank's principals include both the cabinet and the legislature. The bank's multiple principals provide central bankers with the ability to influence policy debates by publicizing their policy disputes with the government. The strategic interaction between an independent central bank and the cabinet can therefore actually enhance the government's accountability for monetary policy, allowing backbench legislators, coalition partners, and the public to have a better understanding of the cabinet's behavior.

Furthermore, I have shown that the institutional status of the central bank actually reflects the interests of political parties. Parties will choose central bank institutions to help them win and retain office. In systems where intraparty conflicts threaten the party's ability to hold office, politicians will choose an independent central bank. The bank's political credibility can help them appeal to constituents with diverse preferences over economic policy and balance divergent policy incentives among party politicians. Where party politicians have similar policy incentives or the party's position is secure, politicians will prefer a dependent central bank.

The wave of central bank reform in the late 1980s and 1990s reflects changes in party systems across the industrial democracies. With the economic developments of the past few decades, the major parties now face constituents with a wider variety of preferences over policy and the potential for intraparty conflicts over economic and monetary policy. These changes have increased the political value of an independent central bank, prompting politicians in many countries to grant their central bank increased autonomy. Central bank institutions, therefore, are not undemocratic. Rather, they both reflect and enhance the democratic process.

APPENDIX

A Model of Monetary Policy-Making

The monetary policy-making game involves three players: the government (G), the central bank bureaucrat (B), and the median legislator of the governing coalition (L). L represents the government's backbench legislators and coalition partners. The government may propose to retain the status quo or initiate a policy change, *P.* The policy change, if enacted, produces a new policy outcome. The central bank bureaucrat also makes a policy recommendation, either endorsing or criticizing the potential policy change. After observing the government's policy choice and the bureaucrat's policy recommendation, the legislator decides whether to approve or veto the policy change. I evaluate two possible scenarios. In the first, the government lacks any ex-post authority over the bureaucrat. In the second, the government can impose a penalty on the central banker.

Information Structure

Before the players, G, B, and L, choose their strategies, Nature selects the value of a random variable, D, which determines the outcome produced by enacting P. Variable D takes on two values, 1 (with probability d) and 0 (with probability $1-d$), where $0 < d < 1$. If $D = 1$, the enactment of P yields outcome p_1, whereas if $D = 0$, the enactment of P produces outcome p_2.

G and B know the value of D, while L does not. That is, the government and the bureaucrat know the consequences of a change in monetary policy, P. The legislator, on the other hand, is unaware of the potential consequences of a change in monetary policy. L's beliefs about the probability of Nature making different choices are as follows:

$$q_1 = p(D = 1)$$
$$q_2 = p(D = 0).$$

Prior to observing the messages sent by G and B, L's beliefs are $q_1 = d$ and $q_2 = (1 - d)$.

Strategies

A strategy for G specifies his policy choice, whether to adopt a new monetary policy, *P*, or retain the status quo, *sq*, as a function of his policy goals and his information about *P*. Formally, G's strategy, denoted G(##), indicates whether he recommends *P* or *sq* given the value of *D*. The first number gives G's action (M = recommend a policy change *P*; Q = retain the status quo) when *P* leads to p_1 (i.e., when $D = 1$). The second number indicates G's action when *P* leads to p_2 (i.e., when $D = 0$).

B's strategy, B(##), indicates her policy recommendation based on her policy goals and her information about the consequences of a policy change *P*. The first number gives B's action (E = endorse a policy change *P*; C = criticize a policy change) when *P* leads to p_1 (i.e., when $D = 1$). The second indicates B's strategy when *P* leads to p_2 (i.e., when $D = 0$).

L's strategy, L(####), specifies his vote, up or down, on a policy change *P*, based on the messages sent by G and B. The first number indicates how L votes (u = approve policy change *P*; d = veto *P* and retain the status quo) given that both G and B evaluate a policy change favorably (i.e., when L sees the messages M and E). The second number indicates L's vote when G approves a policy change (G sends message M), but B criticizes a potential policy change (B sends message C). The third number indicates how L votes given that G recommends retaining the status quo (G sends Q), but B endorses a policy change (B sends E). Finally, the fourth number indicates L's vote when both G and B make a recommendation to retain the status quo (G sends Q, B sends C).

Payoffs

L's payoff, $E(u_L)$, reflects the realized outcome and is denoted by $u_L(.)$. L's policy preferences are $p_1 > sq > p_2$. If $D = 1$ (i.e., if *P* leads to p_1), then L prefers to enact *P*. If $D = 0$ (i.e., if *P* leads to p_2), then L prefers the status quo. Therefore, the three possible payoffs are ordered as follows: $u_L(p_1) > u_L(sq) > u_L(p_2)$.

The payoffs of G, $E(u_G)$, are a function of two elements: the realized outcome, denoted $u_G(.)$, and L's vote on policy. The relative magnitudes of $u_G(p_1)$, $u_G(sq)$, and $u_G(p_2)$ vary according to G's policy preferences:

Order 1: $p_1 > sq > p_2$

Order 2: $sq > p_1 > p_2$
Order 3: $sq > p_2 > p_1$
Order 4: $p_1 > p_2 > sq$
Order 5: $p_2 > p_1 > sq$
Order 6: $p_2 > sq > p_1$.

G also incurs a cost k if L votes against his policy choice. This part of G's payoff reflects the negative consequences of a legislative veto. The magnitude of k is larger than any possible gain in utility from achieving his preferred policy outcome. That is, G prefers to sacrifice his preferred policy outcome to avoid a legislative veto.

B's payoffs, $E(u_B)$, differ between two scenarios, depending on the government's ex-post authority. In the first scenario, $E(u_B)$ is a function of the realized outcome, $u_B(.)$, and L's vote on policy. The relative magnitudes of $u_B(p_1)$, $u_B(sq)$, and $u_B(p_2)$ vary according to B's policy preferences. As with G, B has six possible preference orderings.

B also incurs a cost, c, if L votes against B's policy recommendation. The magnitude of c is larger than any possible gain in utility from attaining her preferred policy outcome. That is, B prefers to avoid a legislative veto even if she could ensure her most preferred policy outcome.

In the second scenario, the government has ex-post authority over the bureaucrat. In this case, B's policy payoffs are a function of three elements: the realized outcome, $u_B(.)$, L's policy vote and G's policy recommendation.The first two components of B's policy payoffs, $u_B(.)$ and c, are the same as in the first scenario. In this scenario, however, B incurs a cost, t, if the substance of B's action differs from G's policy recommendation. That is, if G chooses to pursue a policy change P (and sends a message, M), but B criticizes the policy choice (sends message C), B incurs cost t. If G chooses to retain the status quo (sends message Q), but B endorses a policy change (sends message E), B also incurs cost t. This cost t reflects the cost of ex-post action by the government against the bureaucrat, including dismissal, budget cuts, and so on. As with c, the magnitude of t is larger than any possible gain in utility from attaining her preferred policy outcome.

Sequence of Moves

The sequence of moves is as follows:

1. Nature chooses D (i.e., whether a change in policy, P, leads to p_1 or p_2) and informs G and B.

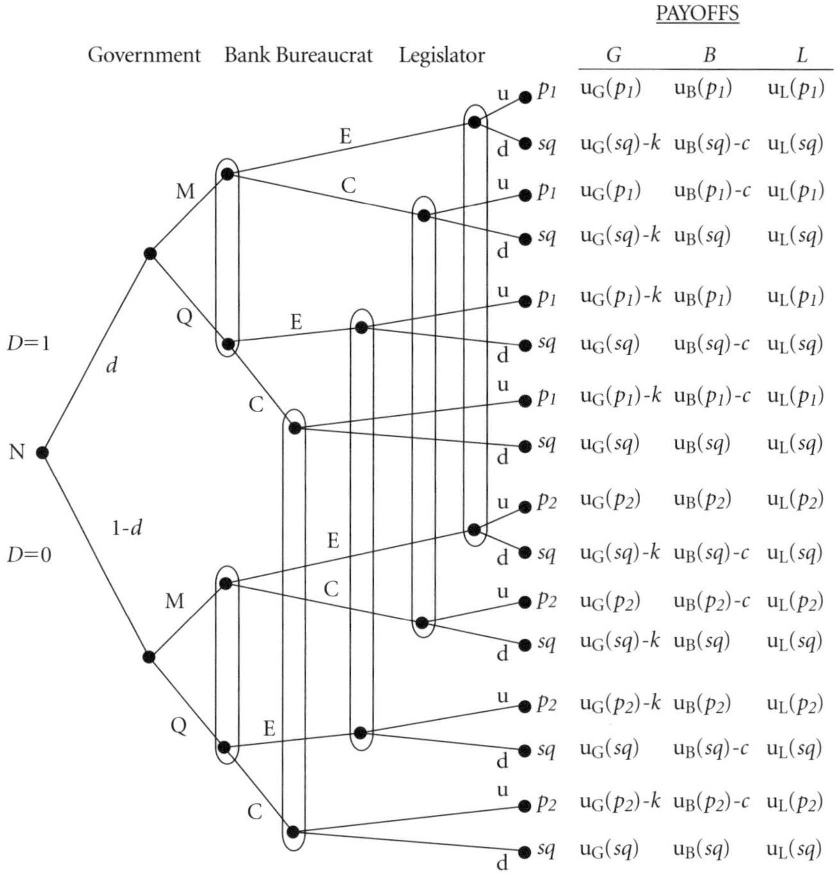

Fig. A1. Game tree: Government has no ex-post authority

2. The government chooses G(.), whether to pursue a policy change (M) or retain the status quo (Q).
3. The bureaucrat chooses B(.), whether to endorse a policy change (E) or criticize a policy change (C).
4. After observing G's action and B's action, the legislator chooses L(.), whether to approve a policy change (u) or veto it (d).
5. The payoffs are distributed to the players.

Figures A1 and A2 give the extensive forms of the policy-making game. Figure A1 indicates the form when the government has no ex-post authority

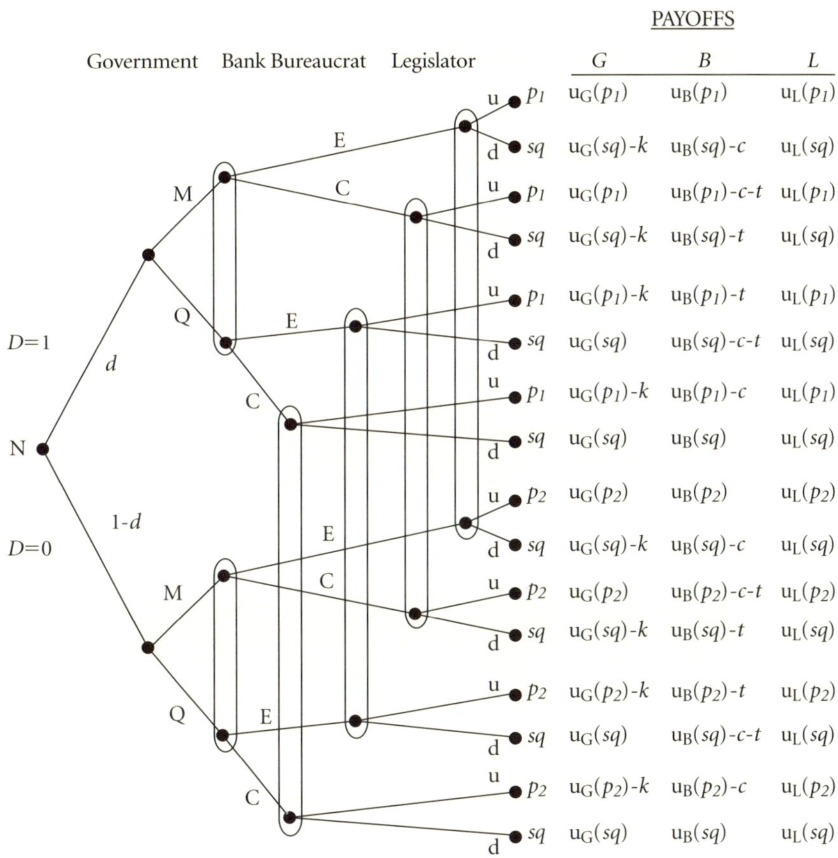

Fig. A2. Game tree: Government has ex-post authority

over the bureaucrat. Figure A2 shows the form when the government has ex-post authority over the bureaucrat. In both scenarios, the extensive form is assumed to be common knowledge.

Equilibrium Concept

The equilibrium concept is sequential equilibrium. A sequential equilibrium in these two games meets the following criteria:

1. G's strategy maximizes $E(u_G)$ given B's and L's strategies and Nature's choice.

2. B's strategy maximizes $E(u_B)$ given G's and L's strategies and Nature's choice.
3. L's strategy maximizes $E(u_L)$ given G's and B's strategies, Nature's choice, and L's beliefs about *P.* L's beliefs are calculated using Bayes' Rule wherever possible.

Additionally, L's off-equilibrium beliefs also satisfy the "intuitive criteria" (Banks and Sobel 1987; Cho and Kreps 1987). That is, L assigns zero probability to types of G and B who certainly lose by deviating from whatever equilibrium strategy they are supposed to be playing. In this game, L's off-equilibrium beliefs differ in three cases, depending on the preference ordering of the senders. In the first two cases, off-equilibrium messages contain new information that may affect L's choice of strategy:

1. If one of the senders has a preference ordering that is completely opposite L's ordering, $p_2 > sq > p_1$, off-equilibrium messages from this sender, say G, contain information about the value of D. If G's equilibrium strategy is to approve a policy change, G(MM), an off-equilibrium message by G, (Q), allows L to infer that the true value of D is 1. Therefore, L's off-equilibrium beliefs are $q_1 = 1$ and $q_2 = 0$. On the other hand, if G's equilibrium strategy is to retain the status quo, G(QQ), an off-equilibrium message, (M), allows L to infer that D = 0. L's off-equilibrium beliefs are $q_1 = 0$ and $q_2 = 1$.

2. If one of the senders has the same preference ordering as L, $p_1 > sq > p_2$, off-equilibrium messages from this sender provide L with information about the value of *D*. For example, if G shares this preference ordering and his equilibrium strategy is to approve a policy change G(MM), an off-equilibrium message by G, (Q), allows L to infer that the true value of *D* is 0. In this case, L's off-equilibrium beliefs are $q_1 = 0$ and $q_2 = 1$. On the other hand, if G's equilibrium strategy is G(QQ), L can interpret an off-equilibrium message, (M), to indicate that $D = 1$. Here, L's off-equilibrium beliefs are $q_1 = 1$ and $q_2 = 0$.

3. If neither sender shares L's preference ordering ($p_1 > sq > p_2$) and neither sender has a preference ordering opposite of L's ($p_2 > sq > p_1$), G's and B's potential off-equilibrium messages provide no new information. L's off-equilibrium beliefs reflect his priors: $q_1 = d$ and $q_2 = 1 - d$.

Equilibrium Behavior: No Ex-Post Authority

In the scenario whereby the government has no ex-post authority over the bureaucrat, three types of outcomes exist. First, if either G or B shares L's preference ordering, the game has separating equilibria. (Recall that L's preference ordering is fixed: $p_1 > sq > p_2$.) In this situation, L is fully informed about the policy consequence and follows the policy prescription of the sender who possesses the same preference ordering. Consequently, the other sender must truthfully reveal the value of D in order to avoid the penalty associated with a legislative veto, regardless of his or her preferences.

In the second and third cases, neither G nor B completely shares L's preference ordering. In this situation, both separating and pooling equilibria exist. Unfortunately, there is no way to determine which equilibria will be played in these circumstances. In the second case, all three players share a partial preference ordering: either $p_1 > sq$ or $sq > p_2$. In equilibrium, both players send the same truthful message about the value of D. L is informed about the consequences of a policy change.

In case 3, pooling equilibria exist if neither sender shares L's preference ordering. In this case, L gains no new information about the state of the world. Instead, G and B send messages that reflect L's beliefs about the value of D.

Case I

G(MQ), B(EC), L(uudd)

Government: When $D = 1$, G receives $u_G(p_1)$ from sending M. Sending Q yields $u_G(sq)$. G's best response is M if $u_G(p_1) > u_G(sq)$. When $D = 0$, G receives $u_G(sq)$ from sending Q. Sending M yields $u_G(p_2)$. Q is a best response if $u_G(sq) > u_G(p_2)$. Therefore, G(MQ) is a best response to B(EC) and L(uudd) if G has the preference ordering $p_1 > sq > p_2$.

Bureaucrat: When $D = 1$, B receives $u_B(p_1)$ from sending E. Sending C yields $u_B(p_1) - c$. B's best response is E if $u_B(p_1) > u_B(p_1) - c$. When $D = 0$, B receives $u_B(sq)$ from sending C. Sending E yields $u_B(sq) - c$. B's best response is C if $u_B(sq) > u_B(sq) - c$. Therefore, B(EC) is a best response to G(MQ) and L(uudd) regardless of B's preferences.

Legislator: If L sees the messages M (from G) and E (from B), L can infer that $D = 1$. L's best response in this case is u: $u_L(p_1) > u_L(sq)$. If L receives the messages Q (from G) and C (from B), L can infer that $D = 0$. L's best response in this case is d: $u_L(sq) > u_L(p_2)$. Therefore, L(uudd) is a best response to G(MQ) and B(EC) under the assumption that L has the preference ordering $p_1 > sq > p_2$.

G(QM), B(EC), L(dduu)

Government: When $D = 1$, G receives $u_G(p_1) - k$ from sending Q. Sending M yields $u_G(sq) - k$. G's best response is Q if $u_G(p_1) - k > u_G(sq) - k$.

When $D = 0$, G receives $u_G(sq) - k$ from sending M. Sending Q yields $u_G(p_2) - k$. M, therefore, is a best response if $u_G(sq) - k > u_G(p_2) - k$. Therefore, G(QM) is a best response to B(EC) and L(dduu) if G has the preference ordering $p_1 > sq > p_2$.

Bureaucrat: When $D = 1$, B receives $u_B(p_1)$ from sending E. Sending C yields $u_B(p_1) - c$. B's best response is E if $u_B(p_1) > u_B(p_1) - c$. When $D = 0$, B receives $u_B(sq)$ from sending C. Sending E yields $u_B(sq) - c$. B's best response is C if $u_B(sq) > u_B(sq) - c$. Therefore, B(EC) is a best response to G(QM) and L(dduu) regardless of B's preferences.

Legislator: If L sees the messages Q (from G) and E (from B), L can infer that $D = 1$. L's best response in this case is u: $u_L(p_1) > u_L(sq)$. If L receives the messages M (from G) and C (from B), L can infer that $D = 0$. L's best response in this case is d: $u_L(sq) > u_L(p_2)$. Therefore, L(dduu) is a best response to G(QM) and B(EC) under the assumption that L has the preference ordering $p_1 > sq > p_2$.

G(MQ), B(EC), L(udud)

Government: When $D = 1$, G receives $u_G(p_1)$ from sending M. Sending Q yields $u_G(p_1) - k$. G's best response is M if $u_G(p_1) > u_G(p_1) - k$. When $D = 0$, G receives $u_G(sq)$ from sending Q. Sending M yields $u_G(sq) - k$. G's best response is Q if $u_G(sq) > u_G(sq) - k$. Therefore, G(MQ) is a best response to B(EC) and L(udud) regardless of G's preferences.

Bureaucrat: When $D = 1$, B receives $u_B(p_1)$ from sending E. Sending C yields $u_B(sq)$. B's best response is E if $u_B(p_1) > u_B(sq)$. When $D = 0$, B receives $u_B(sq)$ from sending C. Sending E yields $u_B(p_2)$. C, therefore, is a best response if $u_B(sq) > u_B(p_2)$. Therefore, B(EC) is a best response to G(MQ) and L(udud) if B has the preference ordering $p_1 > sq > p_2$.

Legislator: If L sees the messages M (from G) and E (from B), L can infer that $D = 1$. L's best response in this case is u: $u_L(p_1) > u_L(sq)$. If L receives the messages Q (from G) and C (from B), L can infer that $D = 0$. L's best response in this case is d: $u_L(sq) > u_L(p_2)$. Therefore, L(udud) is a best response to G(MQ) and B(EC) under the assumption that L has the preference ordering $p_1 > sq > p_2$.

G(MQ), B(CE), L(dudu)

Government: When $D = 1$, G receives $u_G(p_1)$ from sending M. Sending Q yields $u_G(p_1) - k$. G's best response is M if $u_G(p_1) > u_G(p_1) - k$. When $D = 0$, G receives $u_G(sq)$ from sending Q. Sending M yields $u_G(sq) - k$. G's best response is Q if $u_G(sq) > u_G(sq) - k$. Therefore, G(MQ) is a best response to B(CE) and L(dudu) regardless of G's preferences.

Bureaucrat: When $D = 1$, B receives $u_B(p_1) - c$ from sending C. Sending E yields $u_B(sq) - c$. B's best response is C if $u_B(p_1) - c > u_B(sq) - c$. When $D = 0$, B receives $u_B(sq) - c$ from sending E. Sending C yields $u_B(p_2) - c$. E, therefore, is a best response if $u_B(sq) - c > u_B(p_2) - c$. Therefore, B(CE) is a best response to G(MQ) and L(dudu) if B has the preference ordering $p_1 > sq > p_2$.

Legislator: If L sees the messages M (from G) and C (from B), L can infer that $D = 1$. L's best response in this case is u: $u_L(p_1) > u_L(sq)$. If L receives the messages Q (from G) and E (from B), L can infer that $D = 0$. L's best response in this case is d: $u_L(sq) > u_L(p_2)$. Therefore, L(dudu) is a best response to G(MQ) and B(CE) under the assumption that L has the preference ordering $p_1 > sq > p_2$.

Case 2

G(MQ), B(EC), L(uddd)

Government: When $D = 1$, G receives $u_G(p_1)$ from sending M. Sending Q yields $u_G(sq)$. G's best response is M if $u_G(p_1) > u_G(sq)$. When $D = 0$, G receives $u_G(sq)$ from sending Q. Sending M yields $u_G(sq) - k$. G's best response is Q if $u_G(sq) > u_G(sq) - k$. Therefore, G(MQ) is a best response to B(EC) and L(uddd) if G has the preference ordering $p_1 > sq$.

Bureaucrat: When $D = 1$, B receives $u_B(p_1)$ from sending E. Sending C yields $u_B(sq)$. B's best response is E if $u_B(p_1) > u_B(sq)$. When $D = 0$, B receives $u_B(sq)$ from sending C. Sending E yields $u_B(sq) - c$. C, therefore, is a best response if $u_B(sq) > u_B(sq) - c$. Therefore, B(EC) is a best response to G(MQ) and L(uddd) if B has the preference ordering $p_1 > sq$.

Legislator: If L sees the messages M (from G) and E (from B), L can infer that $D = 1$. L's best response in this case is u: $u_L(p_1) > u_L(sq)$. If L receives the messages Q (from G) and C (from B), L can infer that $D = 0$. L's best response in this case is d: $u_L(sq) > u_L(p_2)$. Therefore, L(uddd) is a best response to G(MQ) and B(EC) under the assumption that L has the preference ordering $p_1 > sq > p_2$.

G(MQ), B(EC), L(uuud)

Government: When $D = 1$, G receives $u_G(p_1)$ from sending M. Sending Q yields $u_G(p_1) - k$. G's best response is M if $u_G(p_1) > u_G(p_1) - k$. When $D = 0$, G receives $u_G(sq)$ from sending Q. Sending M yields $u_G(p_2)$. G's best response is Q if $u_G(sq) > u_G(p_2)$. Therefore, G(MQ) is a best response to B(EC) and L(uuud) if G has the preference ordering $sq > p_2$.

Bureaucrat: When $D = 1$, B receives $u_B(p_1)$ from sending E. Sending C yields $u_B(p_1) - c$. B's best response is E if $u_B(p_1) > u_B(p_1) - c$. When $D = 0$, B receives $u_B(sq)$ from sending C. Sending E yields $u_B(p_2)$. C, therefore, is a best response if $u_B(sq) > u_B(p_2)$. Therefore, B(EC) is a best response to G(MQ) and L(uuud) if B has the preference ordering $sq > p_2$.

Legislator: If L sees the messages M (from G) and E (from B), L can infer that $D = 1$. L's best response in this case is u: $u_L(p_1) > u_L(sq)$. If L receives the messages Q (from G) and C (from B), L can infer that $D = 0$. L's best response in this case is d: $u_L(sq) > u_L(p_2)$. Therefore, L(uuud) is a best response to G(MQ) and B(EC) under the assumption that L has the preference ordering $p_1 > sq > p_2$.

Case 3

G(MM), B(EE), L(uuuu)

Government: When $D = 1$, G receives $u_G(p_1)$ from sending M. Sending Q yields $u_G(p_1) - k$. G's best response is M if $u_G(p_1) > u_G(p_1) - k$. When $D = 0$, G receives $u_G(p_2)$ from sending M. Sending Q yields $u_G(p_2) - k$. G's best response is M if $u_G(p_2) > u_G(p_2) - k$. Therefore, G(MM) is a best response to B(EE) and L(uuuu) regardless of G's preferences.

Bureaucrat: When $D = 1$, B receives $u_B(p_1)$ from sending E. Sending C yields $u_B(p_1) - c$. B's best response is E if $u_B(p_1) > u_B(p_1) - c$. When $D = 0$, B receives $u_B(p_2)$ from sending E. Sending C yields $u_B(p_2) - c$. B's best response is E if $u_B(p_2) > u_B(p_2) - c$. Therefore, B(EE) is a best response to G(MM) and L(uuuu) regardless of B's preferences.

Legislator: On equilibrium, where L's beliefs are $q_1 = d$ and $q_2 = 1 - d$, L(uuuu) is a best response if

$$q_1[u_L(p_1)] + q_2[u_L(p_2)] \geq u_L(sq)$$

which implies that

$$q \geq [u_L(sq) - u_L(p_2)]/[u_L(p_1) - u_L(p_2)].$$

L's off-equilibrium beliefs vary across three cases:

1. If either G or B has a preference ordering that is completely opposite L's ordering, $p_2 > sq > p_1$, L's off-equilibrium beliefs are $q_1 = 1$ and $q_2 = 0$. Therefore, L(uuuu) is a best response if $u_L(p_1) > u_L(sq)$, which is true by assumption.

2. If either G or B has the same preference ordering as L, $p_1 > sq > p_2$, L's off-equilibrium beliefs are $q_1 = 0$ and $q_2 = 1$. Therefore, L(uuuu) is not a best response because L would know to veto a policy change if he observed an off-equilibrium message. In this case, vetoing a policy change would yield $u_L(sq)$, which L prefers to $u_L(p_2)$.

3. If neither G or B shares L's preference ordering ($p_1 > sq > p_2$) and neither G or B has a preference ordering opposite of L's ($p_2 > sq > p_1$), L's off-equilibrium beliefs reflect his priors: $q_1 = d$ and $q_2 = 1-d$. L(uuuu) is a best response as long as $q \geq [u_L(sq)-u_L(p_2)]/[u_L(p_1)-u_L(p_2)]$.

Therefore, G(MM), B(EE), L(uuuu) is a sequential equilibrium if (1) $q \geq [u_L(sq)-u_L(p_2)]/[u_L(p_1)-u_L(p_2)]$ and (2) neither G or B has the same preference ordering as L: $p_1 > sq > p_2$.

G(QQ), B(CC), L(dddd)

Government: When $D = 1$, G receives $u_G(sq)$ from sending Q. Sending M yields $u_G(sq)-k$. G's best response is Q if $u_G(sq) > u_G(sq)-k$. When $D = 0$, G receives $u_G(sq)$ from sending Q. Sending M yields $u_G(sq)-k$. G's best response is Q if $u_G(sq) > u_G(sq)-k$. Therefore, G(QQ) is a best response to B(CC) and L(dddd) regardless of G's preferences.

Bureaucrat: When $D = 1$, B receives $u_B(sq)$ from sending C. Sending E yields $u_B(sq)-c$. B's best response is E if $u_B(sq) > u_B(sq)-c$. When $D = 0$, B receives $u_B(sq)$ from sending C. Sending E yields $u_B(sq)-c$. B's best response is E if $u_B(sq) > u_B(sq)-c$. Therefore, B(CC) is a best response to G(QQ) and L(dddd) regardless of B's preferences.

Legislator: On equilibrium, where L's beliefs are $q_1 = d$ and $q_2 = 1-d$, L(dddd) is a best response if

$$u_L(sq) \geq q_1[u_L(p_1)] + q_2[u_L(p_2)]$$

which implies that

$$q \leq [u_L(sq)-u_L(p_2)]/[u_L(p_1)-u_L(p_2)].$$

L's off-equilibrium beliefs vary across three cases:

1. If either G or B has a preference ordering that is completely opposite L's ordering, $p_2 > sq > p_1$, L's off-equilibrium beliefs are: $q_1 = 0$ and $q_2 = 1$. Therefore, L(dddd) is a best response if $u_L(sq) > u_L(p_2)$, which is true by assumption.

2. If either G or B has the same preference ordering as L, $p_1 > sq > p_2$, L's off-equilibrium beliefs are: $q_1 = 1$ and $q_2 = 0$. Therefore, L(dddd) is not a best response because L would know to approve a policy change if he observed an off-equilibrium message. Approving a policy change would yield $u_L(p_1)$, which L prefers to $u_L(sq)$.

3. If neither G or B shares L's preference ordering ($p_1 > sq > p_2$) and neither G or B has a preference ordering opposite of L's ($p_2 > sq > p_1$), L's off-equilibrium beliefs reflect his priors: $q_1 = d$ and $q_2 = 1 - d$. L(dddd) is a best response as long as $q \leq [u_L(sq) - u_L(p_2)]/[u_L(p_1) - u_L(p_2)]$.

Therefore, G(QQ), B(CC), L(dddd) is a sequential equilibrium if (1) $q \leq [u_L(sq) - u_L(p_2)]/[u_L(p_1) - u_L(p_2)]$ and (2) neither G or B has the same preference ordering as L: $p_1 > sq > p_2$.

Equilibrium Behavior: Ex-Post Authority

As in the case with no ex-post authority, separating equilibria exist when G shares L's preference ordering (case 4). In this scenario, B faces a sanction not only from L but also from G if she deviates.

In all other cases, however, both pooling and separating equilibria exist simultaneously. Unfortunately, the game cannot distinguish when these different equilibria will occur. Case 5 demonstrates that a separating equilibrium exists in this scenario regardless of the preferences of the senders. In case 6, separating equilibria also exist when G and L share a partial preference ordering: $p_1 > sq$ or $sq > p_2$. Unlike the scenario with no ex-post authority, however, B's preferences do not affect the existence of these equilibria.

Finally, if G does not share the same preference ordering with L, pooling equilibria exist (case 7). Unlike the scenario in which G lacked ex-post authority over the bureaucrat, there are two sets of pooling equilibria. The first set, G(MM), B(EE), L(uuuu) and G(QQ), B(CC), L(dddd), is the same as in the first scenario. These equilibria exist if neither G or B has the same preference ordering as L. The second set, G(MM), B(CC), L(udud) and G(QQ), B(EE), L(udud), occurs when B shares the same preference ordering as L. Recall that in the game in which G lacked ex-post authority over the bureaucrat, no pooling equilibria existed if B shared L's preference ordering.

Case 4

G(MQ), B(EC), L(uudd)

Government: As in case 1, G(MQ) is a best response to B(EC) and L(uudd) if G has the preference ordering $p_1 > sq > p_2$.

Bureaucrat: When $D = 1$, B receives $u_B(p_1)$ from sending E. Sending C yields $u_B(p_1) - c - t$. B's best response is E if $u_B(p_1) > u_B(p_1) - c - t$. When $D = 0$, B receives $u_B(sq)$ from sending C. Sending E yields $u_B(sq) - c - t$.

B's best response is C if $u_B(sq) > u_B(sq) - c - t$. Therefore, B(EC) is a best response to G(MQ) and L(uudd) regardless of B's preferences.

Legislator: As in case 1, L(uudd) is a best response to G(MQ) and B(EC) under the assumption that L has the preference ordering $p_1 > sq > p_2$.

G(QM), B(CE), L(dduu)

Government: As in case 1, G(QM) is a best response to B(CE) and L(dduu) if G has the preference ordering $p_1 > sq > p_2$.

Bureaucrat: When $D = 1$, B receives $u_B(p_1) - k$ from sending E. Sending C yields $u_B(p_1) - t$. B's best response is E if $u_B(p_1) - k > u_B(p_1) - t$. When $D = 0$, B receives $u_B(sq) - k$ from sending C. Sending E yields $u_B(sq) - t$. B's best response is C if $u_B(sq) - k > u_B(sq) - t$. Therefore, B(EC) is a best response to G(QM) and L(dduu) regardless of B's preferences and if $k < t$.

Legislator: As in case 1, L(dduu) is a best response to G(QM) and B(EC) under the assumption that L has the preference ordering $p_1 > sq > p_2$.

Case 5

G(MQ), B(EC), L(udud)

Government: When $D = 1$, G receives $u_G(p_1)$ from sending M. Sending Q yields $u_G(p_1) - k$. G's best response is M if $u_G(p_1) > u_G(p_1) - k$. When $D = 0$, G receives $u_G(sq)$ from sending Q. Sending M yields $u_G(sq) - k$. Q, therefore, is a best response if $u_G(sq) > u_G(sq) - k$. Therefore, G(MQ) is a best response to B(EC) and L(udud) regardless of G's preference ordering.

Bureaucrat: When $D = 1$, B receives $u_B(p_1)$ from sending E. Sending C yields $u_B(p_1) - c$. B's best response is E if $u_B(p_1) > u_B(p_1) - c$. When $D = 0$, B receives $u_B(sq)$ from sending C. Sending E yields $u_B(sq) - c$. C, therefore, is a best response if $u_B(sq) > u_B(sq) - c$. Therefore, B(EC) is a best response to G(MQ) and L(udud) regardless of B's preference ordering.

Legislator: If L sees the messages M (from G) and E (from B), L can infer that $D = 1$. L's best response in this case is u: $u_L(p_1) > u_L(sq)$. If L receives the messages Q (from G) and C (from B), L can infer that $D = 0$. L's best response in this case is d: $u_L(sq) > u_L(p_2)$. Therefore, L(udud) is a best response to G(MQ) and B(EC) under the assumption that L has the preference ordering $p_1 > sq > p_2$.

Case 6

G(MQ), B(EC), L(uddd)

Government: As in case 2, G(MQ) is a best response to B(EC) and L(uddd) if G has the preference ordering $p_1 > sq$.

Bureaucrat: When $D = 1$, B receives $u_B(p_1)$ from sending E. Sending C yields $u_B(sq) - t$. B's best response is E if $u_B(p_1) > u_B(sq) - t$. When $D = 0$, B receives $u_B(sq)$ from sending C. Sending E yields $u_B(sq) - c - t$. C, therefore, is a best response if $u_B(sq) > u_B(sq) - c - t$. Therefore, B(EC) is a best response to G(MQ) and L(uddd) regardless of B's preferences.

Legislator: As in case 2, L(uddd) is a best response to G(MQ) and B(EC) under the assumption that L has the preference ordering $p_1 > sq > p_2$.

G(MQ), B(EC), L(uuud)

Government: As in case 2, G(MQ) is a best response to B(EC) and L(uuud) if G has the preference ordering $sq > p_2$.

Bureaucrat: When $D = 1$, B receives $u_B(p_1)$ from sending E. Sending C yields $u_B(p_1) - c - t$. B's best response is E if $u_B(p_1) > u_B(p_1) - c - t$. When $D = 0$, B receives $u_B(sq)$ from sending C. Sending E yields $u_B(p_2) - t$. C, therefore, is a best response if $u_B(sq) > u_B(p_2) - t$. Therefore, B(EC) is a best response to G(MQ) and L(uuud) regardless of B's preference ordering.

Legislator: As in case 2, L(uuud) is a best response to G(MQ) and B(EC) under the assumption that L has the preference ordering $p_1 > sq > p_2$.

Case 7

G(MM), B(EE), L(uuuu)

Government: As in case 3, G(MM) is a best response to B(EE) and L(uuuu) regardless of G's preferences.

Bureaucrat: When $D = 1$, B receives $u_B(p_1)$ from sending E. Sending C yields $u_B(p_1) - c - t$. B's best response is E if $u_B(p_1) > u_B(p_1) - c - t$. When $D = 0$, B receives $u_B(p_2)$ from sending E. Sending C yields $u_B(p_2) - c - t$. B's best response is E if $u_B(p_2) > u_B(p_2) - c - t$. Therefore, B(EE) is a best response to G(MM) and L(uuuu) regardless of B's preferences.

Legislator: As in case 3, L(uuuu) is a best response if $q \geq [u_L(sq) - u_L(p_2)]/[u_L(p_1) - u_L(p_2)]$. L's off-equilibrium beliefs are also the same as in case 3.

Therefore, G(MM), B(EE), L(uuuu) is a sequential equilibrium if (1) $q \geq [u_L(sq) - u_L(p_2)]/[u_L(p_1) - u_L(p_2)]$ and (2) neither G nor B has the same preference ordering as L: $p_1 > sq > p_2$.

G(QQ), B(CC), L(dddd)

Government: As in case 3, G(QQ) is a best response to B(CC) and L(dddd) regardless of G's preferences.

Bureaucrat: When $D = 1$, B receives $u_B(sq)$ from sending C. Sending E yields $u_B(sq) - c - t$. B's best response is E if $u_B(sq) > u_B(sq) - c - t$. When $D = 0$, B receives $u_B(sq)$ from sending C. Sending E yields $u_B(sq) - c - t$. B's best response is E if $u_B(sq) > u_B(sq) - c - t$. Therefore, B(CC) is a best response to G(QQ) and L(dddd) regardless of B's preferences.

Legislator: As in case 3, L(dddd) is a best response if $q \leq [u_L(sq) - u_L(p_2)]/[u_L(p_1) - u_L(p_2)]$. L's off-equilibrium beliefs are also the same as in case 3.

Therefore, G(QQ), B(CC), L(dddd) is a sequential equilibrium if (1) $q \leq [u_L(sq) - u_L(p_2)]/[u_L(p_1) - u_L(p_2)]$ and (2) neither G nor B has the same preference ordering as L: $p_1 > sq > p_2$.

G(MM), B(EE), L(udud)

Government: As in case 3, G(MM) is a best response to B(EE) and L(udud) regardless of G's preferences.

Bureaucrat: When $D = 1$, B receives $u_B(p_1)$ from sending E. Sending C yields $u_B(p_1) - c - t$. B's best response is E if $u_B(p_1) > u_B(p_1) - c - t$. When $D = 0$, B receives $u_B(p_2)$ from sending E. Sending C yields $u_B(p_2) - c - t$. B's best response is E if $u_B(p_2) > u_B(p_2) - c - t$. Therefore, B(EE) is a best response to G(MM) and L(udud) regardless of B's preferences.

Legislator: As in case 3, on equilibrium, where L's beliefs are $q_1 = d$ and $q_2 = 1-d$, L(udud) is a best response if $q \geq [u_L(sq) - u_L(p_2)]/[u_L(p_1) - u_L(p_2)]$.

Although L's off-equilibrium beliefs are also the same as in case 3, L's off-equilibrium strategies differ:

1. If G has a preference ordering that is completely opposite L's ordering, L's off-equilibrium beliefs are $q_1 = 1$ and $q_2 = 0$. L should approve the policy change because $u_L(p_1) > u_L(sq)$. Therefore, L(udud) is a best response.

If B has a preference ordering completely opposite L's ordering, L's off-equilibrium beliefs are $q_1 = 1$ and $q_2 = 0$. Therefore, L(udud) is not a best response because L would prefer to vote u ($u_L(p_1) > u_L(sq)$) if B sent an off-equilibrium message.

2. If G has the same preference ordering as L, $p_1 > sq > p_2$, L's off-equilibrium beliefs are $q_1 = 0$ and $q_2 = 1$. If G sends an off-equilibrium message, L(udud) is not a best response because L would prefer d to u ($u_L(sq) > u_L(p_2)$).

If B has the same preference ordering as L, L's off-equilibrium beliefs are $q_1 = 0$ and $q_2 = 1$. Therefore, L(udud) is a best response because L would know to veto a policy change if he observed an off-equilibrium message from B. In this case, vetoing a policy change would yield $u_L(sq)$, which L prefers to $u_L(p_2)$.

3. If G does not share L's preference ordering ($p_1 > sq > p_2$) and does not have a preference ordering opposite of L's ($p_2 > sq > p_1$), L's off-equilibrium beliefs reflect his priors: $q_1 = d$ and $q_2 = 1-d$. Therefore, L(udud) is a best response as long as $q \geq [u_L(sq) - u_L(p_2)]/[u_L(p_1) - u_L(p_2)]$.

If B does not share L's preference ordering ($p_1 > sq > p_2$) and does not have a preference ordering opposite of L's ($p_2 > sq > p_1$), L's off-equilibrium beliefs reflect his priors: $q_1 = d$ and $q_2 = 1-d$. In this situation, L(udud) is not a best response to B's off-equilibrium message. As long as $q \geq [u_L(sq) - u_L(p_2)]/[u_L(p_1) - u_L(p_2)]$, L would prefer to approve the policy than veto it.

Therefore, G(MM), B(EE), L(udud) is a sequential equilibrium if (1) $q \geq [u_L(sq) - u_L(p_2)]/[u_L(p_1) - u_L(p_2)]$, (2) G does not have the same preference ordering as L ($p_1 > sq > p_2$), and (3) B has the same preference ordering as L ($p_1 > sq > p_2$).

G(QQ), B(CC), L(udud)

Government: As in case 3, G(QQ) is a best response to B(CC) and L(udud) regardless of G's preferences.

Bureaucrat: When $D = 1$, B receives $u_B(sq)$ from sending C. Sending E yields $u_B(sq) - c - t$. B's best response is E if $u_B(sq) > u_B(sq) - c - t$. When $D = 0$, B receives $u_B(sq)$ from sending C. Sending E yields $u_B(sq) - c - t$. B's best response is E if $u_B(sq) > u_B(sq) - c - t$. Therefore, B(CC) is a best response to G(QQ) and L(udud) regardless of B's preferences.

Legislator: As in case 3, on equilibrium, where L's beliefs are $q_1 = d$ and $q_2 = 1-d$, L(udud) is a best response if $q \leq [u_L(sq) - u_L(p_2)]/[u_L(p_1) - u_L(p_2)]$.

Although L's off-equilibrium beliefs are also the same as in case 3, L's off-equilibrium strategies differ:

1. If G has a preference ordering that is completely opposite L's ordering ($p_2 > sq > p_1$), L's off-equilibrium beliefs are $q_1 = 0$ and $q_2 = 1$. L should veto the policy change because $u_L(sq) > u_L(p_2)$. Therefore, L(udud) is a best response.

If B has a preference ordering completely opposite L's ordering, L's off-equilibrium beliefs are $q_1 = 0$ and $q_2 = 1$. Therefore, L(udud) is not a best response because L would prefer to vote d ($u_L(sq) > u_L(p_2)$) if B sent an off-equilibrium message.

2. If G has the same preference ordering as L ($p_1 > sq > p_2$), L's off-equilibrium beliefs are $q_1 = 1$ and $q_2 = 0$. If G sends an off-equilibrium message, L(udud) is not a best response because L would prefer u to d ($u_L(p_1) > u_L(sq)$).

If B has the same preference ordering as L, L's off-equilibrium beliefs are $q_1 = 1$ and $q_2 = 0$. Therefore, L(udud) is a best response because L would know to approve a policy change if he observed an off-equilibrium message from B. In this case, approving a policy change would yield $u_L(p_1)$, which L prefers to $u_L(sq)$.

3. If G does not share L's preference ordering ($p_1 > sq > p_2$) and does not have a preference ordering opposite of L's ($p_2 > sq > p_1$), L's off-equilibrium beliefs reflect his priors: $q_1 = d$ and $q_2 = 1 - d$. Therefore, L(udud) is a best response as long as $q \leq [u_L(sq) - u_L(p_2)]/[u_L(p_1) - u_L(p_2)]$.

If B does not share L's preference ordering ($p_1 > sq > p_2$) and does not have a preference ordering opposite of L's ($p_2 > sq > p_1$), L's off-equilibrium beliefs reflect his priors: $q_1 = d$ and $q_2 = 1 - d$. In this situation, L(udud) is not a best response to B's off-equilibrium message. As long as $q \leq [u_L(sq) - u_L(p_2)]/[u_L(p_1) - u_L(p_2)]$, L would prefer to veto the policy than approve it.

Therefore, G(QQ), B(CC), L(udud) is a sequential equilibrium if (1) $q \leq [u_L(sq) - u_L(p_2)]/[u_L(p_1) - u_L(p_2)]$, (2) G does not have the same preference ordering as L ($p_1 > sq > p_2$), and (3) B has the same preference ordering as L ($p_1 > sq > p_2$).

Notes

Chapter 1

1. Throughout the book, I use the terms *cabinet, ministers,* and *government* interchangeably to refer to the executive.

2. Parties in a coalition government divide the portfolios. The party that controls the portfolio on a particular dimension (here, the monetary-policy dimension) is referred to as the *portfolio party* or the *cabinet minister.* The terms *coalition partners* or *nonportfolio parties* refer to parties that participate in the governing coalition but do not hold the portfolio on the monetary-policy dimension.

3. The term *backbench legislators* refers to legislators in the governing party(ies) who are *not* members of the cabinet.

Chapter 2

1. This contracting approach has engendered critics of its own, who note that politicians may be unwilling to punish the central banker (de Haan 1997; McCallum 1997; Waller 1995). That is, the decision to enforce the contract also reflects the strategic interaction of central bankers and politicians. Defenders argue that the announcement of specific goals and targets changes this interaction by increasing the transparency of monetary policy, which may in turn increase the public costs to politicians of reneging on the contract.

2. Research suggests that ex-post measures may be a less-effective method of controlling bureaucrats. Bureaucrats can defy the enacting coalition's preferences by pursuing policies that appeal to a new majority of legislators (McCubbins, Noll, and Weingast 1989). Bureaucrats can also exploit the imperfect relationship between their policy choices and policy outcomes to avoid sanctions (Banks 1989). Finally, politicians may have difficulty punishing bureaucrats without hurting affected constituents; extensive budget cuts or dismantlement of the agency may destroy politically desirable programs.

3. Political economists have also attempted to gauge a bank's independence using behavioral indicators. Cukierman (1992; Cukierman, Webb, and Neyapti 1992), for example, measures independence using the turnover of central bank governors, arguing that high

turnover indicates that the government retains control over monetary policy. A long tenure, however, could reflect the governor's compliance with the policy demands of his political principals. The Bank of France, for example, has had only a few governors in the post–World War II period but is usually classified as dependent by scales of independence based on formal indicators. Behavioral measures of independence are ex-post indicators, themselves a product of the strategic interaction between politicians and central bankers in the policy process—interactions that depend on the institutional environment.

4. All legal rankings of central bank independence share a number of shortcomings (Forder 1996, 1998a; Mangano 1998). Most rankings simply assign equal weight to each component and add them together to form the index. Some factors, however, may carry more weight in the determination of central banks' overall independence. Additionally, some components may be interactive, becoming important only in the presence of other variables. Further, the scales consider only the banks' formal structures, ignoring some behavioral features that may affect the banks' performance (Forder 1996).

5. Ratification of the Maastricht Treaty, however, has changed the constitutional status of central banks not only in Germany but throughout the EU. The treaty calls for each member-state government to grant its central bank formal independence. The constitutional status of the treaty therefore makes the institutional organization of the central bank a constitutional issue.

6. Leftist opponents of the reform challenged its legality in court. The Constitutional Council, France's highest constitutional body, actually struck down the reform in August 1993. The Council argued that under the French Constitution, only the government has the right to determine monetary policy. The Council did acknowledge that the reform would become legal once the Maastricht Treaty came into effect because the treaty commitment would override the constitution (*Wall Street Journal,* 5 August 1993; *Financial Times,* 13 August 1993).

7. Examples of the delegation literature include Banks (1989), Banks and Weingast (1992), Calvert, McCubbins, and Weingast (1989), Lupia and McCubbins (1993), McCubbins, Noll, and Weingast (1987, 1989), McCubbins and Schwartz (1983), Moe (1987), and Weingast and Moran (1983).

8. Although the time-consistency framework dominated macroeconomic approaches to monetary policy in the 1980s, the approach has some critics, who contend that the setup does not accurately characterize the policy process (Blinder 1997; Freedman 1993; McCallum 1995, 1997).

9. The effect of central bank independence on real economic variables remains a point of controversy. One line of research investigates how central bank independence affects the costs of disinflation in terms of lost output and increased unemployment. In theory, the credibility of an independent central bank should lower these costs because economic agents will adjust their inflation expectations more rapidly than with a dependent central bank. Empirical studies, however, show that the costs of disinflation are actually higher under an independent central bank (Posen 1998; Walsh 1995a). A sec-

ond set of political economists has investigated the relationship between central bank independence and labor-market organization. This work demonstrates that systems with highly unionized workforces and coordinated wage bargaining can better respond to the policy actions of an independent central bank, helping to keep unemployment low (Franzese 2000; Hall and Franzese 1998; Iversen 1998, 1999).

10. Moe (1989, 1990) recognizes that political institutions can influence politicians' incentives over bureaucratic structure. In his discussion of the U.S. case, he argues that the president has specific preferences over bureaucratic institutions, preferring a hierarchical top-down structure to enhance the president's ability to control policy. In contrast, Moe assumes that legislators usually act as conduits for interest-group pressures.

Chapter 3

1. In a coalition government, cabinet ministers typically act as agents of their party, rather than as individuals or representatives of factions (Laver and Shepsle 1994).

2. More than one nonportfolio party may exist. For stylistic convenience, however, I refer only to a single nonportfolio party.

3. Backbench legislators and coalition partners need not have perfect information about the cabinet's preferences in order to limit the range of its policy discretion. Under the assumption that cabinet ministers have a lexicographic preference for office, the threat of a veto or dismissal should provide incentive for any government—even one with policy preferences opposed to its supporters—to remain within the range of acceptable policies.

4. Economists have proposed both noncontingent rules and contingent policy rules (Keech 1995). Noncontingent rules specify the policy response regardless of the economic situation. They establish clear standards to evaluate performance, although their inflexibility limits their feasibility. Contingent rules specify different policy responses depending on the economic situation. It may be impossible, however, to specify rules for every possible situation. Further, policymakers might have discretion in defining which situation applied to the rule. Finally, contingent rules may become so complex that it is difficult to determine whether the government has complied with the rule.

5. Typically, the financial sector closely monitors the government's monetary policy choices. But politicians may be reluctant to depend on it for information because the financial sector lacks a broad political constituency.

6. I model the government's and central bank's actions as simultaneous moves. The bureaucrat makes a comment on the government's policy proposal, either endorsing or criticizing potential policy actions. Simultaneous actions are plausible because monetary policy-making is a continuous process.

7. I examined allowing the government to punish the bureaucrat for other reasons, including sending a message that led the legislator to veto the government. The results are qualitatively similar.

Chapter 4

1. Case accounts of the interaction between the German government and the Bundesbank abound. See, for example, Heisenberg (1999), Henning (1994), Goodman (1992), Marsh (1992), Kennedy (1991), and Scharpf (1987).

2. Marsh (1992) suggests that the Bundesbank's actions contributed to the downfall of the Erhard (1966), Keisinger (1969), and Schmidt (1982) governments.

3. In spring 1993, I conducted a number of off-the-record interviews with bank officials regarding the Bundesbank, some of which I draw upon in this chapter.

4. Approximately 78 percent reported that the recommendation by the European Monetary Institute, the forerunner of the European Central Bank, would also be an important source of information.

5. A Belgian central banker noted that as his country's bank had become de facto more independent in the 1980s, the governor had increased his political role, appearing more frequently in newspapers and television.

Chapter 5

1. If the issue does not affect vital Lander interests and the Bundesrat fails to pass the legislation by a simple majority, then a simple Bundestag majority can overturn the Bundesrat veto. In this case, the Bundesrat veto only delays the bill's implementation. If the Bundesrat vetoes the legislation by a two-thirds majority, however, the Bundestag can overturn the veto only with a two-thirds majority. For issues affecting Lander interests, however, a simple majority in the Bundesrat can veto legislation, unless the government can muster a two-thirds majority in the Bundestag to override the veto.

2. *The Economist* noted that it would "take a very nervous heart to register a flutter at what is contained in the Bill. Nothing could be more moderate" (quoted in Fforde 1992, 27).

3. The Alford index subtracts the percentage of voters from non–working classes voting for the Left party(ies) from the percentage of blue-collar workers voting for the Left party(ies). To create an Alford index that covers the same period as the dependent variable, I averaged two indices, one from the 1960s–early 1970s and the other from 1990. For the 1960s–early 1970s Alford index, I employed data from Powell (1982). His data were collected from a variety of sources. Next, I constructed an index using the 1990 World Values Survey. Respondents identified both which party they would support in a hypothetical general election and their occupation. Manual workers (skilled, semiskilled, unskilled), foremen/supervisors, and agricultural workers were coded as blue collar. All others were included as non–working class. Left parties included Socialist, Labor, Communist, and other far Left parties. For each country, I calculated the percentage of voters from non–working classes voting for the Left party(ies) and subtracted that from the proportion of blue-collar workers voting for the Left party(ies).

The correlation between the World Values index and Powell's data is $r = .52$, significant at the 0.05 level.

Although the two sources had many countries in common, the World Values Survey did not include Australia or New Zealand. I imputed the missing values by regressing the World Values Survey index on Powell's data. Using the coefficients from the equation and the values of the missing countries on Powell's data, I computed the missing values for the World Values Survey index. Additionally, Powell does not include data for Spain because it was not a democracy until the mid-1970s. Therefore, I included only the data from the World Values Survey for the Spanish case. Finally, I ran each model using Powell's data and the index created by the World Values Survey separately (results not reported). The results for each index were in the predicted direction and significant ($p < 0.05$), although at lower levels of confidence than the averaged index.

4. According to Powell (1982), extremist parties exhibit one of the following characteristics: (1) a well-developed nondemocratic ideology; (2) a proposal to break up or fundamentally alter the boundaries of the nation; or (3) diffuse protest, alienation, and distrust of the existing political system. I updated Powell's measure to include the average polarization for 1960 to 1990. I follow Powell's classifications with the following exceptions: France (include National Front) and Spain (include Communist, Separatist parties).

5. Following Strom (1990a), Powell and Whitten (1993) define a committee system as strong if it shares two of the three following characteristics: size (over 10 committees), specialization to fit the government bureaucracy, and limitations in the number of committeeships held by individual legislators. Inclusive committee systems require that committee chairmanships be distributed proportionally among all parties, regardless of their participation in government. Countries with strong and inclusive committee systems include Austria, Belgium, Denmark, Germany, the Netherlands, Norway, Sweden, and Switzerland.

6. I calculated the proportion of time a country was governed by a coalition or minority government from 1960 to 1990 using data from Woldendrop, Keman, and Budge (1993). I counted instances of "divided government" in the United States as minority government because the president's party lacks an overall majority in Congress.

7. I also ran the models using the index from Cukierman, Webb, and Neyapti (1992) as the dependent variable. The results were similar (results not reported).

8. The Alford index had a significant negative relationship with the other scales, except for the Cukierman index. There, the coefficient was in the predicted direction but failed to attain conventional levels of significance (t-statistic $= -1.53$, critical value for two-tailed test $= -2.16$).

9. I also ran each of these variables individually. Both committee strength and the coalition/minority government variables were significant and in the predicted direction. Polarization was in the predicted (negative) direction but did not attain conventional levels of significance (t-statistic $= -1.46$, critical value for two-tailed test $= -2.16$). Results not reported.

10. This test is a check for spatial correlation between errors of cases located next to one another.

11. RESET is the regression specification error test proposed by Ramsey (1969). The test uses the predicted values of the dependent variable from the original equation, raised to the second, third, and fourth powers, as additional regressors. The significance of these additional regressors is evaluated with a standard F-test. A significant test indicates that the model is misspecified.

12. I also used a population-adjusted measure of trade openness, based on Taagepera and Hayes (1977). I created the population-weighted variable by regressing the (logged) proportion of trade on the (logged) population for the sample of countries. I then subtracted the predicted proportion of trade from the actual values to form the measure. This measure also failed to attain significance.

13. It can be argued, somewhat counterintuitively, that Left parties will favor independent central banks. Left parties recognize that they possess little anti-inflation credibility with financial and capital markets, contributing to higher risk premia and the possibility of capital flight (Garrett 1998a). To demonstrate their commitment to responsible economic policies, Left parties may institute an independent central bank. Right parties have more credibility with the markets and consequently, less incentive to choose an independent central bank.

14. I employed average measures for other time periods, including 1970–79 and 1980–89. These measures were not significant.

15. Posen's data set did not include Norway and Sweden. Following Posen (1995), I constructed measures for these two countries using a variety of sources. Additionally, Posen's measure of financial sector strength can be broken into two dimensions—a financial-sector dimension, composed of the presence of universal banking and the regulatory role of the central bank, and a political dimension, composed of federalism and party-system fractionalization. The financial dimension is highly correlated with the punishment index ($r = 0.85$). The political dimension is correlated with the presence of strong bicameralism ($r = 0.83$). Both correlations are significant at the 0.001 level.

16. I performed similar analyses for models with other measures of central bank independence as the dependent variable. The other models exhibited some evidence of influential outliers, although Britain was the only outlier common to all four indices.

17. Belsley, Kuh, and Welsch (1980) suggest observations with $|DFBETA_i| > 2/(n^{1/2})$ exert undue influence. This cutoff is stronger than the standard recommended by Bollen and Jackman. For the Alford index, observations failing to meet this standard include Canada (−0.79), Denmark (0.69), and Britain (1.19). For strong bicameralism, Australia (−0.89) exceeds the cutoff. Finally, Australia (0.63), Belgium (−0.49), and Britain (−0.99) exceed the cutoff for the punishment index.

18. I also tried individual dummy variables for Britain, Denmark, and Australia. The Britain dummy variable attained statistical significance. The Denmark dummy was not significant on its own but became significant when used in a model with the Britain dummy. The dummy for Australia was not statistically significant at any point.

19. If the absolute value of DFFITS is less than or equal to 0.34, then the weight is equal to one. If |DFFITS| > 0.34, then the weight is 0.34/|DFFITS|. Weights for the bounded regression are contained in table 5.

Chapter 6

1. Following King, Burns, and Laver (1990) and Warwick (1994), I estimate how different cabinet, party system, and economic system attributes affect expected, rather than actual, cabinet duration. That is, I use the attributes to estimate how long the cabinet is expected to survive on the day it takes office. Actual cabinet duration is, instead, a function of a stochastic process.

2. In alternative specifications, I used (1) a dummy variable for capital controls from Leblang (1997) and (2) a measure of overall capital and current account openness developed by Quinn (1997). The results from all three measures were qualitatively similar, although at varying levels of statistical significance.

3. The source for this data is Golden, Lange, and Wallerstein (1998). In alternative specifications, I also used a measure of the centralization of wage bargaining from Iversen (1999). The results were similar, but I lost almost 25 percent of the sample when this variable was included.

4. I excluded Switzerland due to the permanent oversize status of their executive council. I excluded other countries due to limitations in the availability of data.

5. In alternative specifications, I ran the analysis without this control variable. The results were similar.

6. Ordinary robust estimators are also vulnerable to outlying or influential cases. To overcome this problem, this robust estimator begins by performing an initial screening for high-leverage cases based on Cook's Distance. Cases that have values of Cook's Distance greater than one are dropped from the analysis. The robust estimator then proceeds iteratively and downweights observations based on both Tukey's and Huber's weighting scheme (Hamilton 1992). The results are thus not only robust to departures from normality on the part of the dependent variable but are also shielded from being overly influenced by high-leverage observations.

7. Using the OLS estimates, the mean predicted value of cabinet durability in an open economy increases from 0.93 to 1.12 as central bank independence moves from low (0.2) to high (0.7). Using the estimates obtained via robust regression, the mean predicted value of cabinet durability in an open economy increases from 0.58 to 1.06 over the same range of central bank independence.

8. For clarity of presentation, I omitted the confidence intervals. The graph was simulated using the results obtained via OLS (model III in table 8).

9. To calculate these values, I used the range of central bank independence. For a "dependent" central bank, I restricted the variable to be its lowest level in the sample (0.17). To capture the effect of an independent central bank, I restricted the variable to be its highest

value in the sample (0.69). To measure economic openness, I employed different levels of the capital account and trade openness variables. For a "closed" economy, I restricted capital account openness to be at its lowest level in the sample (1.5) and trade openness to be one standard deviation less than the mean (30 percent of GDP). For an open economy, I restricted capital account openness to be at its highest level in the sample (4) and trade openness to be one standard deviation more than the mean (100 percent of GDP).

10. For the OLS results, the differences in predicted cabinet durability are not statistically significant at the 95 percent confidence level at any point, although the confidence intervals (not shown) do approach significance at lower levels of unionization.

11. For Left government, I restricted the partisanship variable to take on the value of 1, indicating a Left cabinet with a bare majority of legislative seats. For Right government, the partisanship variable takes on a value of 0, indicating no Left parties in the cabinet. The levels of openness were computed as before. The graph was simulated using the results obtained via OLS (model III in table 8).

12. The difference between predicted cabinet durability for Left and Right governments under conditions of economic openness is statistically significant. The difference between Left and Right under a closed economy is not.

Chapter 7

1. Between 1969 and 1972, unions negotiated substantial wage increases, pushing up nominal wages more than 10 percent a year (Goodman 1992). Between 1970 and 1974, unit labor costs increased over 64 percent (Locke 1995).

2. Additionally, in 1975, unions bargained for the *scala mobile,* which indexed wages to price increases, helping to fuel inflation (Lange 1986; Locke 1995).

3. Revenues from the North Sea oil began to flow in 1977, easing the balance-of-payments problems.

4. The Conservatives had previously considered an independent central bank. As a member of the opposition in 1978, future Chancellor Nigel Lawson called for an independent Bank of England. Other Conservatives recalled that in the late 1970s, proposals for an independent central bank had received serious debate within the party (*Financial Times,* 2 November 1989).

5. See, for example, John Maples, former Conservative MP and economic secretary to the Treasury, in the *Guardian* (30 May 1994) and Bryan Gould, Labour MP, in the *Guardian* (5 January 1994).

6. Note that the Westminster system protected the Conservative Party's position in office, even though intraparty conflicts cost Thatcher her job.

7. If the bank missed the target range (if inflation was either above or below the target), it would have to write an open letter to the chancellor, explaining the reasons for missing the target and the actions that the bank would take to correct the problem (*Financial Times* 12 June 1997; 13 June 1997).

8. Abbott had served on the Treasury Select Committee in 1993–94 that had advocated a more independent Bank of England. She was the only member of that committee to vote against that recommendation. She argued that the Labour government's bill destroyed democratic accountability and that academic research had established only correlation, rather than causation, between central bank independence and inflation.

9. Interestingly, in Britain, many proponents of central bank independence also advocated sweeping reforms to Britain's political and electoral institutions. The Liberal Democrats, who supported an independent bank, demanded the adoption of a proportional representation electoral system. Additionally, *The Economist* strongly advocated independence for the Bank of England (see, for example, *The Economist,* 28 October 1989), while endorsing political and electoral reform (for example, in its series, "Britain's Constitution," beginning 14 October 1995). Will Hutton, a columnist for the *Guardian* and an opponent of independence, argued that an independent Bank of England would be ineffective and unaccountable within the current political system. Instead, an independent central bank could work only under a "wider constitutional settlement . . . with reconstructed Houses of Parliament and [a] system of regional government. The Bank of Britain [*sic*] would then become federally constituted like the Bundesbank and the Fed with members from Scotland, Wales, and the English regions, and made accountable to a two-chamber parliament in which, hopefully, the committee system could be more effective" (*Guardian,* 30 August 1993).

10. Institutional reform can also occur if the traditional governing parties do not adjust their policies adequately enough to political and economic shocks. Political entrepreneurs can attempt to capitalize on voter dissatisfaction and appeal to groups unrepresented by the traditional governing party(ies) to press for political reforms that are likely to produce party systems more responsive to the changing demands of voters.

11. I am not arguing that central bank reform and electoral reform necessarily occur together. Both events are far too contingent on a variety of other factors for that to be the case. But if they share a similar underlying cause, then these events are likely to coincide in at least a number of cases.

12. The economic reforms instituted by the Labour government had exacerbated existing divisions within the National Party. Consequently, the new National government had a "somewhat unwieldy caucus of backbenchers with widely differing views on the economy" (*Keesing's Archives* 1991, 37 (11): 38643).

13. In 1993, the Citizen Initiated Referenda Act also gave voters the right to petition for a (nonbinding) referendum to be held on a particular issue, another departure from traditional Westminster political institutions (Mulgan 1994).

Chapter 8

1. Accounts of the Maastricht Treaty abound. Some useful discussions include Eichengreen (1993a), Eichengreen and Frieden (1994), Gros and Thygesen (1998), McNamara (1998), Moravscik (1998), Sandholtz (1993).

2. The debates surrounding the economic effects of EMU have produced a voluminous literature. For helpful reviews, see Eichengreen (1993a; 1997), Gros and Thygesen (1998), and Wyplosz (1997), as well as special issues of *Economic Policy* (*EMU* 1998) and the *Oxford Review of Economic Policy* (Allsopp and Vines 1998).

3. Prior to the advent of the single currency, both the European Monetary Institute (the forerunner of the European Central Bank) and the European Commission would have to issue reports to the Council of Ministers recommending countries for participation based on their compliance with the convergance criteria.

4. For individual level analyses of support for the euro, see Gabel (1999), Kaltenthaler and Anderson (1999), and Gartner (1997).

5. The treaty could have come into effect if it had been approved by a five-sixths majority of the Danish parliament. Although the major parties supported the treaty, they could not assemble such a majority, sending it to a referendum.

6. In October 1992, the Danish government renegotiated the treaty, securing guarantees for Danish autonomy in the areas of defense, citizenship, and the single currency.

7. The possibility of currency speculation prevented member-state governments from justifying a currency realignment to their publics in advance of any action. If governments had attempted to prepare public opinion for a general realignment, their statements would have unleashed an overwhelming wave of speculation in the exchange markets.

8. In an anti-EMU article, Martin Feldstein draws a similar conclusion: "What is clear to me is that the decision [to adopt the euro in 1999] will not depend on the *economic* advantages and disadvantages of a single currency. The decision of whether or not to form a monetary union will reflect deeply held political views about the appropriate future for Europe and the political advantages and disadvantages to the individual countries and even to the individual political decisionmakers themselves" (Feldstein 1997, 23).

References

Aldrich, John H. 1995. *Why Parties? The Origin and Transformation of Political Parties in America.* Chicago: University of Chicago Press.

Alesina, Alberto. 1988a. "Credibility and Policy Convergence in a Two-Party System with Rational Voters." *American Economic Review* 78:796–806.

———. 1988b. "Macroeconomics and Politics." In *NBER Macroeconomic Annual 1988,* 11–15. Cambridge, Mass.: MIT Press.

———. 1989. "Inflation, Unemployment, and Politics in Industrial Democracies." *Economic Policy* 8 (spring): 55–98.

Alesina, Alberto, and Roberta Gatti. 1995. "Independent Central Banks: Low Inflation at No Cost?" *American Economic Review* 85 (2):196–200.

Alesina, Alberto, and Howard Rosenthal. 1995. *Partisan Politics, Divided Government, and the Economy.* New York: Cambridge University Press.

Alesina, Alberto, and Jeffrey Sachs. 1988. "Political Parties and the Business Cycle in the United States: 1948–1984." *Journal of Money, Credit, and Banking* 20 (1): 63–82.

Alesina, Alberto, and Lawrence Summers. 1993. "Central Bank Independence and Macroeconomic Performance: Some Comparative Evidence." *Journal of Money, Credit, and Banking* 25 (2): 151–62.

Alford, Robert. 1963. *Party and Society: The Anglo-American Democracies.* Chicago: Rand MacNally.

Allsopp, Christopher, and David Vines, eds. 1998. *Macroeconomic Policy after EMU.* Special issue, *Oxford Review of Economic Policy* 14 (3).

Allum, Percy A. 1973. *Italy: Republic without Government?* New York: Norton.

Alt, James. 1979. *The Politics of Economic Decline.* New York: Cambridge University Press.

Alt, James, and Michael Gilligan. 1994. "The Political Economy of Trading States: Factor Specificity, Collective Action Problems, and Domestic Political Institutions." *Journal of Political Philosophy* 2 (2): 165–92.

Alt, James, and Gary King. 1994. "Transfers of Governmental Power: The Meaning of Time Dependence." *Comparative Political Studies* 27 (2): 190–210.

Andrews, David. 1994. "Capital Mobility and State Autonomy: Toward a Structural Theory of International Monetary Relations." *International Studies Quarterly* 38:193–218.

Austen-Smith, David, and Jeffrey Banks. 1990. "Stable Governments and the Allocation of Portfolios." *American Political Science Review* 84 (3): 891–906.

Banaian, King, Leroy Laney, and Thomas Willett. 1983. "Central Bank Independence: An International Comparison." *Economic Review: Federal Reserve Bank of Dallas* March: 1–13.

Banks, Jeffrey. 1989. "Agency Budgets, Cost Information, and Auditing." *American Journal of Political Science* 33:670–99.

Banks, Jeffrey, and Joel Sobel. 1987. "Equilibrium Selection in Signaling Games." *Econometrica* 55:647–62.

Banks, Jeffrey, and Barry Weingast. 1992. "The Political Control of Bureaucrats under Asymmetric Information." *American Journal of Political Science* 36:509–24.

Barnes, Samuel. 1984. "Secular Trends and Partisan Realignment in Italy." In *Electoral Change in Advanced Industrial Democracies,* edited by Russell J. Dalton, Scott C. Flanagan, and Paul Allen Beck, 205–30. Princeton: Princeton University Press.

———. 1997. "Electoral Behavior and Comparative Politics." In *Comparative Politics: Rationality, Culture, and Structure,* edited by Mark Lichbach and Alan Zuckerman, 115–41. New York: Cambridge University Press.

Barro, Robert, and David Gordon. 1983. "Rules, Discretion, and Reputation in a Model of Monetary Policy." *Journal of Monetary Economics* 12:101–21.

Bayoumi, Tamim, and Barry Eichengreen. 1993. "Shocking Aspects of European Monetary Integration." In *Growth and Adjustment in the European Monetary Union,* edited by Francisco Torres and Francesco Giavazzi, 193–229. New York: Cambridge University Press.

———. 1997. "Ever Closer to Heaven? An Optimum Currency Area Index for European Countries." *European Economic Review* 41 (3–5): 761–70.

Bayoumi, Tamim, and Paul Masson. 1995. "Fiscal Flows in the United States and Canada: Lessons for Monetary Union in Europe." *European Economic Review* 39:253–75.

Beck, Nathaniel. 1987. "Elections and the Fed: Is There a Political Monetary Cycle?" *American Journal of Political Science* 31 (1): 194–216.

———. 1990a. "Congress and the Fed: Why the Dog Does Not Bark in the Night." In *The Political Economy of American Monetary Policy,* edited by Thomas Mayer, 131–50. New York: Cambridge University Press.

———. 1990b. "Political Monetary Cycles." In *The Political Economy of American Monetary Policy,* edited by Thomas Mayer, 115–30. New York: Cambridge University Press.

Beck, Nathaniel, and Jonathan Katz. 1995. "What to Do (and Not to Do) with Time-Series Cross-Section Data." *American Political Science Review* 89:634–47.

———. 1996. "Nuisance vs. Substance: Specifying and Estimating Time-Series–Cross-Section Models." *Political Analysis* 6:1–36.

Beckner, Steven. 1996. *Back from the Brink: The Greenspan Years.* New York: Wiley.

Belden, Susan. 1989. "Policy Preferences of FOMC Members as Revealed by Dissenting Votes." *Journal of Money Credit and Banking* 21:432–41.

Belsley, David A., Edwin Kuh, and Roy E. Welsch. 1980. *Regression Diagnostics: Identifying Influential Data and Sources of Collinearity.* New York: Wiley.

Berger, Helge. 1997. "The Bundesbank's Path to Independence: Evidence from the 1950s." *Public Choice* 93:427–53.

Berger, Helge, and Jakob de Haan. 1999. "A State within the State? An Event Study on the Bundesbank (1948–1973)." *Scottish Journal of Political Economy* 46 (1): 17–39.

Berger, Helge, and Ulrich Woitek. 1997a. "How Opportunistic Are Partisan German Central Bankers?" *European Journal of Political Economy* 13:807–22.

———. 1997b. "Searching for Political Business Cycles in Germany." *Public Choice* 91:179–97.

Bergsten, C. Fred. 1999. "America and Europe: Clash of the Titans?" *Foreign Affairs* (March/April): 20–34.

Berman, Sheri, and Kathleen McNamara. 1999. "Bank on Democracy: Why Central Banks Need Public Oversight." *Foreign Affairs* (March/April): 2–8.

Bernhard, William. 1998. "Political Accountability in the European Monetary System." University of Illinois at Urbana-Champaign. Typescript.

Betz, Hans-Georg. 1994. *Radical Right-Wing Populism in Western Europe.* New York: St. Martin's Press.

Blinder, Alan. 1997. "What Central Bankers Could Learn from Academics—and Vice Versa." *Journal of Economic Perspectives* 11 (2): 3–19.

Boix, Carles. 1998. *Political Parties, Growth, and Equality: Conservative and Social Democratic Economic Strategies in the World Economy.* New York: Cambridge University Press.

Bollen, Kenneth, and Robert Jackman. 1990. "Regression Diagnostics: An Expository Treatment of Outliers and Influential Cases." In *Modern Methods of Data Analysis,* edited by John Fox and J. Scott Long, 257–91. Newbury Park, Calif.: Sage.

Britton, Andrew. 1991. *Macroeconomic Policy in Britain 1974–1987.* New York: Cambridge University Press.

Broz, J. Lawrence. 1997. *The International Origins of the Federal Reserve System.* Ithaca: Cornell University Press.

Budge, Ian, and Dennis Farlie. 1983. "Party Competition—Selective Emphasis or Direct Confrontation? An Alternative View with Data." In *Western European Party Systems: Continuity and Change,* edited by H. Daadler and P. Mair, 267–306. Beverly Hills, Calif.: Sage.

Buiter, Willem. 1999. "Alice in Euroland." *Journal of Common Market Studies* 37 (2): 181–209.

Buiter, Willem, Giancarlo Corsetti, and Paolo Pesenti. 1998. *Financial Markets and European Monetary Cooperation.* New York: Cambridge University Press.

Buiter, Willem, Giancarlo Corsetti, and Nouriel Roubini. 1993. "Excessive Deficits: Sense and Nonsense in the Treaty of Maastricht." *Economic Policy* (April): 57–100.

Burdekin, Richard, and Thomas Willett. 1991. "Central Bank Reform: The Federal Reserve in International Perspective." *Public Budgeting and Financial Management* 3 (3): 531–51.

Buti, Marco, Daniele Franco, and Hedwig Ongena. 1998. "Fiscal Discipline and Flexibility in EMU: The Implementation of the Stability and Growth Pact." *Oxford Review of Economic Policy* 14 (3): 81–97.

Cairncross, Alec. 1988. "The Bank of England: Relationships with the Government, the Civil Service, and the Parliament." In *Central Banks' Independence in Historical Perspective,* edited by Gianni Toniolo. New York: W. de Gruyter.

Calvert, Randall L. 1985. "The Value of Biased Information: A Rational Choice Model of Political Advice." *Journal of Politics* 47:530–55.

Calvert, Randall L., Mathew D. McCubbins, and Barry Weingast. 1989. "Theory of Political Control and Agency Discretion." *American Journal of Political Science* 33 (3): 588–611.

Cameron, David. 1978. "The Expansion of the Public Economy: A Comparative Analysis." *American Political Science Review* 72 (4): 1243–61.

———. 1984. "Social Democracy, Corporatism, Labour Quiescence, and the Representation of Economic Interest in Advanced Capitalist Society." In *Order and Conflict in Contemporary Capitalism,* edited by John H. Goldthorpe, 143–78. Oxford: Clarendon Press.

———. 1993. "British Exit, German Voice, French Loyalty: Defection, Domination, and Cooperation in the 1992–93 ERM Crisis." Yale University. Typescript.

Chang, Kelly. 1997. "Appointments at the U.S. Federal Reserve." Ph.D. diss., Stanford University.

Chappell, Henry, Thomas Havrilesky, and Rob Roy MacGregor. 1993. "Partisan Monetary Policies: Presidential Influence through the Power of Appointment." *Quarterly Journal of Economics* 108:185–219.

Cho, In-Koo, and David Kreps. 1987. "Signaling Games and Stable Equilibria." *Quarterly Journal of Economics* 102:179–222.

Clarida, Richard, Jordi Gali, and Mark Gertler. 1999. "The Science of Monetary Policy: A New Keynesian Perspective." *Journal of Economic Literature* 37 (December): 1661–1707.

Clark, William Roberts. 1999. "Structuring Strategies: Capital Mobility, Central Bank Independence, and the Political Control of the Economy." New York University. Typescript.

Clark, William Roberts, and Mark Hallerberg. 2000. "Mobile Capital, Domestic Institutions, and Electorally Induced Monetary and Fiscal Policy." *American Political Science Review* 94 (2): 323–46.

Clarke, Harold, and Marianne Stewart. 1995. "Economic Evaluations, Prime Ministerial Approval, and Governing Party Support: Rival Models Reconsidered." *British Journal of Political Science* 25:145–70.

Cobham, David, ed. 1994. *European Monetary Upheavals.* Manchester: Manchester University Press.

Conradt, David P. 1989. *The German Polity.* New York: Longman Press.

Cook, R. D., and S. Weisberg. 1983. "Diagnostics for Heteroskedasticity in Regression." *Biometrika* 70 (1): 1–10.

Cox, Gary, and Mathew D. McCubbins. 1993. *Legislative Leviathan: Party Government in the House.* Berkeley: University of California Press.

Craig, Fred W. S., ed. 1982. *Conservative and Labour Party Conference Decisions, 1945–1981.* Chichester: Parliamentary Research Services.

Crewe, Ivor. 1985. "Great Britain." In *Electoral Change in Western European Democracies,* edited by Ivor Crewe and David Denver, 100–150. New York: St. Martin's Press.

Cukierman, Alex. 1992. *Central Bank Strategy, Credibility, and Independence: Theory and Evidence.* Cambridge, Mass.: MIT Press.

Cukierman, Alex, Pantelis Kalaitzidakis, Lawrence Summers, and Steven Webb. 1993. "Central Bank Independence, Growth, Investment, and Real Rates." *Carnegie-Rochester Conference Series on Public Policy* 39:95–140.

Cukierman, Alex, and Allan Meltzer. 1986. "A Positive Theory of Discretionary Policy, the Cost of Democratic Government, and the Benefits of a Constitution." *Economic Inquiry* 24:367–88.

Cukierman, Alex, Steven B. Webb, and Bilin Neyapti. 1992. "Measuring the Independence of Central Banks and Its Effect on Policy Outcomes." *World Bank Economic Review* 6 (3): 353–98.

D'Alimonte, Roberto. 1999. "Party Behavior in a Polarized System: The Italian Communist Party and the Historic Compromise." In *Policy, Office, or Votes? How Political Parties in Western Europe Make Hard Decisions,* edited by Wolfgang C. Muller and Kaare Strom, 141–71. New York: Cambridge University Press.

Dalton, Russell, Scott Flanagan, and Paul Allen Beck, eds. 1984. *Electoral Change in Advanced Industrial Economies.* Princeton: Princeton University Press.

Dalziel, Paul. 1993. "The Reserve Bank Act: Reflecting Changing Relationships between State and Economy in the Twentieth Century." In *State and Economy in New Zealand,* edited by Brian Roper and Chris Rudd. New York: Oxford University Press.

de Boissieu, Christian, and Jean Pisani-Ferry. 1998. "The Political Economy of French Economic Policy in the Perspective of EMU." In *Forging an Integrated Europe,* edited by Barry Eichengreen and Jeffry Frieden, 49–90. Ann Arbor: University of Michigan Press.

de Haan, Jakob. 1997. "The European Central Bank: Independence, Accountability, and Strategy." *Public Choice* 93:395–426.

de Haan, Jakob, Wim Moessen, and Bjorn Volkerink. 1999. "Budgetary Procedures—Aspects and Changes: New Evidence for Some European Countries." In *Fiscal Institutions and Fiscal Performance,* edited by James Poterba and Jurgen von Hagen, 265–99. Chicago: University of Chicago Press.

de Haan, Jakob, and Jan-Egbert Sturm. 1994. "Political and Institutional Determinants of Fiscal Policy in the European Community." *Public Choice* 80:157–72.

———. 1997. "Political and Economic Determinants of OECD Budget Deficits and Government Expenditures: A Reinvestigation." *European Journal of Political Economy* 13:739–50.

de Haan, Jakob, and Gert Jan Van't Hag. 1995. "Variation in Central Bank Independence across Countries: Some Provisional Empirical Evidence." *Public Choice* 85:335–51.

Deane, Marjorie, and Robert Pringle. 1995. *The Central Banks.* New York: Viking.

Debelle, Guy, and Stanley Fischer. 1994. "How Independent Should a Central Bank Be?" In *Goals, Guidelines, and Constraints Facing Monetary Policymakers,* edited by Jeffrey C. Fuhrer, 195–221. Federal Reserve Bank of Boston Conference Series, no. 38. Boston: Federal Reserve Bank of Boston.

Della Sala, Vincent. 1988. "The Italian Budgetary Process: Political and Institutional Constraints." *West European Politics* 11 (3): 110–25.

Deutsche Bundesbank. 1989. *The Deutsche Bundesbank: Its Instruments and Functions.* 3d ed. Frankfurt: Deutsche Bundesbank.

Dinan, Desmond. 1999. *Ever Closer Union: An Introduction to European Integration.* 2d ed. Boulder, Colo.: Lynne Rienner.

Downs, Anthony. 1957. *An Economic Theory of Democracy.* New York: Harper and Row.

Drazen, Allan. 2000. *Political Economy in Macroeconomics.* Princeton: Princeton University Press.

The Economics of EMU. European Economy, special edition, no. 1. Luxembourg: Office for Official Publications of the European Communities.

Eichengreen, Barry. 1992. *Should the Maastricht Treaty Be Saved?* Princeton Studies in International Finance no. 74.

———. 1993a. "European Monetary Unification" *Journal of Economic Literature* 31 (September): 1321–57.

———. 1993b. "Labor Markets and European Monetary Unification" In *Policy Issues in the Operation of Currency Unions,* edited by Paul Masson and Mark Taylor, 130–62. New York: Cambridge University Press.

———. 1997. *European Monetary Unification: Theory, Practice, and Analysis.* Cambridge, Mass.: MIT Press.

———. 1998. "European Monetary Unification: A Tour d'Horizon." *Oxford Review of Economic Policy* 14 (3): 24–40.

Eichengreen, Barry, and Jeffry Frieden, eds. 1994. *The Political Economy of European Monetary Unification.* Boulder, Colo.: Westview Press.

Eichengreen, Barry, and Charles Wyplosz. 1998. "The Stability Pact: More Than a Minor Nuisance?" *Economic Policy* 26 (April): 65–104.

Eijffinger, Sylvester, and Jakob de Haan. 1996. *The Political Economy of Central Bank Independence.* Princeton Special Papers in International Economics no. 19.

Eijffinger, Sylvester, Eric Schaling, and Marco Hoeberichts. 1998. "Central Bank Independence: A Sensitivity Analysis." *European Journal of Political Economy* 14:73–88.

Eizenga, Weitze. 1987. *The Independence of the Deutsche Bundesbank and the Nederlandsche Bank with regard to Monetary Policy: A Comparative Study.* SUERF Papers on Monetary Policy and Financial Systems no. 2. Tilburg: Societe Universitaire Europeenne de Recherches Financieres.

Elgie, Robert, and Helen Thompson. 1998. *The Politics of Central Banks.* New York: Routledge.

Emerson, Michael, Daniel Gros, Alexander Italianer, Jean Pisani-Ferry, and Horst Reichenbach. 1991. *One Market, One Money.* Special issue, *European Economy* 44. Oxford: Oxford University Press.

EMU. 1998. Special issue, *Economic Policy* 26 (April).

Epstein, Gerald, and Juliet Schor. 1989. "The Divorce of the Banca d'Italia and the Italian Treasury: A Case Study of Central Bank Independence." In *State, Market, and Social Regulation: New Perspectives on Italy,* edited by Peter Lange and Mario Regini, 147–64. Cambridge: Cambridge University Press.

Esping-Andersen, Gosta. 1999. "Politics without Class: Postindustrial Cleavages in Europe and America." In *Continuity and Change in Contemporary Capitalism,* edited by Herbert Kitschelt, Peter Lange, Gary Marks, and John D. Stephens, 293–316. New York: Cambridge University Press.

Fair, Don. 1979. "The Independence of Central Banks." *Banker* 129 (October): 31–41.

Fatas, Antonio. 1998. "Does EMU Need a Fiscal Federation?" *Economic Policy* 26 (April): 163–92.

Fay, R. 1988. *Portrait of an Old Lady.* London: Penguin Books.

Feldstein, Martin. 1997. "The Political Economy for the European Economic and Monetary Union: Political Sources of an Economic Liability." *Journal of Economic Perspectives* 11 (4): 23–42.

Ferejohn, John, and Charles Shipan. 1990. "Congressional Influence on Bureaucracy." *Journal of Law, Economics, and Organization* 6 (1): 1–20.

Ferrara, Maurizio. 1989. "Politics, Institutional Features, and the Government of Industry." In *State, Market, and Social Regulation: New Perspectives on Italy,* edited by Peter Lange and Mario Regini, 111–28. Cambridge: Cambridge University Press.

Fforde, John. 1992. *The Bank of England and Public Policy 1941–1958.* New York: Cambridge University Press.

Fischer, Stanley. 1995. "Central Bank Independence Revisited." *American Economic Review* 85 (2): 201–6.

Forder, James. 1996. "On the Assessment and Implementation of 'Institutional' Remedies." *Oxford Economic Papers* 48:39–51.

———. 1998a. "The Case for an Independent European Central Bank: A Reassessment of Evidence and Sources." *European Journal of Political Economy* 14:53–71.

———. 1998b. "Central Bank Independence: Conceptual Clarifications and Interim Assessment." *Oxford Economic Papers* 50:307–34.

Frankel, Jeffrey, and Andrew Rose. 1996. "Economic Structure and the Decision to Adopt a Common Currency." Center for International and Development Economics Research Working Paper C96–073.

Franzese, Robert. 1999. "Partially Independent Central Banks, Politically Responsive Governments, and Inflation." *American Journal of Political Science* 43 (3): 681–706.

———. 2000. "Comparative Democratic Mismanagement of the Keynesian Welfare State." University of Michigan. Typescript.

Fratianni, Michele, Jurgen von Hagen, and Christopher Waller. 1997. "Central Banking as a Political Principal-Agent Problem." *Economic Inquiry* 35 (April): 378–93.

Freedman, Charles. 1993. "Designing Institutions for Monetary Stability: A Comment." *Carnegie-Rochester Conference Series on Public Policy* 39:85–94.

Frieden, Jeffry. 1991. "Invested Interests: The Politics of National Economic Policies in a World of Global Finance." *International Organization* 45:425–51.

——-. 1994. "Making Commitments: France and Italy in the European Monetary System, 1979–1985." In *The Political Economy of European Monetary Unification,* edited by Barry Eichengreen and Jeffry Frieden, 25–46. Boulder, Colo.: Westview Press.

———. 1998. "The Euro: Who Wins? Who Loses?" *Foreign Policy* (fall): 24–40.

Frieden, Jeffry, and Ronald Rogowski. 1996. "The Impact of the International Economy on National Policies: An Analytical Overview." In *Internationalization and Domestic Politics,* edited by Robert Keohane and Helen Milner, 25–47. Cambridge: Cambridge University Press.

Friedman, Milton. 1968. "The Role of Monetary Policy." *American Economic Review* 58 (1): 1–17.

Gabel, Matthew. 1999. "Divided Opinion, Common Currency: The Political-Economy of Public Support for EMU." University of Kentucky. Typescript.

Garrett, Geoffrey. 1992. "The Political Consequences of Thatcherism." *Political Behavior* 14:361–82.

———. 1995. "Capital Mobility, Trade, and the Domestic Politics of Economic Policy." *International Organization* 49 (4): 657–87.

———. 1998a. *Partisan Politics in the Global Economy.* New York: Cambridge University Press.

———. 1998b. "The Transition to Economic and Monetary Union." In *Forging an Integrated Europe,* edited by Barry Eichengreen and Jeffry Frieden, 21–48. Ann Arbor: University of Michigan Press.

Garrett, Geoffrey, and Peter Lange. 1996. "Internationalization, Institutions, and Political Change." In *Internationalization and Domestic Politics,* edited Robert Keohane and Helen Milner, 48–78. New York: Cambridge University Press.

Gartner, Manfred. 1997. "Who Wants the Euro—and Why? Economic Explanations of Public Attitudes towards a Single European Currency." *Public Choice* 93:487–510.

Gildea, John. 1990. "Explaining FOMC Members' Votes." In *The Political Economy of American Monetary Policy,* edited by Thomas Mayer, 211–28. Cambridge: Cambridge University Press.

Gilligan, Thomas, and Keith Krehbiel. 1989. "Asymmetric Information and Legislative Rules with a Heterogenous Committee." *American Journal of Political Science* 33:459–90.

———. 1990. "Organization of Informative Committees by a Rational Legislature." *American Journal of Political Science* 34:531–64.

Golden, Miriam, Peter Lange, and Michael Wallerstein. 1998. "Union Centralization among Advanced Industrial Societies: An Empirical Study." Dataset available at <http://www.shelley.polisci.ucla.edu/data>.

———. 1999. "Postwar Trade-Union Organization and Industrial Relations in Twelve Countries." In *Continuity and Change in Contemporary Capitalism,* edited by Herbert Kitschelt, Peter Lange, Gary Marks, and John D. Stephens, 194–230. New York: Cambridge University Press.

Goodhart, Charles. 1994. "Central Bank Independence." *Journal of International and Comparative Economics* 3:1–12.

Goodman, John. 1991. "The Politics of Central Bank Independence." *Comparative Politics* 23 (3): 329–49.

———. 1992. *Monetary Sovereignty.* Ithaca: Cornell University Press.

Goodman, John, and Louis B. Pauly. 1993. "The Obsolescence of Capital Controls? Economic Management in an Age of Global Markets." *World Politics* 46:50–82.

Granato, Jim. 1996. "The Effect of Policymaker Reputation and Credibility on Public Expectations: An Application to Macroeconomic Policy Changes." *Journal of Theoretical Politics* 8 (4): 449–70.

———. 2000. "Transitions to Policy Accountability: American Inflation 1970–1995." Michigan State University. Typescript.

Granato, Jim, Ronald Inglehart, and David Leblang. 1996. "The Effect of Cultural Values on Economic Development: Theory, Hypotheses, and Some Empirical Tests." *American Journal of Political Science* 40 (3): 607–31.

Granato, Jim, and Mitoshi Suzuki. 1996. "The Use of the Encompassing Principle to Resolve Empirical Controversies in Voting Behavior: An Application to Voter Rationality in Congressional Elections." *Electoral Studies* 15 (3): 383–98.

Greider, William. 1987. *Secrets of the Temple: How the Federal Reserve Runs the Country.* New York: Touchstone.

Grier, Kevin. 1989. "On the Existence of a Political Monetary Cycle." *American Journal of Political Science* 33:376–89.

Grilli, Vittorio, Donato Masciandaro, and Guido Tabellini. 1991. "Political and Monetary Institutions and Public Finance Policies in the Industrialized Democracies." *Economic Policy* 10 (October): 342–92.

Gros, Daniel, and Alfred Steinherr. 1992. "EMS Is Dead: Long Live EMU!" Brussels: Centre for European Policy Studies. Typescript.

Gros, Daniel, and Neils Thygesen. 1998. *European Monetary Integration: From the European Monetary System to European Monetary Union.* 2d ed. New York: Longman Press.

Hall, Peter. 1986. *Governing the Economy: The Politics of State Intervention in Britain and France.* New York: Oxford University Press.

Hall, Peter, and Robert Franzese. 1998. "Mixed Signals: Central Bank Independence, Coordinated Wage-Bargaining, and European Monetary Union." *International Organization* 52 (3): 505–35.

Hallerberg, Mark. 1999. "The Importance of Domestic Political Institutions: Why and How Belgium and Italy Qualified for EMU." University of Pittsburgh. Typescript.

Hallerberg, Mark, and Jurgen von Hagen. 1999. "Electoral Institutions, Cabinet Negotiations, and Budget Deficits within the European Union." In *Fiscal Institutions and Fiscal Performance,* edited by James Poterba and Jurgen von Hagen, 209–32. Chicago: University of Chicago Press.

Hallett, Andrew, Michael Hutchison, and Svend Hougaard Jensen, eds. 1999. *Fiscal Aspects of European Monetary Integration.* New York: Cambridge University Press.

Hamilton, Lawrence. 1992. *Regression with Graphics: A Second Course in Applied Statistics.* Pacific Grove, Calif.: Brooks/Cole.

Hammond, Thomas, Jeffrey Hill, and Gary Miller. 1986. "Presidents, Congress, and the 'Congressional Control of Administration' Hypothesis." Paper presented at the Annual Convention of the American Political Science Association.

Havrilesky, Thomas. 1987. "A Partisanship Theory of Fiscal and Monetary Regimes." *Journal of Money, Credit, and Banking* 20 (3): 308–25.

———. 1988. "Monetary Policy Signaling from the Administration to the Federal Reserve." *Journal of Money, Credit, and Banking* 20:83–101.

———. 1993. *The Political Pressures on American Monetary Policy.* Norwell, Mass.: Kluwer Academic.

———. 1994a. "A Model of Optimal European Central Bank Restructuring." Duke University. Typescript.

———. 1994b. "The Political Economy of Monetary Policy." *European Journal of Political Economy* 10 (1): 111–34.

Havrilesky, Thomas, and John Gildea. 1992. "Reliable and Unreliable Partisan Appointees to the Board of Governors." *Public Choice* 73:397–417.

Havrilesky, Thomas, and Jim Granato. 1993. "Determinants of Inflationary Performance: Corporatist Structure vs. Central Bank Autonomy." *Public Choice* 76 (3): 249–61.

Havrilesky, Thomas, and Robert Schweitzer. 1990. "A Theory of FOMC Dissent Voting with Evidence from the Time Series." In *The Political Economy of American Monetary Policy,* edited by Thomas Mayer, 197–210. Cambridge: Cambridge University Press.

Heisenberg, Dorothee. 1998. "German Parliament Members' Opinions about European Monetary Union." Centre for European Policy Studies Working Document no. 115.

———. 1999. *The Mark of the Bundesbank: Germany's Role in European Monetary Cooperation.* Boulder, Colo.: Lynne Rienner.

Henning, C. Randall. 1994. *Currencies and Politics in the United States, Germany, and Japan.* Washington, D.C.: Institute for International Economics.

———. 1998. "Systemic Conflict and Regional Monetary Integration: The Case of Europe." *International Organization* 52 (3): 537–73.

Herron, Michael. 2000. "Estimating the Economic Impact of Political Party Competition in the 1992 British Election." *American Journal of Political Science* 44 (2): 320–31.

Hibbs, Douglas. 1987. *The American Political Economy.* Cambridge, Mass.: Harvard University Press.

Huber, John. 1996. "The Vote of Confidence in Parliamentary Democracies." *American Political Science Review* 90 (2): 269–82.

Inglehart, Ronald. 1997. *Modernization and Postmodernization: Cultural, Economic, and Political Change in 43 Societies.* Princeton: Princeton University Press.

Inglehart, Ronald, and Paul Abramson. 1994. "Economic Security and Value Change." *American Political Science Review* 88:336–54.

Issing, Otmar. 1999. "The Eurosystem: Transparent and Accountable or 'Willem in Euroland.'" *Journal of Common Market Studies* 37 (3): 503–19.

Iversen, Torben. 1996. "Power, Flexibility, and the Breakdown of Centralized Wage Bargaining: The Cases of Denmark and Sweden in Comparative Perspective." *Comparative Politics* 28 (3): 399–436.

———. 1998. "Wage Bargaining, Central Bank Independence, and the Real Effects of Money." *International Organization* 52 (summer): 469–504.

———. 1999. *Contested Economic Institutions: The Politics of Macroeconomics and Wage Bargaining in Advanced Democracies.* New York: Cambridge University Press.

Iversen, Torben, and Thomas Cusack. 2000. "The Causes of Welfare State Expansion: Deindustrialization or Globalization?" *World Politics* 52 (3): 313–49.

Iversen, Torben, and Anne Wren. 1998. "Equality, Employment, and Budgetary Restraint: The Trilemma of the Service Economy." *World Politics* 50 (4): 507–46.

Jackman, Robert. 1987. "The Politics of Economic Growth in Industrialized Democracies, 1974–1980." *Journal of Politics* 49 (1): 242–56.

Johnson, Christopher, and Stefan Collignon, eds. 1994. *The Monetary Economics of Europe: Causes of the E.M.S. Crisis.* London: Pinter.

Kaltenthaler, Karl. 1996. "The Restructuring of the German Bundesbank: The Politics of Institutional Change." *German Politics and Society* 14 (4): 23–48.

Kaltenthaler, Karl, and Christopher Anderson. 1999. "Europeans and Their Money: Explaining Public Support for the Common European Currency." SUNY-Binghamton. Typescript.

Kane, Edward. 1980. "Politics and Fed Policymaking: The More Things Change the More They Remain the Same." *Journal of Monetary Economics* 6:199–211.

Kapstein, Ethan. 1994. *Governing the Global Economy: International Finance and the State.* Cambridge, Mass.: Harvard University Press.

Katzenstein, Peter. 1985. *Small States in World Markets: Industrial Policy in Europe.* Ithaca: Cornell University Press.

Kavanaugh, Dennis. 1987. *Thatcherism and British Politics: The End of Consensus?* New York: Oxford University Press.

Keech, William. 1995. *Economic Politics: The Costs of Democracy.* New York: Cambridge University Press.

Keefer, Philip, and David Stasavage. 2000. "Checks and Balances, Private Information, and the Credibility of Monetary Commitments." The World Bank. Typescript.

Keesing's Archives. 1991. New York: Longman.

Kennedy, Ellen. 1991. *The Bundesbank: Germany's Central Bank in the International Monetary System.* London: Pinter.

Keohane, Robert, and Helen Milner, eds. 1996. *Internationalization and Domestic Politics.* New York: Cambridge University Press.

Kettl, Donald. 1986. *Leadership at the Fed.* New Haven: Yale University Press.

Kiewiet, D. Roderick, and Mathew D. McCubbins. 1991. *The Logic of Delegation.* Chicago: University of Chicago Press.

King, Gary, James Alt, Nancy Burns, and Michael Laver. 1990. "A Unified Model of Cabinet Dissolution in Parliamentary Democracies." *American Journal of Political Science* 34 (3): 846–71.

King, Gary, Michael Tomz, and Jason Wittenberg. 2000. "Making the Most of Statistical Analyses: Improving Interpretation and Presentation." *American Journal of Political Science* 44 (2): 347–61.

Kirchheimer, Otto. 1966. "The Transformation of Western European Party Systems." In *Political Parties and Political Development,* edited by Joseph LaPalombara and Myron Weiner, 177–200. Princeton: Princeton University Press.

Kitschelt, Herbert. 1989. *The Logics of Party Formation.* Ithaca: Cornell University Press.

———. 1994. *The Transformation of European Social Democracy.* New York: Cambridge University Press.

———. 1997. *The Radical Right in Western Europe.* Ann Arbor: University of Michigan Press.

———. 1999. "European Social Democracy between Political Economy and Electoral Competition." In *Continuity and Change in Contemporary Capitalism,* edited by Herbert Kitschelt, Peter Lange, Gary Marks, and John D. Stephens, 317–45. New York: Cambridge University Press.

Kletzer, Kenneth. 1998. "Macroeconomic Stabilization with a Common Currency: Does European Monetary Unification Create a Need for Fiscal Insurance or Federalism." In *Forging an Integrated Europe,* edited by Barry Eichengreen and Jeffry Frieden, 91–128. Ann Arbor: University of Michigan Press.

Krehbiel, Keith. 1991. *Information and Legislative Organization.* Ann Arbor: University of Michigan Press.

Krugman, Paul. 1994. *Peddling Prosperity.* New York: Norton.

Kydland, Finn, and Edward Prescott. 1977. "Rules Rather Than Discretion: The Inconsistency of Optimal Plans." *Journal of Political Economy* 83:473–91.

Kynaston, David. 1995. "The Bank of England and the Government." In *The Bank of England: Money, Power, and Influence 1694–1994,* edited by Richard Roberts and David Kynaston, 19–55. Oxford: Clarendon Press.

Lange, Peter. 1980. "Crisis and Consent, Change and Compromise: Dilemmas of Italian Communism in the 1970s." In *Italy in Transition,* edited by Peter Lange and Sidney Tarrow, 110–32. London: Cass.

———. 1986. "The End of an Era: The Wage Indexation Referendum of 1985." In *Italian Politics: A Review,* edited by Robert Leonardi and Raffaella Nanetti, 29–46. London: Pinter.

Lange, Peter, and Geoffrey Garrett. 1985. "The Politics of Growth: Strategic Interaction and Economic Performance in the Advanced Industrial Democracies, 1974–1980." *Journal of Politics* 47:792–827.

Lange, Peter, and Sidney Tarrow, eds. 1980. *Italy in Transition.* London: Cass.

Lange, Peter, and Maurizio Vannicelli. 1982. "Strategy under Stress: The Italian Union Movement and the Italian Crisis in Developmental Perspective." In *Unions, Change, and Crisis,* edited by Peter Lange, George Ross, and Maurizio Vannicelli, 95–206. Boston: George Allen and Unwin.

LaPalombara, Joseph. 1981. "Two Steps Forward, One Step Back: The PCI's Struggle for Legitimacy." In *Italy at the Polls, 1979,* edited by Howard R. Penniman, 104–40. Washington, D.C.: American Enterprise Institute.

Laver, Michael, and Ben Hunt. 1992. *Policy and Party Competition.* New York: Routledge.

Laver, Michael, and Norman Schofield. 1990. *Multiparty Government: The Politics of Coalition in Europe.* New York: Oxford University Press.

Laver, Michael, and Kenneth Shepsle. 1996. *Making and Breaking Governments.* Cambridge: Cambridge University Press.

———, eds. 1994. *Cabinet Ministers and Parliamentary Government.* Cambridge: Cambridge University Press.

Lawson, Nigel. 1992. *The View from No. 11: Memoirs of a Tory Radical.* London: Bantam Press.

Leblang, David. 1997. "Are Capital Controls Obsolete? Domestic and Systemic Determinants of Capital Controls in the Developed and Developing World." *International Studies Quarterly* 41 (3): 435–54.

Leblang, David, and William Bernhard. 2000. "The Politics of Speculative Attacks in Industrial Democracies." *International Organization* 54 (2): 291–324.

LeLoup, Lance, and John Woolley. 1991. "Legislative Oversight of Monetary Policy in France, Germany, Great Britain, and the United States." In *Legislatures in the Policy Process: The Dilemmas of Economic Policy,* edited by David M. Olson and Michael L. Mezey, 25–58. Cambridge: Cambridge University Press.

Leonardi, Robert. 1987. "The Changing Balance: The Rise of the Small Parties in the 1983 Elections." In *Italy at the Polls, 1983,* edited by Howard Penniman, 100–119. Washington, D.C.: American Enterprise Institute.

Lewis-Beck, Michael S. 1988. *Economics and Elections: The Major Western Democracies.* Ann Arbor: University of Michigan Press.

Lewis-Beck, Michael S., Helmut Norpoth, and Jean-Dominique Lafay, eds. 1991. *Economics and Politics: The Calculus of Support.* Ann Arbor: University of Michigan Press.

Lijphart, Arend. 1984. *Democracies.* New Haven: Yale University Press.

Lipset, Seymour Martin, and Stein Rokkan. 1967. "Cleavage Structures, Party Systems, and Voter Alignments: An Introduction." In *Party Systems and Voter Alignments: Cross National Perspectives,* edited by Seymour Martin Lipset and Stein Rokkan, 1–64. New York: Free Press.

Locke, Richard. 1995. *Remaking the Italian Economy.* Ithaca: Cornell University Press.

Lohmann, Susanne. 1992. "Optimal Commitment in Monetary Policy: Credibility versus Flexibility." *American Economic Review* 82 (1): 273–86.

———. 1994. "Designing a Central Bank in a Federal System: The Deutsche Bundesbank, 1957–1992." In *Varieties of Monetary Reforms: Lessons and Experiences on the Road to Monetary Union,* edited by Pierre Siklos, 247–78. Boston: Kluwer Academic.

———. 1997. "Partisan Control of the Money Supply and Decentralized Appointment Powers." *European Journal of Political Economy* 13:225–46.

———. 1998a. "Federalism and Central Bank Independence: The Politics of German Monetary Policy, 1957–1992." *World Politics* 50:401–46.

———. 1998b. "Institutional Checks and Balances and the Political Control of the Money Supply." *Oxford Economic Papers* 50:360–77.

Loriaux, Michael. 1991. *France after Hegemony: International Change and Financial Reform.* Ithaca: Cornell University Press.

Lucas, Robert. 1972. "Expectations and the Neutrality of Money." *Journal of Economic Theory* 4:103–24.

Ludlow, Peter. 1982. *The Making of the European Monetary System.* London: Butterworth.

Lupia, Arthur. 1992. "Busy Voters, Agenda Control, and the Power of Information." *American Political Science Review* 86:390–404.

Lupia, Arthur, and Mathew McCubbins. 1993. "Learning from Oversight: Fire Alarms and Police Patrols Reconstructed." University of California at San Diego. Typescript.

Maes, Ivo. 1992. "Comparing the Werner Report and the Maastricht Treaty." National Bank of Belgium. Typescript.

Maguire, Maria. 1983. "Is There Still Persistence? Electoral Change in Western Europe, 1948–1979." In *Western European Party Systems: Continuity and Change,* edited by Hans Daalder and Peter Mair, 67–94. Beverly Hills, Calif.: Sage.

Mangano, Gabriel. 1998. "Measuring Central Bank Independence: A Tale of Subjectivity and of Its Consequences." *Oxford Economic Papers* 50:468–92.

Marsh, David. 1992. *The Bundesbank: The Bank That Rules Europe.* London: Heinemann.

Maxfield, Sylvia. 1994. "Financial Incentives and Central Bank Authority in Industrializing Nations." *World Politics* 46 (4): 556–88.

———. 1997. *Gatekeepers of Growth: The International Political Economy of Central Banking in Developing Countries.* Princeton: Princeton University Press.

McCallum, Bennett. 1995. "Two Fallacies concerning Central Bank Independence." *American Economic Review* 85 (2): 207–11.

———. 1997. "Crucial Issues concerning Central Bank Independence." *Journal of Monetary Economics* 39:99–112.

McCubbins, Mathew, Roger Noll, and Barry Weingast. 1987. "Administrative Procedures as Instruments of Political Control." *Journal of Law, Economics, and Organization* 3:243–77.

———. 1989. "Structure and Process, Politics and Policy: Administrative Arrangements and the Political Control of Agencies." *Virginia Law Review* 75 (2): 431–82.

McCubbins, Mathew, and Thomas Schwartz. 1983. "Congressional Oversight Overlooked: Police Patrols versus Fire Alarms." *American Journal of Political Science* 28 (1): 165–79.

McGregor, Rob B. 1996. "FOMC Voting Behavior and Electoral Cycles." *Economics and Politics.*

McKinnon, Ronald. 1963. "Optimum Currency Areas." *American Economic Review* 53 (4): 717–25.

McNamara, Kathleen. 1998. *The Currency of Ideas: Monetary Politics in the European Union.* Ithaca: Cornell University Press.

———. 2000. "Globalization, Fiscal Adjustment, and EMU: Race to the Bottom or Room for Maneuver?" Princeton University. Typescript.

Milner, Helen, and Robert Keohane. 1996. "Internationalization and Domestic Politics: An Introduction." In *Internationalization and Domestic Politics,* edited by Robert Keohane and Helen Milner, 3–24. New York: Cambridge University Press.

Moe, Terry. 1987. "An Assessment of the Positive Theory of Congressional Dominance." *Legislative Studies Quarterly* 12:475–520.

———. 1989. "The Politics of Bureaucratic Structure." In *Can the Government Govern?* edited by John Chubb and Paul Peterson, 267–329. Washington, D.C.: Brookings Institution.

———. 1990. "The Politics of Structural Choice: Toward a Theory of Public Bureaucracy." In *Organization Theory: From Chester Barnard to the Present and Beyond,* edited by Oliver Williamson, 116–53. New York: Oxford University Press.

Mooney, Christopher Z. 1996. "Bootstrap Statistical Inference: Examples and Evaluations for Political Science." *American Journal of Political Science* 40 (2): 570–602.

Mooney, Christopher Z., and Robert Duval 1993. *Bootstrapping: A Nonparametric Approach to Statistical Inference.* Sage University Paper Series on Quantitative Applications in the Social Sciences, 07-095. Newbury Park, Calif.: Sage.

Moravscik, Andrew. 1991. "Negotiating the Single European Act." *International Organization* 45 (1): 19–56.

———. 1998. *The Choice for Europe: Social Purpose and State Power from Messina to Maastricht.* Ithaca: Cornell University Press.

Morgan, Kenneth. 1984. *Labour In Power, 1945–1951.* New York: Oxford University Press.

Morris, Irwin. 2000. *Congress, the President, and the Federal Reserve.* Ann Arbor: University of Michigan Press.

Mulgan, Richard. 1994. *Politics in New Zealand.* Auckland: Auckland University Press.

Muller, Wolfgang, and Kaare Strom, eds. 1999. *Policy, Office, or Votes? How Political Parties in Western Europe Make Hard Decisions.* New York: Cambridge University Press.

Mundell, Robert. 1961. "A Theory of Optimum Currency Areas." *American Economic Review.* 51 (4): 657–65.

Munger, Michael, and Brian Roberts. 1990. "The Federal Reserve and Its Institutional Environment: A Review." In *The Political Economy of American Monetary Policy,* edited by Thomas Mayer, 83–98. New York: Cambridge University Press.

Neumann, Manfred J. 1991. "Central Bank Independence as a Prerequisite for Price Stability." In *The Economics of EMU. European Economy,* special edition, no.1, 79–92. Luxembourg: Office for Official Publications of the European Communities.

New Zealand Parliamentary Debates. 1989. Auckland: Government of New Zealand.

Nokken, Timothy, and Brian Sala. 2000. "Confirmation Dynamics: Presidential Appointments to Independent Agencies." *Journal of Theoretical Politics* 12 (1): 91–112.

Nordhaus, William. 1975. "The Political Business Cycle." *Review of Economic Studies* 42:169–90.

Oatley, Thomas. 1997. *Monetary Politics: Exchange Rate Cooperation in the European Union.* Ann Arbor: University of Michigan Press.

———. 1999. "How Constraining Is Capital Mobility? The Partisan Hypothesis in an Open Economy." *American Journal of Political Science* 43 (4): 1003–27.

Obstfeld, Maurice, and Giovanni Peri. 1998. "Regional Non-Adjustment and Fiscal Policy." *Economic Policy* 26 (April): 205–59.

Olson, Mancur. 1982. *The Rise and Decline of Nations: Economic Growth, Stagflation, and Social Rigidities.* New Haven: Yale University Press.

Ordeshook, Peter. 1986. *Game Theory and Political Theory.* New York: Cambridge University Press.

Padoa-Schioppa, Tommaso. 1987. "Reshaping Monetary Policy." In *Macroeconomics and Finance: Essays in Honor of Franco Modigliani,* edited by Rudiger Dornbusch, Stanley Fischer, and John Bossons, 265–86. Cambridge, Mass.: MIT Press.

Pearce, Robert. 1994. *Attlee's Labour Governments, 1945–1951.* New York: Routledge.

Pedersen, Mogens. 1983. "Changing Patterns of Electoral Volatility in European Party Systems, 1948–1977: Explorations in Explanation." In *Western European Party Systems: Continuity and Change,* Hans Daalder and Peter Mair, 29–66. Beverly Hills, Calif.: Sage.

Pempel, T. J. 1998. *Regime Shift: Comparative Dynamics of the Japanese Political Economy.* Ithaca: Cornell University Press.

Penniman, Howard, ed. 1981. *Italy at the Polls, 1983.* Washington, D.C.: American Enterprise Institute.

Persson, Torsten, and Guido Tabellini. 1990. *Macroeconomic Policy, Credibility, and Politics.* London: Harwood Academic.

———. 1993. "Designing Institutions for Monetary Stability." *Carnegie-Rochester Conference Series on Public Policy* 39:53–84.

Pitruzello, Salvatore. 1997. "Social Policy and the Implementation of the Maastricht Fiscal Convergence Criteria: The Italian and French Attempts at Welfare and Pension Reforms." *Social Research* 64 (4): 1589–1642.

Pollard, Patricia. 1993. "Central Bank Independence and Economic Performance." *Federal Reserve Bank of St. Louis Review* (July/August): 21–36.

Posen, Adam. 1993. "Why Central Bank Independence Does Not Cause Low Inflation: The Politics behind the Institutional Fix." In *Finance and the International Economy,* vol. 7, edited by Richard O'Brien, 40–65. New York: Oxford University Press.

———. 1995. "Declarations Are Not Enough: Financial Sector Sources of Central Bank Independence." In *NBER Macroeconomics Annual.* Cambridge, Mass.: MIT Press.

———. 1998. "Central Bank Independence and Disinflationary Credibility: A Missing Link?" *Oxford Economic Papers* 50:335–59.

Powell, G. Bingham. 1982. *Contemporary Democracies: Participation, Stability, and Violence.* Cambridge, Mass.: Harvard University Press.

Powell, G. Bingham, and Guy Whitten. 1993. "A Cross-National Analysis of Economic Voting Taking Account of the Political Context." *American Journal of Political Science* 37 (2): 391–414.

Prast, Henriette. 1996. "Commitment Rather Than Independence: An Institutional Design for Reducing the Inflationary Bias of Monetary Policy." *Kyklos* 49:377–405.

Przeworski, Adam, and John Sprague. 1986. *Paper Stones: A History of Electoral Socialism.* Chicago: University of Chicago Press.

Putnam, Robert. 1993. *Making Democracy Work.* Princeton: Princeton University Press.

Quinn, Dennis. 1997. "The Correlates of Change in International Financial Regulation." *American Political Science Review* 91 (3): 531–552.

Quinn, Dennis, and Carla Inclan. 1997. "The Origins of Financial Openness: A Study of Current and Capital Account Liberalization." *American Journal of Political Science* 41 (3): 771–813.

Rae, Douglas. 1971. *The Political Consequences of Electoral Laws.* 2d ed. New Haven: Yale University Press.

Ramsey, James B. 1969. "Tests for Specification Errors in Classical Linear Least Squares Regression Analysis." *Journal of the Royal Statistical Society,* series B, 31 (2): 350–71.

Ramseyer, J. Mark, and Frances Rosenbluth. 1993. *Japan's Political Marketplace.* New York: Cambridge University Press.

Reyneri, Emilio. 1989. "The Italian Labor Market: Between State Control and Social Regulation." In *State, Market, and Social Regulation: New Perspectives on Italy,* edited by Peter Lange and Mario Regini, 129–46. Cambridge: Cambridge University Press.

Richardson, Dick, and Chris Rootes, eds. 1995. *The Green Challenge: The Development of Green Parties in Europe.* New York: Routledge.

Rogoff, Kenneth. 1985. "The Optimal Degree of Commitment to an Intermediate Monetary Target." *Quarterly Journal of Economics* 100 (4): 1169–89.

Rogoff, Kenneth, and Anne Sibert. 1988. "Elections and Macroeconomic Policy Cycles." *Review of Economic Studies* 55 (1): 1–16.

Rogowski, Ronald. 1987. "Trade and the Variety of Democratic Institutions." *International Organization* 41 (2): 203–33.

———. 1989. *Commerce and Coalitions: How Trade Affects Domestic Political Alignments.* Princeton: Princeton University Press.

Rosenbluth, Frances. 1996. "Internationalization and Electoral Politics in Japan." In *Internationalization and Domestic Politics,* edited by Robert Keohane and Helen Milner, 137–58. New York: Cambridge University Press.

Roubini, Nouriel, and Jeffrey Sachs. 1989a. "Government Spending and Budget Deficits in the Industrial Democracies." *Economic Policy* 8:99–132.

———. 1989b. "Political and Economic Determinants of Budget Deficits in the Industrial Democracies." *European Economic Review* 33 (2): 903–33.

Sala-i-Martin, Xavier, and Jeffrey Sachs. 1992. "Federal Fiscal Policy and Optimum Currency Areas." In *Establishing a Central Bank: Issues in Europe and Lessons from the US,* edited by Matthew Canzoneri, Vittorio Grilli, and Paul Masson, 195–220. New York: Cambridge University Press.

Sandholtz, Wayne. 1993. "Choosing Union: Monetary Politics and Maastricht." *International Organization* 47 (1): 1–39.

Sandholtz, Wayne, and John Zysman. 1989. "1992: Recasting the European Bargain." *World Politics* 42:95–128.

Sani, Giacomo. 1981. "Italian Voters, 1976–1979." In *Italy at the Polls, 1979,* edited by Howard Penniman, 34–63. Washington, D.C.: American Enterprise Institute.

———. 1987. "The Electorate: An Ambiguous Verdict." In *Italy at the Polls, 1983,* edited by Howard Penniman, 18–34. Washington, D.C.: American Enterprise Institute.

Sargent, Thomas J. 1999. *The Conquest of American Inflation.* Princeton: Princeton University Press.

Sartori, Giovanni. 1976. *Parties and Party Systems.* New York: Cambridge University Press.

Scharpf, Fritz. 1987. *Crisis and Choice in European Social Democracy.* Ithaca: Cornell University Press.

Shoch, Jim. 2000. *Trading Blows: Party Politics and American Trade Policy in the Twentieth Century.* Chapel Hill: University of North Carolina Press.

Shull, Tad. 1999. *Redefining Red and Green: Ideology and Strategy in European Political Ecology.* Albany: State University of New York Press.

Simmons, Beth. 1994. *Who Adjusts? Domestic Sources of Foreign Economic Policy during the Interwar Years, 1924–1939.* Princeton: Princeton University Press.

———. 1996. "Rulers of the Game: Central Bank Independence during the Interwar Years." *International Organization* 50:407–43.

———. 1999. "The Internationalization of Capital." In *Continuity and Change in Contemporary Capitalism,* edited by Herbert Kitschelt, Peter Lange, Gary Marks, and John D. Stephens, 36–69. New York: Cambridge University Press.

Soskice, David, and Torben Iversen. 1998. "Multiple Wage-Bargaining Systems in the Single European Currency Area." *Oxford Review of Economic Policy* 14 (3): 110–24.

Spotts, Frederic, and Theodor Weiser. 1986. *Italy: A Difficult Democracy.* New York: Cambridge University Press.

Strøm, Kaare. 1990a. "A Behavioral Theory of Competitive Political Parties." *American Journal of Political Science* 34 (2): 565–98.

———. 1990b. *Minority Government and Majority Rule.* New York: Cambridge University Press.

Sturm, Roland. 1989. "The Role of the Bundesbank in German Politics." *West European Politics* 12 (2): 1–11.

Swinburne, Mark, and Marta Castello-Branco. 1991. "Central Bank Independence: Issues and Experience." International Monetary Fund Working Paper.

Taagepera, Rein, and James Hayes. 1977. "How Trade/GNP Ratio Decreases with Country Size." *Social Science Research* 6 (1): 108–32.

Tabellini, Guido. 1987. "Central Bank Reputation and the Monetization of Deficits: The 1981 Italian Monetary Reform." *Economic Inquiry* 25:185–200.

———. 1988. "Monetary and Fiscal Policy Coordination with a High Public Debt." In *High Public Debt: The Italian Experience,* edited by Francesco Giavazzi and Luigi Spaventa, 90–126. Cambridge: Cambridge University Press.

Tarrow, Sidney. 1981. "Three Years of Italian Democracy." In *Italy at the Polls, 1979,* edited by Howard Penniman, 1–33. Washington, D.C.: American Enterprise Institute.

———. 1989. *Democracy and Disorder: Protest and Politics in Italy, 1965–1975.* New York: Oxford University Press.

———. 1990. "Maintaining Hegemony in Italy: 'The Softer They Rise, the Slower They Fall!'" In *Uncommon Democracies: The One-Party Dominant Regimes,* edited by T. J. Pempel, 306–32. Ithaca: Cornell University Press.

Tavelli, Henry, Giuseppe Tullio, and Franco Spinelli. 1998. "The Evolution of European Central Bank Independence: An Updating of the Masciandaro and Spinelli Index." *Scottish Journal of Political Economy* 45 (3): 341–44.

Tavlas, George. 1993. "The 'New' Theory of Optimum Currency Areas." *World Economy* 16 (6): 663–85.

Temperton, Paul. 1991. *UK Monetary Policy.* New York: St. Martin's Press.

Thatcher, Margaret. 1993. *The Downing Street Years.* New York: Harper Collins.

Thompson, Noel. 1996. *Political Economy and the Labour Party: The Economics of Democratic Socialism, 1884–1995.* London: UCL Press.

Tufte, Edward. 1978. *Political Control of the Economy.* Princeton: Princeton University Press.

United Kingdom. House of Commons. 1945. *Sessional Papers, 1945–46.* Vol. 5.

United Kingdom. *Parliamentary Debates,* Commons, 5th ser. vols. 294, 295, 300 (1997).

Vaubel, Roland. 1997. "The Bureaucratic and Partisan Behavior of Independent Central Banks: German and International Evidence." *European Journal of Political Economy* 13:201–24.

von Hagen, Jurgen. 1992. *Budgeting Procedures and Fiscal Performance in the European Communities.* Economic Papers. Brussels: Commission of the European Communities.

Waller, Christopher. 1989. "Monetary Policy Games and Central Bank Politics." *Journal of Money, Credit, and Banking* 21:422–31.

———. 1991. "Bashing and Coercion in Monetary Policy." *Economic Inquiry* 29:1–13.

———. 1992a. "A Bargaining Model of Partisan Appointments to the Central Bank." *Journal of Monetary Economics* 29:411–28.

———. 1992b. "The Choice of a Conservative Central Banker in a Multisector Economy." *American Economic Review* 82 (4): 1006–12.

———. 1995. "Performance Contracts for Central Bankers." *Federal Reserve Bank of St. Louis Review* 77 (5): 3–14.

Waller, Christopher, and Carl Walsh. 1996. "Central Bank Independence, Economic Behavior, and Optimal Term Lengths." *American Economic Review* 86 (5): 1139–53.

Wallerstein, Michael. 1998. "The Impact of Economic Integration on European Wage-Setting Institutions." In *Forging an Integrated Europe,* edited by Barry Eichengreen and Jeffry Frieden, 185–210. Ann Arbor: University of Michigan Press.

Walsh, Carl. 1993. "Central Bank Strategies, Credibility, and Independence." *Journal of Monetary Economics* 32:287–302.

———. 1995a. "Central Bank Independence and the Short-Run Output-Inflation Trade-Off in the European Community." In *Monetary and Fiscal Policy in an Integrated Europe,* edited by Barry Eichengreen, Jeffry Frieden, and Jurgen von Hagen, 12–35. New York: Springer.

———. 1995b. "Is New Zealand's Reserve Bank Act of 1989 an Optimal Central Bank Contract?" *Journal of Money, Credit, and Banking* 27 (4): 1179–91.

———. 1995c. "Optimal Contracts for Central Bankers." *American Economic Review* 85 (1): 150–67.

———. 1999. "Announcements, Inflation Targeting, and Central Bank Incentives." *Economica* 66:255–69.

Warwick, Paul. 1994. *Government Survival in Parliamentary Democracies.* New York: Cambridge University Press.

Weingast, Barry, and Mark Moran. 1983. "Bureaucratic Discretion or Congressional Control? Regulatory Policymaking by the Federal Trade Commission." *Journal of Political Economy* 91:765–800.

Welsch, Roy. 1980. "Regression Sensitivity Analysis and Bounded-Influence Estimation." In *Evaluation of Econometric Models,* edited by Jan Kmenta and James Ramsey, 153–67. New York: Academic Press.

Wertmann, Douglas A. 1981. "The Christian Democrats: Masters of Survival." In *Italy at the Polls, 1979,* edited by Howard Penniman, 64–103. Washington, D.C.: American Enterprise Institute.

———. 1987. "The Christian Democrats: The Big Losers." In *Italy at the Polls, 1983,* edited by Howard Penniman, 35–59. Washington, D.C.: American Enterprise Institute.

Western, Bruce. 1995. "Concepts and Suggestions for Robust Regression Analysis." *American Journal of Political Science* 39 (3): 786–818.

Woldendrop, Jaap, Hans Keman, and Ian Budge, eds. 1993. *Political Data 1945–1990: Party Government in 20 Democracies.* Special issue, *European Journal of Political Research* 24 (1).

Woolley, John. 1984. *Monetary Politics: The Federal Reserve and the Politics of Monetary Policy.* New York: Cambridge University Press.

Woolley, John, and Lance LeLoup. 1989. "The Adequacy of the Electoral Motive in Explaining Legislative Attention to Monetary Policy." *Comparative Politics* (October): 63–82.

Wyplosz, Charles. 1997. "EMU: Why and How It Might Happen." *Journal of Economic Perspectives* 11 (4): 3–22.

Zysman, John. 1983. *Governments, Markets, and Growth.* Ithaca: Cornell University Press.

Index